# *Romans*

# *Romans*

An Exposition of Chapter 11
To God's Glory

*D. M. Lloyd-Jones*

THE BANNER OF TRUTH TRUST

THE BANNER OF TRUTH TRUST

*Head Office*
3 Murrayfield Road
Edinburgh, EH12 6EL
UK

*North America Office*
PO Box 621
Carlisle, PA 17013
USA

banneroftruth.org

First published 1998

Reprinted 2005, 2009, 2015, 2018, 2021

*

ISBN
This volume: 978 0 85151 748 3
14-volume set: 978 0 85151 756 8

*

Typeset in 10/12 Stempel Garamond

Printed in the USA by
Versa Press Inc.,
East Peoria, IL

*The sermons in this volume*
*were originally preached at Westminster Chapel*
*between October 1964 and May 1965*

# *Contents*

# *One*

*

*I say then, Hath God cast away his people? God forbid.*
Romans 11:1a

The eleventh chapter of Paul's Epistle to the Romans is one of the great and notable chapters in the whole of the Bible. I know that I have a tendency to say that about every chapter which we consider, but there are certain chapters which stand out as one reads through the Bible. Romans chapter eight would surely be one of those, perhaps mainly from a literary standpoint, but there are other chapters whose importance is only properly recognized when one comes to study them in detail. It is then that one realizes how wonderful and profound they are and also how ashamed one is not to have seen this before. Romans 11 – and here I am giving my own experience – is one of those chapters.

However, it has its difficulties. In many ways I would say that it is much more difficult than either chapter 9 or 10. Certainly, there has been disagreement about some of its content and it is therefore essential that as we come to consider it we should begin with a kind of general introduction.

But before we do that there is something which is even more important. It relates to the spirit in which we approach this chapter. We must come with reverence and humility. Of course, the Scriptures are always to be approached in that way but it is necessary at times and for particular reasons to enforce that requirement and one of those relates to the fact there are matters in this chapter which are the subject of great dispute. Let us therefore resolve at the outset that our object in examining this chapter is not going to be to prove that we are right while others are wrong. We must avoid a spirit of controversy. There are several differing points of view here and they are all conscientiously held.

We must also be careful that our proper interest in the content of this chapter does not become carnal excitement. There is more than one way of being excited. We can be excited intellectually as well as emotionally. I warn those who are keen to find out what is going to be said on this matter or that and particularly on 'So all Israel shall be saved'. This attitude is quite inappropriate when one comes to study the Scriptures.

Let us remind ourselves at the outset of two things which we find in this chapter. The first is that the Apostle refers in it to a mystery. If therefore we think that we have this chapter all sorted out and tabulated and that there can be no other view worth considering, we are already wrong. But the second is the way in which the Apostle concluded this chapter. Having written it he finds himself in a state of mind and heart in which he can think of and do nothing else but praise and worship God – 'O the depth of the riches both of the wisdom and knowledge of God.' The consideration of this truth had that effect on him. So it should on us and on all who consider it and that is what we now begin to do.

I have indicated how important it is to realize that chapters 9, 10 and 11 of this great Epistle constitute a section on their own and that they must always be taken together. What is their theme? Well, it is, of course, the whole question of the case and the condition of the Jews at the time of our Lord and of the Apostle. Speaking generally, they were rejecting the gospel, were outside the church and the Gentiles were streaming in. Now the Apostle is concerned about this for many reasons. He is undoubtedly concerned about it because he was a Jew himself. He has shown that at the beginning of the previous two chapters. The Christian is not unnatural, and we should all be concerned about our relatives, about our fellow-countrymen.

But not only that; he had a much deeper and greater concern, and that was about the great question of the purpose and the plan of God. He had ended chapter 8 on a tremendous note of assurance and of certainty. He had thrown out his mighty challenges: 'What shall we then say to these things? If God be for us, who can be against us?' and he had worked it out, you remember, ending up with the triumphant statement: 'For I am persuaded, that neither death, nor life, nor angels, nor principalities, nor powers, nor things present, nor things to come, nor height, nor depth, nor any other creature, shall be able to separate us from the love of God, which is in Christ Jesus our Lord'. The purpose of God is so certain that nothing can frustrate it.

But a question is immediately begged. It is: 'How can that be said in the light of the position and the condition of the Jews, God's own people? Is not their condition a proof, in and of itself, that the purpose of God is not sure? Has it not broken down completely?

The purpose of these three chapters is to answer that question and to show plainly and clearly that the purpose of God has not collapsed, and that if these things are properly understood, then there is ultimately no problem at all. Indeed, they are to show that the exact opposite is the case, that God's purpose always has been carried out, is being carried out and always will be to an absolute perfection and a final consummation.

The Apostle starts on this great demonstration in chapter 9 and the key to it all is in the second half of the sixth verse where he says, 'They are not all Israel, which are of Israel'. This is the secret. There is an Israel within Israel. There is a literal, national Israel, but there is a spiritual 'Israel' within that larger body. And what he goes on to say is that it was never God's purpose or promise that the whole of physical Israel was going to be saved. God never said that. His purpose was only to save the spiritual Israel, and that purpose He has been carrying on throughout the running centuries.

He illustrates this in what he says about Isaac and Ishmael, Jacob and Esau, showing how God made this distinction and acted in the one He had already chosen, bringing His great purpose to pass and carrying it right through. And that leads him to emphasize the fact that salvation is entirely the result of the sovereign will of God. There is a great statement in the eleventh verse of the ninth chapter: 'For the children being not yet born, neither having done any good or evil that the purpose of God according to election might stand, not of works, but of Him that calleth'. So he emphasizes that the fact that anybody is saved is solely the result of the election of God, God's great sovereign purpose. We are all saved by that. But he equally emphasizes that we are responsible if we are in a state of condemnation. We are not responsible for our salvation, but we are responsible for our condemnation.

We must not go into these details again, but he works out his case so as to make it abundantly clear to any who object to it that they are, in reality, questioning God. He says 'O man, who art thou that repliest against God?'. The great principle is that God saves, but man is responsible for his own rejection. So the ninth chapter ends with its being asserted that the Jews are responsible for their position because they have rebelled against God, substituting their own ideas for God's sovereign purpose and seeking salvation by the works of the law instead of accepting it by faith as the free gift of God.

So the important thing to remember is the distinction within Israel and that God's purpose has been worked out through the spiritual Israel. There is nothing missing, nothing lacking because that is all God ever purposed to do and He has done it.

In chapter 10 the Apostle takes up that point and works it out in detail. He shows the utter folly of the Jews by pointing out that God's way of salvation has always been by faith and that there is no other way at all. That is God's method universally. Salvation is therefore not dependent upon a man's works, nor on anything in man, but upon God and His sovereign will, and, as it is obtained by faith, is as open to Gentiles as to Jews. He sums that up in his resounding statement in the thirteenth verse of the tenth chapter: 'Whosoever shall call upon the name of the Lord shall be saved'. It does not matter who a person is. People are not saved because they are Jews, or because they do good works and are religious. No, no, it is God's calling that saves, and therefore the gospel is to be preached to all and the one thing that matters is whether a man believes it and obeys it.

Again, the two sides come in. Salvation is all of God, and yet a man can bring down upon himself condemnation. In the sixteenth verse he says: 'But they have not all obeyed the Gospel', and again clinches this whole argument with regard to the Jews. The offer was made to them before it was ever made to the Gentiles. The apostles started in Jerusalem before they went down to Samaria and the uttermost parts of the earth, but the Jews rejected the message because they completely misunderstood God's way of salvation. They sought it by keeping the law instead of realising that it is always by faith. And as in the ninth chapter so in the tenth, the Apostle proves by numerous quotations from the Scriptures that all this was not only true, but that it had all been predicted and prophesied. There is no need therefore for anybody to stumble at this because these great quotations from Moses and from Isaiah show that all along the purpose of God is being carried out. There is no problem, there is no failure: what God said He would do, He has been doing, is doing and will do. At the end of chapter 10 he comes back to the same point exactly as at the end of chapter 9, which is once more to show these two sides – God's free grace according to His sovereign will, and man's responsibility for his own condemnation because he rejects God's way.

So the point we have arrived at is this: God's purpose is certainly and surely being carried out although at the present time, he says, it is mainly through the Gentiles rather than the Jews. This is due to the blindness of the Jews and their inability to understand their own Scriptures about which they had boasted so much. They had been blinded by the god of this world. There was a veil over their eyes so that, although the Scriptures were read every Sabbath in the synagogues, they did not understand them and that led to all their trouble. That is how he ends chapter 10 just as he ended chapter 9.

But that gives rise to the question which is found at the beginning of this eleventh chapter – 'I say then, Hath God cast away His people?'. 'Are you arguing', somebody may say to the Apostle, 'that God has now finished completely with the Jews, and that henceforth the only people to consider are the Gentiles?'. It is that specific question which he takes up and answers in this chapter.

The Apostle had not dealt with this in chapters 9 and 10 which are simply concerned to show us why the Jews were in the condition which they were in his day. It was an amazing thing to both Jews and Gentiles, once they became Christians, that the Jewish people should be outside. The Apostle had to explain that but also he had to explain how the Gentiles could come in. That is what he does in chapters 9 and 10. He shows why the Jews are outside; he shows how the Gentiles have come in, and how this is just a fulfilment of everything that had been prophesied; but he does not take the argument any further in those chapters.

But in chapter 11 he does go further. He looks into the future and shows how this great and grand purpose of God is going to be carried out in its glorious fulness, both as regards Gentiles and Jews. So there is a new theme here. The present has been explained but the question now is, What of the future? The Jews are outside, are they always to be there? Is this the end of the Jews as regards salvation? Has God's purpose with respect to the Jew finished? Paul answers that and shows that that is not the case. So he gives us this great preview of history – the ultimate purpose of God in all its fulness with respect to both the Jews and the Gentiles. That is a summary of the three chapters which shows the setting of this eleventh chapter.

We are now in a position to give a general analysis of the contents of this chapter. There is no difficulty about doing this because it divides itself up for us. There are three sections in it.

The first section is from verses 1 to 10. It begins with the words 'I say then' which are also found in verse 11 at the beginning of the second section. The question dealt with in this first section is, 'Hath God cast away his people?'. A negative answer is expected which he gives in the words, 'God forbid!'.

Now, what he does here is to show that this rejection of the Jews, which he has been dealing with in chapters 9 and 10 is not a *total* rejection – in the sense that all Jews have been rejected. There are some who do believe and are Christians, as he has hinted in that tenth chapter in the sixteenth verse: 'But they have not all obeyed the gospel'. Some have, but not all. He takes up that point and he elaborates it.

Then we come to the second section which begins at verse 11. The question he asks here is, 'Have they stumbled that they might fall?'. A negative answer is again implied. In this section which continues to verse 32 he shows that the rejection of Israel – the nation – is not *final*. It was not total in verses 1 to 10; in these verses it is not final. We shall see that verses 11–23 point to a possibility of the Jews being restored. Verse 24 says that it is a probability. Verse 25 says that it is a certainty. You see the argument develops. It is not a total rejection; it is not a final rejection; indeed, something tremendous is going to take place.

That leaves the third and the last section, verses 33 to verse 36, and this, of course, is nothing but a great doxology, an expression of amazement, and of worship and praise. This, then, is our division or analysis of the contents of the chapter.

# *Two*

*

*I say then, Hath God cast away his people? God forbid. For I also am an Israelite, of the seed of Abraham, of the tribe of Benjamin. God hath not cast away his people which he foreknew. Wot ye not what the scripture saith of Elias? how he maketh intercession to God against Israel, saying, Lord, they have killed thy prophets, and digged down thine altars; and I am left alone, and they seek my life. But what saith the answer of God unto him? I have reserved to myself seven thousand men, who have not bowed the knee to the image of Baal.* Romans 11:1–4

---

We come now to the detailed working out of the first section of this chapter. It runs from verse 1 to verse 10 and in it the Apostle is setting out to prove that the rejection of Israel is not total. He puts that in the form of the question: 'I say then, Hath God cast away his people?' which you could take like this: 'I am asking, Is it possible that God has cast away His people?'

What is he really asking? What does this 'casting away' amount to? It means a rejection which is complete, a resolve to have nothing more to do with those referred to. That is the term which the Apostle uses and he puts it in a prominent position in his sentence in order to emphasize it. He is saying in effect, 'Is it therefore my teaching that God has finished with His people, that is the Jews?' So that is the question which he is putting up and he does so in such a way that there is only one answer to it. That answer as given in the Authorized Version is, 'God forbid' which means 'may it not be' – the thing is unthinkable!

Now then, why does he say that this is something which is quite impossible? I want to suggest to you that he gives three reasons for that in verses 1 to 10, which I propose to sub-divide as follows.

The first explanation of why he says 'unthinkable' is found in the first verse and in the first half of the second, and that is, his own case.

The second explanation has to do with the doctrine of the remnant and that begins halfway through the second verse and goes on to the end of the sixth verse. Thirdly, in verses seven to ten the Apostle sums up by referring to the doctrine of election. Finally, to prove his argument he clinches it with scriptural quotations in his usual manner.

Let us look, then, at these three sub-divisions of this first section. Why does he in effect say 'God forbid that anybody should come to the conclusion that I am teaching that God has finished with the nation of Israel'? Well, he says, here is my first answer: 'I also am an Israelite, of the seed of Abraham, and of the tribe of Benjamin. God hath not cast away His people which He foreknew'.

This is a most interesting statement. There are two particular matters in it to which I must call your attention. He says, 'I also am an Israelite', and then to underline that he says, 'of the seed of Abraham, of the tribe of Benjamin'. He says, If anybody thinks I am teaching that when God sent His son into this world with the gospel as a way of salvation it meant that no Jew was ever to be brought in, that God had finished with Israel and that He is only interested in Gentiles henceforward, I alone am sufficient to answer that, because I myself am an Israelite'. And not being content with stating it in general, he adds, 'I am of the seed of Abraham'.

In previous chapters, and particularly in chapter 9 verse 6, Paul had made a great deal of this matter of descent from Abraham. He says: 'Not as though the Word of God hath taken none effect. For they are not all Israel, which are of Israel: Neither, because they are of the seed of Abraham, are they all children'. The great boast of the Israelites and the Jews was 'We are the children of Abraham, we are Abraham's seed', and you will find that running as a refrain through the pages of the Gospels. So he says, 'I am of the seed of Abraham'.

He also says that he is an 'Israelite' and that brings Jacob into view because it was to Jacob that the name Israel was given. In other words, he is out to prove that he comes in the right line. In accord with the argument of chapter 9, Paul says, 'I am not only descended from Abraham, I belong to this line that comes down through Jacob; I am an Israelite'. And then he particularizes it still more by saying that he was 'of the tribe of Benjamin'. He is obviously anxious to say that he is not a proselyte, but not only that. By telling us that he is of the tribe of Benjamin, he reminds us how Benjamin stood with Judah in remaining true to God's covenant with David whereas, following the death of Solomon, the other ten tribes set up their own kingdom in Samaria, only to be carried away into captivity.

So what he is really doing is setting out to prove his point which is that if anyone were to say that God has completely finished with Israel, that must mean that not a single Israelite could ever have believed the gospel and been saved by it. But he says 'I am an Israelite, and I have been saved by it'. Very well; there he has made this personal statement and it is a very cogent and powerful argument.

But then he adds the words 'God hath not cast away his people which he foreknew'. This is an important statement but there is some disagreement about it. It is a kind of quotation of Psalm 94 verse 14 which reads: 'For the Lord will not cast off his people, neither will he forsake his inheritance'. That was obviously in the Apostle's mind as he utters this phrase. But there are two ways of construing his statement. Here is the first. 'God hath not cast away his people, which he foreknew'. The second way of reading it is this: 'God hath not cast away his people which he foreknew'. Now do you see the difference? It lies in the comma. The first reading means the nation of Israel; the second only the elect within it.

Now there are the two points of view and, as I say, it is not only interesting but important that we should be clear about this and that the rest of our exposition should be consistent with our understanding at this point. Paul is either referring to the elect within the nation or to the nation as a whole. Let us take these views in that order because the two great commentators on this Epistle – Charles Hodge and Robert Haldane – both take the first view and they say something like this: In the first verse of this chapter 'his people' means the nation, but in the second he is obviously not referring to the nation as such, but only to the elect as within it. They understand it as saying that God has cast away all beside His elect, 'his people whom he foreknew'.

We will confine ourselves to Hodge because he presents three arguments for this particular exposition. What are they? First, he says that by referring only here to the 'elect', the Apostle is saying something that is in line with what he has already said in chapter 9 verses six to eight about the true Israel. Secondly, he says, that this interpretation is what Paul says in verse five of this chapter: 'Even so then at this present time also there is a remnant according to the election of grace'. His third argument is this: 'The Apostle's use of the illustration of what happened in the time of Elias, and what was said to Elias himself, fits in also with this statement', because at that time the nation as a whole, as it were, was apostate and there was just a small company that still believed.

Once more, with considerable trepidation and hesitation, I venture to dissent from this exposition of both Hodge and Haldane and those who agree with them. Why do I reject it? Here are my reasons. First, it always seems to me that to give different meanings to a word or expression when it recurs as closely as 'his people' does in verse 1 and 2 is a very doubtful thing to do. Surely, we are entitled to assume that a word used in the same context and as a part of the same argument has the same connotation, unless there is some overwhelming reason to the contrary.

But secondly, it seems to me that to adopt their exposition is really to suggest that Paul is guilty of what is called 'tautology', that is, pointless repetition. What they are making the Apostle say is this: 'God has not cast away the people whom He has chosen'. Now how could He cast away people if He had chosen them? There is obviously no need to say such a thing. It is not adding to the meaning. It is sheer repetition and the Apostle is never guilty of that. That is what their interpretation makes him say: 'God has not cast away His people whom He has elected, whom He foreknew'. Well of course He has not!

But thirdly, it seems to me that their exposition entirely forgets the real object of the whole of this chapter. I remind you that in chapter 11 the Apostle is not merely repeating what he said in chapter 9 and finally worked out in chapter 10. He is adding to it, going beyond it and is saying something new and fresh. In chapters 9 and 10 he had to reconcile the fact that the majority of the Jews were not believing the gospel with the teaching of the Old Testament, and also to justify the fact that the Gentiles were coming in. That was the object of chapters 9 and 10 – and he did that, of course, in his own admirable and perfect manner. But now in chapter 11 he is going further, he is now looking into the future, he is now going to tell us what is going to happen to this nation.

Now it is an extraordinary thing that both Hodge and Haldane agree that this is the great object of the chapter, and yet at this point they forget that the Apostle has finished with the theme of chapter 9 and is going on to a fresh subject altogether. He is looking at the position of the nation as such in the light of God's ultimate plan and purpose. That, it seems to me, is sufficient in and of itself to put their exposition entirely out of court.

But what about the reference to Elijah in verse 2 and following? Why does Paul include this? Surely the answer is this: to argue that God had finished with the nation because the majority of the Jews were not believing the gospel, is to be like poor Elijah. He fell into exactly the same trap and thought that he alone remained. But of course the answer of God to him was, that there were many others who were all right also. Surely that is the force of Paul's argument. And so the Apostle is really saying, 'Not only am I a believer, but there are many others also at this present time'. 'Even so then at this present time also there is a remnant according to the election of grace' and that is the exact opposite of Hodge's deduction from Paul's employment of this case of Elijah.

So I come to my last reason for rejecting this exposition. It is that the whole purpose of this chapter is to deal with the nation as such, and this is what makes it so astonishing to me that they can have misinterpreted this particular statement. Both Hodge and Haldane agree that from here on the Apostle is interested in the nation as such. You read through the chapter again for yourself and you will find that all along Paul has his eye on the Jewish nation – a phenomenon – and what is going to happen to them in the future.

Look at the terms which he uses, which prove this beyond any misunderstanding whatsoever. He says, 'I say then, Have they stumbled that they should fall?' Who are they? It is the nation. He is not talking about the elect. The 'they' refers to this 'people' of God. 'Have "they" stumbled that they should fall?' This is not the elect believers, it is the nation. 'God forbid', he says: 'but rather through their fall salvation is come unto the Gentiles'. Then this great argument: 'Now if the fall of them be the riches of the Gentiles'. This is not the elect remnant: it is the nation. And so it goes on right through. He says that 'blindness in part is happened to Israel'. He is still talking about the nation. Verse 25: 'I would not, brethren, that ye should be ignorant of this mystery, lest ye should be wise in your own conceits; that blindness in part is happened to Israel, until the fulness of the Gentiles be come in'.

Now the whole chapter is dealing with 'Israel', and Hodge and Haldane are very eloquent about this. They are the keenest in saying that 'blindness in part is happened to Israel'. And then you have these other phrases which say that they can be 'grafted in' again. Who are these? Well, it is the nation that is now outside; it is not the elect he is talking about. He is not dealing with them at all!

Then there is this other great statement in verse 28: 'As concerning the gospel, they are enemies for your sakes: but as touching the election, they are beloved for the fathers' sake'. Who are these? Well, it is the nation of Israel. Not merely the saved remnant in the nation, not merely the 'Israel within Israel'. This is Israel considered as a physical nation, as a theocratic people of God, they are the people who are 'beloved for the fathers' sake'. Right through the chapter in this phrase as everywhere else the Apostle is talking about them, the theocratic nation of Israel, the people as a totality, the people as a whole.

We need not stay with the word 'foreknew' because we have already come across it so often in this great Epistle. What does it mean? Well the better translation here is 'foreordained'. It is exactly the same word as is used in 1 Peter 1:20, where the Apostle Peter is referring to our Lord's death and says that he was 'foreordained before the foundation of the world, but was manifest in these last times for you'. In our verse it therefore means the people whom God 'foreordained'. It does not just mean that God who knows everything knows who is going to believe and who is going to reject the gospel. Anybody who has worked his way through the Epistle to the Romans could not believe that for a second. The whole argument in chapter 9 was, that while these two children were still in the womb of their mother, Jacob and Esau, God said, 'Jacob have I loved, but Esau have I hated'. They had not done anything at all. That is foreordination, and that is the word that we have here.

It means that God has taken a special interest in this nation. He had set His heart and affection upon them. Indeed it goes further: God made and prepared this nation for Himself. In Amos 3:2 God addresses these people and says, 'You only have I known of all the families of the earth'. Now that can only have one meaning. It does not mean that He knew about them, because God knows about all the nations of the earth. It means, 'You only have I known with a special affection and interest; you alone are a people who are a peculiar possession to Me; I am in this intimate relationship to you. I have known you as I have known nobody else. I recognize you, you are My people'. That is what it means, and that is what God, of course, tells us everywhere in the Bible about His people. It is the teaching of the whole Bible about the children of Israel. They had not just come into being like the other nations; they were not a nation like other nations. God had prepared them as a special people for Himself, for His own peculiar possession. He knows them – 'I will be your God, and you shall be My people'. He pledges Himself to them. All that is included in the idea of 'foreknowledge' meaning 'foreordination'.

So the Apostle's statement is this: Why do I say God forbid? I say God forbid for this reason, that God has made this nation for Himself; if therefore He casts them away in the way you are suggesting, it means that God is contradicting Himself, it means that God is going back upon His own purpose! Such a thing is unthinkable. The purposes of God are always sure. He sees the end from the beginning. God is immutable, He is unchangeable, He is the everlasting God. So the Apostle has given us here in and of itself a sufficient explanation of why he speaks so strongly and says, 'God forbid'!

Before we leave this first explanation there is one thing I must just mention in connection with the word 'Israelite' in verse 1. Part of the marvel of the Scriptures is the way in which every every word counts and here is something which is important at the present time in relation to the teaching of the so-called 'British Israelites'. What do they teach? They say that the mistake people have always made is to pay such attention to the Jews that, seeing their current condition, they are in trouble over the prophecies of the Old Testament, they are at a loss to relate this to the great promises of the Old Testament. But this is because they do not realise that there is all the difference in the world between a Jew and an Israelite. They say that the key to the understanding of the whole of Scripture is to see this difference and to realise that the promises are made entirely to Israel and not to the Jews.

Who then is Israel? They say that 'Israel' is the ten lost tribes referred to often in the Scriptures as 'Ephraim'. And who are they now? People of British stock, they say. The British people are Ephraim; the Americans are 'Manasseh'; and they say these glorious promises in the Scriptures are really all for the British people and the British Empire.

Now that is their teaching and I mention it to you because there is a possibility that you may meet someone who teaches these things and who will claim that you have misunderstood the whole of your Scriptures. What will your answer be? What I am concerned to show you is that this one verse of Romans is enough by itself to give the lie direct to all that monstrous teaching. How? Because the Apostle Paul, who gives us his Jewish pedigree here, says also 'I am an Israelite'. That proves that the suggested distinction between Jew and

Israelite is ridiculous and meaningless. You read the case for British Israelism and you will find that it not only does not correspond to biblical teaching, it does not correspond to history and all that is dragged in by way of anthropology. It has no facts, it is theory, suppositions, manipulation of Scripture and so on; but here, I say, we have enough in and of itself. Here is a Jew, glorying, as they all did, in the fact that he is an 'Israelite', and that is, of course, the truth with respect to this matter.

We have only touched on the first part of the Apostle's argument in this opening section, but I do trust that I have persuaded any who may have felt doubtful about this that this is not only glorious Scripture and an introduction to a great theme, it is also of great practical importance and usefulness and relevance, and the more we know the Scripture the more we shall find that it deals with our modern and contemporary problems.

# *Three*

*

*I say then, Hath God cast away his people? God forbid. For I also am an Israelite, of the seed of Abraham, of the tribe of Benjamin. God hath not cast away his people which he foreknew. Wot ye not what the scripture saith of Elias? how he maketh intercession to God against Israel, saying, Lord, they have killed thy prophets, and digged down thine altars; and I am left alone, and they seek my life. But what saith the answer of God unto him? I have reserved to myself seven thousand men, who have not bowed the knee to the image of Baal. Even so then at this present time also there is a remnant according to the election of grace. And if by grace, then is it no more of works: otherwise grace is no more grace. But if it be of works, then is it no more grace: otherwise work is no more work.* Romans 11:1–6

---

We resume our study of the first section of this chapter which runs from verse 1 to verse 10 in which the Apostle is pointing out that although the Jews are largely outside the church, God has not *totally* rejected the nation. Paul gives his reasons for that. The first is that he says 'I am an Israelite' – meaning that as he has become a Christian that is sufficient by itself to prove that God's rejection of His people is not total.

We move on now to the second argument which he presents. It is found in the second half of the second verse through to verse 6. There is a very obvious and natural division in these verses. The Apostle first of all states a case, and he does that from the second half of verse 2 to the end of verse 4; and then in verses 5 and 6 he applies it and shows the relevance of what he is saying.

First of all, we must deal with pure exposition in order that we may get our facts straight. He introduces this matter by saying in effect, 'Are you not aware?' This is how the great Apostle often proceeds. He appeals to what his readers already know. He says: 'Do you not know what the Scriptures say?'. Now why does he do that? Well, he is anxious to show that he is not presenting his own theory or ideas. The Apostle never bases his position upon his own thinking. He always wants them to see and to know that what he is saying is based upon the authority of the Word of God.

In other words, as we have seen so often in his reasoning and argumentation, a point that he makes, perhaps more frequently than any others in these three chapters, 9, 10 and 11, is that there was nothing new in what was happening among the Jews in his own day. The self-same thing had occurred repeatedly in the history of the children of Israel in the Old Testament.

Now this is a very important argument, because the charge that was levelled against the great Apostle was that, in teaching the gospel and in the whole notion of the Christian church, he was saying something which could not in any way be linked with the teaching of the Old Testament. Nothing is so important to the great Apostle as to be able to show that he taught nothing new in principle but that it had all been foretold in the Old Testament. God has only one great method; there is only one way of salvation. You see it in the Old Testament as well as in the New Testament. So it is obviously very germane to the whole argument at this point that the great Apostle should be able to demonstrate this by an example and an illustration from Old Testament history.

'Do you not know', he says, 'what the Scripture saith of Elias?' A better translation of this would be: 'Do you not know what the Scripture saith "in" Elias?' Why do I make that point? Because it shows us how Scripture refers to Scripture. There is no book of 'Elias' (that is the Greek form of Elijah) so why does he say 'in Elias'? Well, that is a way of saying, 'Do you not know what God has said in the portion of Scripture dealing with the story of Elijah, and, for short, he says, 'in Elias'. What God said 'in Elias' is what we have in 1 Kings 19 in the account of Elijah and in particular what he said in prayer to God.

Recall the facts of this remarkable story. Elijah had just been on Mount Carmel and there, alone, he had been facing eight hundred and fifty false prophets. This one man stood against them like a lion, and, of course, he routed them and defeated them. But having done that, he hears about the intention of Queen Jezebel to put him to death and he escapes for his life. And there we see him sitting under a juniper tree and making supplication to God against Israel. He was praying to God to do something about the people of Israel and said in effect, 'They have broken your laws, they have killed your prophets, they have dug down thine altars; and I am left, and they are now threatening to kill me. Why don't you do something about these people, why don't you smite them?'. He called upon God to act in a judicial manner with respect to them. He not only runs away himself and sits down and speaks as he does and feels as he does, but he actually goes as far as that.

Now then what is the point? The whole trouble was that Elijah misjudged the situation, completely, and God pointed that out to him by saying: 'I have reserved to myself seven thousand men, who have not bowed the knee to Baal' and the whole object of the Apostle is to show a parallel between those times and his own, saying that it is not the case that he alone is saved and is a Christian. He has claimed to be a Christian but wants to make it clear that he is not in the position of Elijah, thinking that he alone is left. He knows he is one of a great number. In the time of Elijah there was a real apostasy on the part of the nation of Israel and if you had looked at the situation superficially you might very well have come to the conclusion that Elijah was right; but the point is that he was absolutely wrong. And, says the apostle, it is exactly the same now. I who am an Israelite, am a Christian – but I am not the only one.

But we are not left in the realm of opinion on this. Paul writes: 'What saith the answer of God unto him?' and there he uses a significant word, one which is not used elsewhere in the New Testament. There are those who would translate it like this: 'What saith the Oracle of God?'. The word refers to a very special pronouncement by God, a divine response, and what God said was, 'I have left me seven thousand in Israel, all the knees which have not bowed to Baal'. Paul says 'I have reserved to myself seven thousand men, who have not bowed the knee to the image of Baal'.

I draw attention to this difference because there are people who think that this variation in words challenges the doctrine of the verbal inspiration of Scripture. They say, what is the use of claiming that this man was divinely inspired when he misquotes or adds to Scripture; how can you still hold to your doctrine of its divine inspiration? Well, as I have had occasion to point out many times, this kind of thing is a proof of inspiration rather than the reverse. It is the same Holy Spirit who inspired the writers in the Old Testament who inspired the Apostle Paul and it is He alone who has a right to add, or change or give a different shade of meaning. Paul, as a former Pharisee, would never venture to quote the Old Testament in a manner which was not word perfect, but he does so quite frequently and this is because he was an apostle, and inspired. So when we have God saying 'I have left', the Apostle understands this by the Spirit to mean 'I have reserved to myself'. As the Spirit is the author and the inspirer of the whole of Scripture, it is He alone who knows what particular meaning He wants to bring out at any particular point. So, far from this variation militating against divine inspiration, it is an argument in favour of it.

Finally, we must note the numbers which are mentioned and the great difference between them. One and seven thousand! Poor Elijah says, 'I am left alone'. God, by an oracle, says to him 'I have seven thousand who have not bowed the knee to Baal'. What a contrast! It gives force to Paul's conclusion in verse 5,'Even so then at this present time also there is a remnant according to the election of grace!'

Now in the time of Elijah it was only a remnant that God had reserved unto Himself. The bulk of the nation had gone into a state of apostasy, but God had reserved a 'remnant'. And what the Apostle is saying is, that God has still reserved a remnant. A superficial view of the first-century situation might result in the conclusion that the Christian church consists only of Gentiles. That is wrong, says Paul. I am in it. But not only I, there are others; as there was in the days of Elijah there is still a remnant according to the election of grace.

I think it is important that we should bear in mind that in Paul's day, there were more Jews who had become Christians than we sometimes realize. For instance, James and the elders in the Jerusalem church said to Paul that there were ' many thousands of Jews . . . which believe; and they are all zealous of the law' [*Acts* 21:20]. Notice that – 'how many thousands of Jews there are which believe'. So what the Apostle is saying here was strictly accurate. Therefore the idea that God has finished with his people is something that is entirely wrong. It is wrong from every standpoint, even on the factual level, but it is also a proof that 'there is a remnant according to the election of grace'.

Having said that the Apostle adds 'If by grace, then it is no more of works: otherwise grace is no more grace. But if it be of works, then is it no more grace: otherwise work is no more work'. Two points need to be mentioned here. The first relates to the second part of the statement which, as many commentators point out, is absent from the best and the oldest manuscripts. Now this does not matter, of course, at all. I take it you are all clear that this is not 'higher criticism'; it is textual criticism. There are many manuscripts, and some are more important than others. In the best manuscripts, the second half of the verse is not present. Even so, it makes no material difference because it is simply the exact reverse of what is said in the first half which really contains all the meaning. 'If it is by grace, then is it no more of works: otherwise grace is no more grace' inevitably carries the corollary that, 'If it be of works, then is it no more grace: otherwise work is no more work'. In other words, the main point is it has to be either 'grace' or 'works'. It cannot be the two at the same time. These are eternal antitheses and if it is one, it cannot be the other.

But secondly, some commentators wonder why Paul even said the first half of verse 6. This is very important. Some seem to feel that the Apostle repeats this because he was a preacher and a preacher likes to repeat his points. He had been making a great deal of the 'works – grace' antithesis from the very beginning of this Epistle (indeed, the whole Epistle is in a sense a treatise on salvation being by grace and not works) and so they think that, having said 'election of grace' Paul cannot resist saying 'If by grace, then it is no more of works'.

Now I am prepared to grant that there may be some force in that argument – just another final blow of the hammer on the nail to make sure that it is permanently fixed. But there is something still more important here. It is that Paul is intent on demonstrating the absolute certainty of all this; that what is happening in Israel is not out of hand as it were, but that God is in control. It is this great over-arching doctrine of the election of grace, found in such detail in chapter 9, that he is reminding us of once more.

Now let us come on to the lessons for ourselves, to the application of this teaching. First of all, let us draw an important theological or a doctrinal lesson. What is it? It is this doctrine of the remnant which existed in the days of Elijah. The argument really is that the remnant, in a sense, gives a kind of guarantee for the nation. The remnant is after all a part of the nation, and because a 'remnant' is saved you cannot say, and must not say, that the whole nation is rejected. The remnant is a part of the whole and if it is saved, that tells us something about the whole.

Of course, we must not press this too far as some do who say that the remnant constitutes the whole. We must not say that, because it is not what the Apostle teaches. He is saying it is a remnant 'of' the whole that has been saved, and that was the position also in the time of Elijah. But, this is the really important point, it is God who preserves the remnant. Now you see this is put to us in several words: 'reserved', 'election' and 'grace'. Now you could not have anything stronger than this. Paul could not have chosen three other words to bring out this point with greater force. The principle in operation is one of grace. Here again is, of course, something that is quite fundamental to the whole of the biblical teaching. You find it in Isaiah 1:9; 7:3 and 2 Timothy 2:17–19. Here is something that we ought to grapple with and we ought to understand. It is the great message of God's plan and saving purpose.

Were there no doctrine of the remnant the children of Israel would have vanished long ago, even before the time of our Lord. Were it not for God's purpose the Christian church would long since have disappeared altogether. There is only one reason why the church goes on, and that is because she is the church of God. If it were our church we would long since have ruined her. But it is not, you see. The remnant is the result of God's choice. The election! There is no other explanation. It does not depend upon man at all. It is not that a few have decided to hold on to the truth. No, they would not. Nobody would hold on to it if God did not hold on to them as he has shown in such detail in chapter 9. It is to me one of the most inexplicable things that any Christian person should ever object to the doctrine of the election of God. My dear friends, the Christian church would have perished centuries ago, probably in the first century without the election of God. It is He who preserves the Church, as He had preserved the children of Israel. The Word of God would have taken none effect were it not that God had kept it going, and He keeps it going by the principle of election, and election is entirely a matter of grace. Nobody is chosen because he is good or because he believes. If you take credit to yourself because you believe the gospel you are denying the essential teaching of the New Testament.

No! You do not believe because you are a better person than the unbeliever who is out in the world – not at all. We are all the same, 'we have all sinned and come short of the glory of God'. That any man is saved at all is solely due to the election of grace. And as he says, 'If it is of grace, well then it is no more of works'; it has got to be one or the other. 'Grace' means that we are saved in spite of ourselves; it is altogether of God's goodness; it means favour shown to people who do not deserve any favour at all. It is favour shown to criminals, to people who deserve to be destroyed everlastingly. Grace is entirely of God. It is not God's response to anything that we do, it is initiated by

God, it all comes from God. Grace! And the point that is emphasized here is, of course, that the remnant is preserved solely because it is the purpose of God. 'If he had not left unto us a very small remnant' – yes and it was He alone who could leave it. All would have gone but for Him.

Let me give you the classical example of this if you like; what happened in Sodom and Gomorrah to which Isaiah refers. Lot and his family had gone there, as you know; they should never have gone there. That is where Lot made his great mistake. He chose the cities of the plain, he wanted to make money and Abram is left farming a few sheep on top of the mountains. That was the initial mistake of Lot. And then things went from bad to worse, and God decides to destroy them because of the terrible life that was lived in those cities of the plain. He sent his angels, you remember, to warn Lot and his family and in Genesis 19 verse 16 there is a great statement which I sometimes think is one of the most dramatic statements in the whole of Scripture. Here is Lot being urged to leave by the messenger of God and the statement is, 'While he lingered . . . !' If it had been left to Lot he would have been destroyed and his family with the cities of the plain, with Sodom and Gomorrah, but the angel of God put his hand upon him and he led him out. While he was lingering, he was led out and so was saved by the action of God. The warning was not enough, he had to be pressed out, as it were, and so the remnant was saved out of Sodom and Gomorrah. It was so in the time of Elijah and of Isaiah, and the Apostle is saying that it is still the same. It is God who keeps it going, it is the election of grace! And if it is grace, it is no more of works: otherwise grace is no more grace. It is altogether of God.

Let us now draw a few practical conclusions and deductions for ourselves out of all this, and I thank God for it. This passage makes me thank God for the Scriptures more than ever. How wonderful they are! Not only the teaching but even the history. I like the history in the Scriptures; I like these examples and illustrations of the men of God and God's prophets and chosen servants. What a comfort it is to read about a man like Elijah, that he could ever be found sitting under a juniper tree. What a comfort to us lesser mortals who spend a lot of our time in such places. Look at this mighty man of God, this blazing prophet, the first of the great prophets of God in Israel. Elijah! – the Mount Carmel man, the man of courage, the rock-like character who can defy the eight hundred and fifty. I nearly said thank God that, in this next chapter, he is to be found sitting under the tree feeling very sorry for himself and grumbling and complaining. Oh the comfort and consolation of the Scriptures!

But let me draw some detailed lessons. Here is the first lesson that I draw from all this. We must learn to face every situation in life in a scriptural manner. What I mean by that is this: whatever happens to us let us not merely look at the thing itself, let us not merely apply our own reason to it; let us think of it scripturally. Say to yourself, 'Has anything like this happened to anyone in the Scriptures? Can I find an analogy there?' That is what Paul was doing. He says, 'Wot ye not what the Scripture saith of Elias?' He says, Look here, you should not be in trouble about what is happening now, do you not see there is a perfect illustration of it there.

Another practical very personal lesson that I draw is this: Let us be careful that we never become involved too personally in these matters. What do I mean? Well, I do not mean that you should take a detached, theoretical attitude to the things of God and the life and work of the church, I do not mean that at all. That is all wrong, of course; in that sense you must be personally involved. But what I do mean is this: never let the devil persuade you that the church is yours. Do not get involved personally like that. That was the trouble with Elijah, was it not? You see, Israel was his: 'O Lord, I am left alone, they are trying to kill me', as if God were not there and as if Israel did not belong to God. It was his concern, it was his institution as it were, it was his nation. He had become involved personally in the wrong sense, and so he becomes depressed.

In other words, there is nothing more important for us to remember especially at a time like this than just this simple fact: 'The battle is not yours, but God's'. This is one of the great troubles. People think of it in terms of themselves, as if the church were their possession, and they become involved personally, they become hurt and they become offended, and so on. We must not become involved in that wrong sense. It is not ours, it belongs to the everlasting and eternal God.

Then, let us note a warning here which is much-needed at the present time. It is, 'Do not be carried away by numbers. Do not follow the crowd'. In the time of Elijah, almost everybody was on the wrong side; the king and queen and all the prophets. (No one knew about the seven thousand). But Elijah did not say, Well, I must be wrong; I cannot alone be right and all those men wrong. That is what people are trying to get us to think today about the Ecumenical Movement! 'Who are you to stand against this?' I say, thank God for this story of Elijah! It does not matter if the whole world says the other thing; do not follow the crowd, do not assume that the numbers are always right. Remember:

*Truth for ever on the scaffold,*
*Wrong for ever on the throne*

is as true today as it has ever been. You do not judge these matters by numbers; it is truth that matters. I stand out with a man like Elijah, Martin Luther standing alone – standing against fifteen centuries of Roman Catholic tradition and teaching, all the great doctors of the church arrayed against him. It does not matter, he knows what is true so he says, 'Here I stand, I can do no other; so help me God'. Very well, I think we need to learn this great lesson which comes out of this doctrine of the remnant at the present time. The whole atmosphere is against this at the present time. They do not like remnants, they are thinking in terms of amalgamations, numbers, World Church and so on, and who are you to stand out? So you will get vilified and criticized. Don't worry, my friends; don't think in terms of numbers. It is truth that matters – not numbers, not popularity, not any one of these things. There is a great warning to us here.

And then there is a rebuke to us here, and it is, of course, that we must not become pessimistic, we must never feel a sense of despair: still less must we become cynical. Oh, it is so easy to say that, but it is is very difficult to put it into practice. We are living in days of great discouragement and especially for evangelical people who value truth. The whole climate of opinion today is to the effect, 'Oh, what does it matter in the end, it is a man's general spirit that matters; what does it matter what you know or whether you believe or not?' The whole climate is against us and it becomes easy to be pessimistic, even to despair. You see the whole cause going and you say, 'I alone am left' and you sit down under your juniper tree or you run away and you say, 'Well, let them get on with it. I have done my best. I can do no more. If that is what they want let them have it, they will soon discover, they will find it eventually, I cannot do any more about them'. Terrible temptations have come sometimes to those who suffer discouragement – when you have given yourself, your soul as it were, and you see the same masses of people listening to the false prophets.

The temptation is to turn away, to run away like Elijah did, and to say, 'Let them stew in their own juice'. And you sit under your juniper tree and you feel very sorry for yourself. But, my friends, this incident rebukes us. When you sit there God will come to you, as He came to Elijah, and what He will say to you is this: 'What are you doing here?' This is not your place, this is no place for the Elijah of Mount Carmel. Elijahs do not run away from women – even if they are queens. 'What are you doing here, Elijah? Get back to your place, get back to your work'. There is a rebuke here. And, my friends, you and I need this in these difficult, trying, testing times through which we are passing.

But let me end with the comfort; the comfort of this great incident. And the comfort of the great incident is this, God's purposes are sure. And that is why the Apostle, you see, brings in this 'remnant according to the election of grace. And if by grace, then it is no more of works'. You see this is the comfort and that is why he makes the point. That is why the expositors should not say, 'Why does he bring this in here?' The answer is this: He said, Look here, thank God this matter does not depend on us at all: 'not of works'! It is all of the grace of God. God will keep His church going. The remnant may become a very small one, it does not matter; God's purposes are sure, nothing can stop them, nothing can frustrate them. It does not matter how many wander away and fall by the wayside, God will always have His remnant, God will always keep His work going. We do not know how but He always will. That is the great doctrine. And He always has, of course. History is full of proofs of this. In the worst period of the darkness of Roman Catholicism you had people like the Waldensians in Northern Italy, and the 'Brethren of the Common Life' in Moravia and Bohemia and in parts of Holland and in places like that. God has always had His remnant, always had a people and He has kept it going; and He will keep it going. That is why we need not finally be troubled nor worried about all that is happening in the modern world. All this notion of a great World Church which will not leave very much room for the evangelical faith; my friends, you need not worry. You need not worry about God's cause. He will keep it going!

What is important for us is not to be worried about God's cause, but to make sure that we belong to His people, so that when the day comes we shall not have that awful feeling of shame that we just 'followed the crowd', took the easy way. We were ready to belong to a despised remnant, however small; we were interested in nothing but the truth.

But let us remember this: that does not mean that you just sit down in inactivity and say, 'We are the remnant', and you do not care what happens to the rest. Not at all! That was not the Apostle's attitude, as we shall see as we go on through this chapter. He says, he was doing his best to 'provoke the majority to jealousy'. He did not say, we are all right, come into my little circle, we are the orthodox, let the world go to hell. Not at all! He was concerned about them. We have seen that at the beginning of chapter 9 and at the beginning of chapter 10. He will repeat it. He is doing his best to create a 'jealousy' within them that they may come back and believe the gospel.

So you see, while you do take comfort from the doctrine of the remnant you must not take the wrong comfort, just saying, 'We are right! We alone are right and we can do nothing'. Not at all; it is our business to open the eyes of others, it is our business to be concerned about them. The doctrine of the remnant according to the election of grace should preserve us from pessimism and despair, but it should never lead to inactivity. Being confident and sure of God's plan and purpose we should exert our every effort to make the truth known and to persuade others to believe it and to accept it.

# *Four*

*

*What then? Israel hath not obtained that which he seeketh for; but the election hath obtained it, and the rest were blinded (according as it is written, God hath given them the spirit of slumber, eyes that they should not see, and ears that they should not hear;) unto this day. And David saith, Let their table be made a snare, and a trap, and a stumblingblock, and a recompence unto them: let their eyes be darkened, that they may not see, and bow down their back alway.* Romans 11:7–10

In these solemn verses the Apostle sums up what he has previously said in this chapter. We certainly are entering into the realm of ultimate mystery. Let us therefore 'take off our shoes from off our feet, for the place on which we stand is holy ground'. This is a passage that must be approached with reverence, with humility and with care. It does indeed hold us face to face with some of the most mysterious elements of biblical teaching, and of Christian teaching in particular. Let us bear in mind what the Apostle says at the end of the chapter. It is very applicable at this point – 'O the depth of the riches both of the wisdom and knowledge of God!'

Now that is the spirit and the way in which we must approach this. We are dealing with the mind and the ways of God and we must therefore anticipate that we shall not be able to understand it fully. But a man who rebels because he does not understand the mind of God is one who puts himself immediately into the very category, I say, of these Jews whose tragic case and condition we are considering. Let us be careful. We are all too ready to speak our opinions and when we do not understand the mind of God we say that something seems to us to be wrong. That was the whole trouble with the Jews. God forbid, therefore, that we should be guilty of the terrible thing of which they were.

First of all, let us get clearly in our minds the basic point which the

Apostle is making. He starts off by saying, 'What then?' – which means, 'What therefore?' In other words, 'What is the position in the light of what I have been saying?' His answer is that 'Israel' – that is to say the nation as a whole, 'Israel hath not obtained that which he seeketh for'.

The word 'seeketh' is most important because it means 'earnest seeking'. The Apostle fixed a preposition to the word that he used in order to give it emphasis. It was not a casual 'looking at' but 'an earnest and persistent seeking'. In addition, he uses the present tense to indicate that Israel was still doing so. What was being sought? Well, there is no question but that it must be 'righteousness'. They wanted to be right with God.

But he says that though they were 'earnestly and persistently seeking that, they had not got it, whereas, on the other hand 'the election hath obtained it'. Now here is a most interesting expression. He does not say 'the elect' have obtained it but 'the election'. Why? If he had said 'the elect hath obtained it' we would tend to think of the elect as individuals, and we might fall into the error of thinking that it was as the result of what they were in themselves and what they had done. But in order to obviate any such possibility the Apostle refers to them as 'the election'. This brings out the great point that it was because of what someone else had done that they had obtained it. This term emphasizes the one who 'elects' rather than any choice made by the people and so all the glory is to be given to God alone. The term also describes people corporately rather than individually and that is relevant to the whole argument.

The statement goes on to say 'and the rest' which means all in the nation apart from those chosen, 'were blinded'. We must look at this word 'blinded' because all the commentators point out that it really should be translated 'hardened'. While that is so, the Authorized Version translators had a good reason for translating it as 'blinded' as they did in 2 Corinthians 3:14, a parallel chapter, where we read, 'But their minds were blinded'. I think we can justify this rendering in Romans by pointing out that in the quotation which the Apostle immediately adduces there is a reference to blindness: 'According as it is written, God hath given them the spirit of slumber, eyes that they should not see'. It means, you see, that a callous mask has come over the eyes, and prevented their seeing. Why should there not be an opacity in the eye as well as hardening of the heart? There is, and he goes on from his quotations to elaborate that point. But the thing for us to notice is that this verb is in the passive voice, they 'were blinded'. We will have to come back to this.

In verses 8 to 10 the Apostle substantiates his basic statement and he does a most extraordinary thing. In the eighth verse he takes a number of quotations from the Scripture and out of them he produces one fresh kind of statement. Here again is another instance of the divine inspiration of the Apostle. The same Spirit who had indited the original statements is here governing this great Apostle, and He is bringing the same meaning out of the three in the form of this one composite declaration. The verses quoted are Isaiah 29:10; Deuteronomy 29:4 and Isaiah 6:9.

Now what does Paul say? He says that 'God hath given them the spirit of slumber'. This means that God had produced a kind of torpor or numbness in them. The meaning of the word he uses refers to an inability to use one's faculties. If you are under the influence of a drug, you will be dimly aware of things happening around you, but you will not be able to understand them. You are not completely unconscious but you are not fully conscious either and it is the highest faculties of seeing, hearing, and understanding that are affected.

What the Apostle is saying is this: Israel has been in this condition before. We have these examples of it even in the time of Moses and the time of Isaiah, and it was still happening in Paul's day. He says there was nothing new about this; and unfortunately, it is still happening. It is the explanation of the fact that the majority of the nation of Israel, all indeed apart from the remnant according to the election of grace, are refusing the gospel and are outside the Christian church.

He quotes from Psalm 69 verses 22 and 23 in verses 9 and 10 which read, 'And David saith, Let their table be made a snare, and a trap, and a stumblingblock, and a recompence unto them: Let their eyes be darkened, that they may not see, and bow down their back alway'. Now here again is a most important, and, at the same time, difficult statement. David refers to their table which of course means the things that are on it and not the table as such. They have a table laden with food and drink, everything that could be desired. David says let all that become a trap to them, and here, of course, he uses illustrations that an agricultural community would understand so well, the gins and the traps used for catching birds and other animals. These traps would be set and the poor animal would go along unsuspectingly, and suddenly the trap or the snare would catch them. There is no point in going into the distinction between the two words. They are used in order to bring out the imagery in its fulness.

But the significant word is 'recompence' rather than ' trap' or 'snare', or even 'stumblingblock'. A recompence means that what is happening is by way of a reward for evil done. In other words, what is in view is that they might reap the consequences of their own recalcitrance and obduracy towards the truth of God. What David was praying was that the very benefits that they were receiving from God might become a punishment and a hindrance to them.

Now what does he mean by the table? Well I think this is most important for us. He is saying something like this. Confronted with this kind of condition, David asked God to turn His blessings into a curse. The table stands for the material benefits and spiritual blessing.

There are terrible instances of this very thing in the Old Testament. One reads like this: 'And he gave them their request; but sent leanness into their soul'. That is found in Psalm 106:15, where the psalmist was reviewing the long story of the children of Israel. 'They believed his words; they sang his praise. They soon forgot his works; they waited not for his counsel: But lusted exceedingly in the wilderness, and tempted God in the desert'. This was the cry for meat, you remember, and the quails were sent to them and so on, but this is how he sums it up – 'He gave them their request; but sent leanness into their soul'. He gave them prosperity. Their bodies became fat but their souls became lean.

Now that is a part of this statement before us, 'Let their table become a snare and a trap, and a stumblingblock, and a recompence unto them'. Now I do not think that we can confine this only to the material benefits associated with God's taking of them into the land of Canaan, 'a land flowing with milk and honey'. Their table was loaded. But it became a curse to them.

But God had given them spiritual blessings. As Paul has said, they were given God's 'lively oracles'. Indeed, he had given them 'the adoption, and the glory, and the covenants, and the giving of the law, and the service of God, and the promises' [*Rom.* 9:4–5]. All that is included too. And David's petition is, that these things which they have abused and misused 'may become a snare and a trap' and a kind of evil recompence to them. And this is the very thing, of course, that was true of the children of Israel. It had been partially fulfilled in the past but the Apostle's point is that the real fulfilment was in his day.

He then adds to that this picture: 'Let their eyes be darkened that they may not see' – this is spiritual blindness; and then, 'bow down their back alway' – this is the picture of an old man, bent, having lost his strength.

Now then what does this mean? The principle that he is putting before us is this; if we do not obey God, God's very blessings will become a curse to us. Is not that a part of the explanation of the state of the church and of this country at the present time? The Christian church became big, important and wealthy in the nineteenth century and was no longer a despised little sect. I believe that became a curse to her and that we are inheriting something of the consequences of that. The terrible thing is this – that even God's blessings, if you look at them in the wrong way and abuse them, they will become a curse to you. That is why tradition is something about which we always ought to be most careful. You look at the long history of the church and you will generally find this, that places which at one time enjoyed unusual blessings are today some of the most barren places in the universe.

Now I happen to know particular instances of that. I was brought up in a place where a mighty man of God was preaching two hundred years ago, the great Daniel Rowland of whom Bishop Ryle said that he was the greatest preacher since the Apostles. Daniel Rowland preached there for fifty years and that place used to experience heaven upon earth, Sunday by Sunday and on other occasions. Now I find it very difficult to think of any place known to me at the present time that is so spiritually dead, and I have no doubt that the explanation is that they tended to live on the tradition. I could name you other places. This has happened to many individual chapels. They have been blessed, God has loaded the table, but the very blessing has become a curse to them, even though the blessing has been the Word of God – the law, the gospel, God's own Word!

So you see it includes all that. The 'table' may mean not only material gifts and blessings from God, it may mean God's own Word, God's richest blessing – that can become a curse to the people. These were the very people to whom the 'oracles of God' were given, yet they were much more blind than the Gentiles who did not have them and were without any knowledge or instruction whatsoever. This is the terrible thing that is being taught here! And I think this is a word to modern evangelical people. God forbid, my friends, that when God chooses to revive his work again evangelicals should be the people who should be by-passed because they are living on a tradition rather than on a living experience of God; because they have become proud of their knowledge of the Scriptures but have lost the Spirit; because they have enjoyed a kind of affluence, material as well as spiritual.

This is an appalling thought! Is the decline, the declension in this country today not due largely to these things? Our very affluence may be the greatest curse. The danger with an affluent society always is to be content and to slacken, and the poorer nations are working hard. While we become slack they are putting energy into it and so our very blessing becomes a curse to us. I think this has been seen since the last war. The recovery of Germany has been a phenomenon, an amazing phenomenon. She is one of the leading industrial nations. Why? Well, because she was so down that she had to work, whereas the other nations, the more prosperous nations, tend to rest upon their oars. That is the principle that is involved here. And it can happen to a church, it can happen to a Christian individual; and it can apply, I say, not only to material benefits and blessings and affluence, it can even apply to an understanding of the Word and the possession of the truth. The moment we begin to rest upon it and to take pride in it and to think that 'we are the people', we have fallen into this very error that brought down this terrible calamity upon the children of Israel.

Now it is important that we should grasp this because our Lord himself said this very thing in his teaching. It is seen in the Parable of the Vineyard in Matthew 21:42 and in the judgment announced in Matthew 23:24. Stephen did the same when he stood before the Sanhedrin. He took them through their whole history and said: 'Ye stiffnecked and uncircumcised in heart and ears, ye do always resist the Holy Ghost: as your fathers did, so do ye. Which of the prophets have not your fathers persecuted? and they have slain them which shewed before of the coming of the Just One; of whom ye have been now the betrayers and murderers: Who have received the law by the disposition of angels, and have not kept it' [*Acts* 7:51]. And that is the very thing that the Apostle is saying here. This had been the tendency of this people from the very beginning, but now the final calamity has come upon them. All that had been predicted and prophesied has come to a head. They were but suggestions of what was coming. It has now come.

And so, you see, this statement helps us to understand the whole of the teaching of the Old Testament. The whole of the Old Testament is, in a sense, a prophecy of this climactic point when the Son of God came and the chosen people did not recognize Him but crucified Him, preferring Barabbas to Him. So, the judgment of God comes down upon them. And the terrifying thing about that is that it all happened to them because they were the people of God, because they did have the promises when nobody else had them, because they alone had the 'oracles', the Word of God, and all the ceremonial and the temple and all that it taught and suggested. These very blessings that God had given to them were the things that had blinded them to the truth as it is in Christ Jesus.

What are the lessons taught here? I suggest there are four of them. First: the great lesson about the wrong way of seeking God's blessing; secondly: judicial blindness; thirdly and fourthly, how to understand the Imprecatory and the Messianic psalms respectively.

First of all: Why is it true to say that 'Israel hath not obtained that which he seeketh for?' The whole answer is because they were not seeking it in the right way. It is because of their complete misunderstanding of the law and the Prophets and especially of the Messiah in His character and His work when He did come. The Apostle has really said this at the end of chapter 9 where we read: 'What shall we say then? That the Gentiles, which followed not after righteousness, have attained to righteousness, even the righteousness which is of faith. But Israel, which followed after the law of righteousness, hath not attained to the law of righteousness. Wherefore? Because they sought it not by faith, but as it were by the works of the law. For they stumbled at that stumblingblock: As it is written, Behold, I lay in Sion a stumblingstone and a rock of offence: and whosoever believeth on him shall not be ashamed'. Their whole tragedy was due to the fact that they did not seek the thing they were seeking in the right way. What they were seeking was right; but here is the terrible lesson, you can be seeking the right thing and yet miss it entirely because you are not seeking it in the right way.

Are we all clear about this? This is where the danger of religion comes in. There are very genuine people who say, 'I want to know God, I want to be blessed of God' – but they do not know Him, and if they remain as they are they never will. But they are zealous, they are keen, they read their Bibles, they pray, they do good works, they will do almost anything, some of them make great sacrifices; but they do not know Him!

Now let us not forget what the Apostle has said about these people. 'Brethren, my heart's desire and prayer to God for Israel is, that they might be saved. I bear them record that they have a zeal for God'. They did have it. They really were seeking intensely, persistently, energetically. The Pharisee was not a man who merely said 'I fast twice in the week and give a tenth of my goods to the poor'. He did it. It was true. That was the whole tragedy of these people. It is the tragedy of all people who trust to their own religion, or their own seeking of God, or their own good works. There is only one way in which this blessing can be obtained. It is entirely by faith. The tragedy of Israel is that she did not seek it 'by faith'. She thought she could keep the law; she felt that she could obtain righteousness and get the blessing of God by the possession of the temple and attendance there and the possession of the law and her works. That is why Stephen had to say to them, Do not tell me, 'We have got the Temple'; God does not dwell in temples made with hands. They thought every time they went into the temple that they were getting a blessing. They did not realize that you could have a heart of stone even in the temple, and the moment you look at the temple in this wrong way. And people are still doing it in their religious life, in their great cathedrals which they think is the worship of God. 'This mountain', as the woman of Samaria said, which was Gerizim; the Jews said 'No, in Jerusalem'. Our Lord says, Neither in this mountain nor in Jerusalem. The time cometh, and now is, when the Father shall seek the true worshippers. God is a Spirit: and they that worship him must worship him in spirit and in truth.

If you are relying upon the fact that you have a Bible or that you are a church member or that you go to a particular building or that you are doing certain good works, you are like the Jews. You are outside, you are blind and you have not got it, and you will never get it along that line. There is only one way of salvation – this is the message of the whole Bible – it is Jesus Christ and Him crucified. It is simple faith in Him, nothing else. If you bring anything else in you have not got it, you will never obtain it. You may get great personal satisfaction, as the Jews had, but the test is this: How do you react to the preaching of justification by faith only? Are you annoyed or irritated by it? Do you feel it is unfair to you? If so, you are like the Jews. That is the tragedy of this people.

I believe we are witnessing something like this at the present time. It is a terrible thing to say, but is it not true that the greatest hindrance to true knowledge of God in Christ and salvation in this country today is the so-called Christian church? It is the greatest hindrance to the people because she is representing a false Christianity. Those who still believe in justification by faith are a very small remnant. Thank God there are still 'seven thousand who have not bowed the knee'. But we are a remnant and there is no question but that the official church, 'Christendom', as it is called, is today the greatest hindrance to the true faith not only in this country but in the whole world. It is a terrifying thing, but it has been true in the past and I believe it is true today.

But let us also be careful if we believe that we belong to the remnant not to boast. We all need to examine ourselves and to be careful. There is only one safe position and it is when we can say honestly, 'I am nothing. Thou art all'. Here is this terrible lesson of this nation of Israel. She has not obtained it. Why? Well, 'because she had a zeal of God, but not according to knowledge'. And the knowledge is, Jesus Christ, and Him crucified. May God have mercy upon us all and give us understanding in these great mysterious matters.

# *Five*

*

*What then? Israel hath not obtained that which he seeketh for; but the election hath obtained it, and the rest were blinded (according as it is written, God hath given them the spirit of slumber, eyes that they should not see, and ears that they should not hear;) unto this day. And David saith, Let their table be made a snare, and a trap, and a stumblingblock, and a recompence unto them: let their eyes be darkened, that they may not see, and bow down their back alway.* Romans 11:7–10

These verses have profound lessons for us which we have begun looking at. The first of these is the terrible danger of wrong seeking. The whole tragedy of the Jews is that, not seeking the blessing of God in the right way, they did not obtain it. We saw that the big lesson this holds for the Christian is, whether at the beginning or even at the end of his life, he is nothing but a sinner, saved only by the grace of God in Jesus Christ. The moment we begin to rely on anything in ourselves, our upbringing, our background, or anything, we have already departed from the true position.

We move on now to our second lesson which is that of 'judicial blindness'. It is referred to at the end of the seventh verse where we read 'the rest were blinded' and it is elaborated in the remaining verses of this portion. The phrases that we must pick out in connection with this are 'the rest were blinded' and 'God hath given them the spirit of slumber'.

Now this is, of course, where we come to the most difficult doctrine which we must approach with fear and trembling because we would never deal with it, were it not that it is in the Scriptures. Let us be careful that we do not allow any human wisdom and understanding to intrude itself in any shape or form. There are those who dislike this doctrine and who reject it and there are others who react against them and are almost proud of it. But both are equally wrong. This is a doctrine that ought to fill us all with a sense of awe and of astonishment. Any partisan spirit that comes in on any side with regard to it makes it clear that people do not realize that they are dealing with the inscrutable mind and purpose of the everlasting God.

What then is this doctrine? It has already been stated in the fifteenth verse of chapter nine where we read that God will 'have mercy on whom he will have mercy and whom he will he hardeneth'. To the objection which is raised that if he hardens, he cannot find fault, there is only one answer and it is 'Nay but, O man, who art thou that repliest against God?'. Do not argue with God! Remember, God is in heaven and you are on earth – and soon you will not be on earth. O! the daring of man in replying against God, venturing to put up his criticisms! 'Shall the thing formed say to him that formed it, why hast thou made me thus? Hath not the potter power over the clay, of the same lump to make one vessel unto honour, and another unto dishonour?' Now that is really the same argument but the Apostle comes back to it, and he does so because he wants to help these people.

But this is something that is taught not only by the Apostle. It is a terrible thing to have to say this but we are surrounded by people in the Christian church who are never tired of contrasting the teaching of Paul with that of our Lord. This has been so popular now for over a hundred years. It is a major result of the so-called 'higher critical' treatment of the Scriptures. People say that they like the teaching of Jesus, but this man, Paul, was an ex-Pharisee who had not shed his legalistic notions and ideas. The tragedy is, they say, that he came along and foisted them all on to this gloriously simple gospel of Jesus Christ.

This is so pathetic because I remind you that our blessed Lord and Saviour Himself taught exactly the same thing. In Matthew 13: 13 we read: 'Therefore speak I to them in parables: because seeing they see not; and hearing they hear not, neither do they understand. And in them is fulfilled the prophecy of Esaias, which saith, By hearing ye shall hear, and shall not understand; and seeing ye shall see, and shall not perceive: for this people's heart is waxed gross, and their ears are dull of hearing, and their eyes they have closed: lest at any time they should see with their eyes, and hear with their ears, and should understand with their heart, and should be converted, and I should heal them'. That is exactly the same quotation as the Apostle Paul gives us here.

But is there not a difference between the two quotations? As our Lord puts it, it is this: 'This people's heart is waxed gross, and their ears are dull of hearing, and their eyes they have closed'. But the Apostle says, 'God hath given them a spirit of torpor' and they have been blinded. Is that not an important difference between our Lord and the Apostle Paul?'

How then do we reconcile these different statements? It is quite simple. There are two elements in all this – there is the human and the divine. The statement in Romans, also found in Acts 28:25 and John 12:37, stresses the divine side whereas it is the human side that is to the fore in Matthew.

Taking what Paul wrote, the important question is 'How does God do this?' The first way in which he does it, quite clearly, is that he ceases to strive with the rebellious. You remember that God said before the flood, 'My Spirit shall not always strive with man' [*Gen.* 6:3]. Clearly, there is a point at which God through the Holy Spirit ceases to strive with people who resist His promptings. Another way in which this happens is described in the first chapter of this very Epistle from verse 19 to the end. There is that thrice-repeated statement to the effect that God has 'given them up', or handed them over to the power of the sin which they will not renounce.

The teaching in other words is this: when man fell and became the slave of Satan and of sin, God did not abandon man. The devil became the god of this world, but that does not mean that God 'abandoned' the world. God introduced what has been called the principle of 'common grace'. This restraining influence results in the effects of sin being kept within bounds. That is why Scripture makes clear that it is God who has ordained the family, law and order in magistrates and government, art, music and culture in civilization and so on. All this has been introduced by God and its main object is to restrict the effects of evil.

Now the world does not know anything about this, but the Bible teaches it very clearly. In other words, if God had not done this, if man had been allowed just to live as he wanted without God's imposing any restraint upon him, he would, beyond any question, have destroyed himself, the whole of humanity and the world. There have been some terrifying epochs and periods in the history of the world. But God has always kept a restraint. It is a wonderful thing to trace this in the Bible especially in the Old Testament, how God allows dictators to arise but only to go so far, never beyond a certain point. God always intervened and stopped them and the biblical teaching is that He has continued to do this.

But it is equally plain that, at certain times, God has, up to a point, withdrawn such restraints in order to teach people a lesson. Whenever He did it with the children of Israel it was always to teach them that He had protected them and shielded them, and given them rulers, but when they kept on rebelling and refusing, God allowed an enemy to conquer them, and they were carried away to captivity. They were in Egypt, then later they were in Babylon, and there they suffered terrible things simply because God had withdrawn His protection.

But there is even a step beyond the withdrawing of restraint and it is the process of actual hardening. This is the sort of thing that the Apostle, you see, was teaching in chapter 9 that God did with Pharaoh. When Pharaoh persisted in his refusal, God did to him what is called 'hardening'. He, as it were, makes Pharaoh worse than he is and Pharaoh becomes incapable of doing anything other than what he did. As the Apostle argues, God raised Pharaoh up in order that a great lesson might be given to the whole world through him.

So there are methods and ways in which God brings about this condition of 'judicial blindness', which means that people in this condition are totally incapable of believing. That is what Paul is really saying. 'What then?' – what is the position? Well it is this: 'Israel hath not obtained that which he seeketh for; the election hath obtained it, but the rest were blinded' because 'God hath given them a spirit of slumber. God hath given them eyes that they should not see, and ears that they should not hear'.

Now our Lord, you see, says exactly the same thing about the Pharisees. In Matthew 13 He says that He spoke in parables in order that those people might not understand what He was saying. It was not given to them to understand as it was to others. They did not know the meaning because they were not meant to know it. This is a judicial blindness that was imposed upon them.

Now is this something which is only punitive? Is this an action which God takes with certain people when He sees obduracy and obstinacy? Is it only a form of punishment? Well the answer to that. I feel, is that it is mainly punitive. In other words, it works like this: that light rejected in and of itself produces hardening and hardness. This is the great characteristic of sin. Sin always tends to produce hardening. You may hesitate a long time before you do a thing for the first time. Once you have done it, it is not so difficult the second time. That is a part of the process of hardening looked at from the reverse side. And so it is with resistance to the work of the Spirit, and to the light and the knowledge of the truth as it is in Christ Jesus.

Now, if you like, in terms of the heart, the same thing happens. If we do not allow ourselves to respond to, and to yield to the truth, the more we hear the truth the harder we shall become. 'Take heed', says the author of the Epistle to the Hebrews, 'lest there be in any of you an evil heart of unbelief, in departing from the living God. But exhort one another daily, while it is called Today; lest any of you be hardened through the deceitfulness of sin' [*Heb.* 3:12–13]. This is seen so perfectly in the story of Pharaoh, how he becomes harder and harder, more and more furious; and he reaches a stage in which he is virtually mad in his unbelief and in his resistance to God.

Now although it is the case that this is something which is chiefly punitive, there is a suggestion in the Scriptures that there is something more than that. At this point I freely confess that we are in a realm where we have to walk unusually carefully. But 1 Peter 2:7 makes this remarkable statement: 'Unto you therefore which believe he is precious: but unto them which be disobedient, the stone which the builders disallowed, the same is made the head of the corner. And a stone of stumbling, and a rock of offence, even to them which stumble at the word, being disobedient: whereunto also they were appointed'. Those last words – 'whereunto also they were appointed'. What were they appointed unto? Well, they were appointed to this – that the Lord Jesus Christ should be to them 'a stone of stumbling, and a rock of offence, even to them which stumble at the word, being disobedient'. We must bear that in mind.

Furthermore there are these words in the fourth verse of the Epistle of Jude. 'For there are certain men crept in unawares, who were before of old ordained to this condemnation, ungodly men, turning the grace of God into lasciviousness, and denying the only Lord God, and our Lord Jesus Christ'. Now this is not as difficult a verse as the last one, because this should be translated: 'who were before of old written down unto this condemnation'. 'Written down' is the translation of the word used by the Apostle. It points to the fact that what they were doing was already known and so it was recorded. But it really does not explain the difficulty. How can a thing be written down unless it is not only known but actually certain?

Putting it at its very least and lowest those two statements suggest this extraordinary thing: that there were people who were appointed to stumble at the Word, being disobedient. What do we say about that? We begin by affirming that God did not create sin. It is impossible that He should so do. 'God is Light, and in him is no darkness at all'. God has never made anybody sin. That is impossible; it is inconceivable. As James reminds us, 'God neither tempteth, nor can be tempted'; this is a fundamental postulate.

What then is the resolution of the problem? Surely this: that it is God, as we have seen so abundantly in these three chapters of the Epistle to the Romans, and God alone, who saves anybody. Nobody is saved apart from the election of God. If you take credit for the fact that you are a believer in Jesus Christ I almost suggest to you that you are not saved. I must not say that; you can be a very ignorant Christian, and a very unscriptural Christian. But the teaching of the Scripture is that no man can contribute anything to his own salvation, it is all according to the election of God.

So that we see this: as God has elected some to salvation, He has not elected others to salvation. And that seems to me to be the explanation of these statements. They are 'ordained unto this condemnation' only in the sense that they have not been elected to salvation. So you see it works like this: Pharaoh is not among the elect. He therefore refuses and disobeys and he rejects. But remember that it is possible for a man to do that in a very quiet and almost inoffensive manner, looked at from the human standpoint.

Now God knows that about Pharaoh, so He raises up Pharaoh as an illustration and example of the horrible nature of unbelief, increasing by His action the natural unbelief and disobedience of Pharaoh. God does not create it, He simply draws it out and makes it more manifest by a violent resistance on Pharaoh's part – and, says Paul, on the part of the children of Israel. God gave them the spirit of slumber. They had been recalcitrant; they had been murdering God's prophets as He sent them to them one after another, and even when He sends His Son they do the same thing. But God is there showing this terrible thing called unbelief. He has given them the spirit of slumber. In other words you may say that they were 'appointed unto this'. The sin is already there; the sin is produced entirely by man. All that God does in this process of judicial blindness is that He exaggerates it, as it were. It is like putting a microscope upon him so that the thing that does not appear plain and clear to mankind normally is magnified so that everybody can see it.

In other words we all look at Pharaoh and we say, 'What a terrible attitude towards God'. We look at the children of Israel at the time of our Lord and at the time of Paul even until this day, and we say, 'What a terrible thing unbelief is. It can lead this very nation of God, the chosen people, not to recognize their own Messiah and even to cry "Away with him; crucify him"'. There it is, magnified and exaggerated. God has produced that in order to make this condition of sin and unbelief clear and obvious to the whole human race. That is what the Apostle is really saying. That seems to me to be the only explanation of these passages quoted from the Old Testament, and also the use of them made by our Lord Himself, Luke in his book of Acts, Jude in his epistle and the apostles Paul and Peter. God is always righteous. He has not made these people sinners but He has chosen not to save them and at the same time He has demonstrated in them and through them the enormity of sin, its terrible character, and how it renders a man finally incapable of worshipping God, of serving Him and receiving His blessings.

Now then what has all this to do with us today? Well, there are just a few practical lessons that I want to put to you at this point. The first lesson that I would draw is this: Is not something like this happening today? Is not this the real explanation of the state of affairs today? Look at the attitude of this country, generally speaking, to the gospel. Why is it so unusual to attend church? What is the matter with the bulk of our fellow-countrymen and women? Why should we be such a small remnant? Only ten per cent of people claim to be Christian in this country, and only half of those take it at all seriously and attend a place of worship regularly – five per cent of the nation. Why do ninety-five per cent not only not believe the gospel but ridicule it?

We are all familiar with all this but how can it be explained? We have open Bibles, endless translations, all sorts of instruction, and evangelistic efforts. But nothing seems to make any difference at all. How do you explain it?

Well I think part of the explanation, you know, is the very thing that the Apostle is telling us here, and even adding the thing that he goes on to quote from David. 'David saith, Let their table be made a snare'. I think the religious situation in this country is mainly to be explained by 'affluence', the 'table'. 'Never had it so good', you see, the table is full. Plenty of money in our pockets, plenty of drink, motor-cars . . . 'Let their table be made a snare'. And off they go in their cars on a Sunday to the seaside or the mountain-top or to play golf or to do this or that – 'Let the table be made . . .' The table is being made a snare. The very blessing of God is becoming a curse. Poverty is a terrible thing but, you know, affluence is a more dangerous thing in a spiritual sense. The table has so often been the snare, and I believe that we are seeing something of this at this present time; that this country and other countries are under this process of judicial blindness. You and I, we see the gospel so clearly. Do you not say sometimes, 'What can be the matter with people? How is it that they cannot see it?' And you have to explain that, and there is no other explanation but this. There is one lesson then.

But then let me follow to a second, a still more practical one. I say this with considerable hesitation and fear, but I am quite sure that it is right. There is a point at which it is better for us to stop presenting the truth of the gospel to certain people. If you find that somebody whom you are trying to bring to a knowledge of the truth begins to blaspheme, I say, stop doing it. Stop doing it! Just tell them that you are not going to talk to them about it any more. You are only driving them to a kind of insane and insensate opposition to the truth. A point comes, I say, when if you see that you are dealing with such obduracy and resistance that it only seems to infuriate them and inflame them, a point comes when you cease talking to them. You go on praying still but I think at that point you stop talking.

Let me give you a third lesson which, again, I think you will find to be very profitable if you consider it. I believe we have here the ultimate answer to the teaching of a man like Charles G. Finney on the question of revival. Now you remember what Finney teaches in his lectures on revival. Finney was a man who had a most amazing conversion and who received the baptism of the Spirit the day after he was converted. He was an astonishing and a brilliant, able man. But as I have often suggested from this pulpit it is possible for a man who has a most amazing experience to go wrong in his teaching, and I believe that Charles G. Finney is wrong in his teaching on revivals. He says in his *Lectures on Revivals* that you can really have a revival almost whenever you like. There are certain things which you have to do; if you do these things you will get a revival. So in his lectures he tells ministers what to do; you get people to make confession of their sins and this and that, 'you do these things', he says, 'and revival is bound to happen'. To which there is only one answer – it not only is not bound to happen but it does not happen. You see, Finney was in the midst of a revival, he did not seem to realize that, he thought it was his technique that did it. It was not! There was a revival, there was an outpouring of the Spirit of God and in those conditions certain things were done. So he then draws this whole deduction, 'Do these things and you will get revival'. Now I know many ministers who having believed Finney have done their utmost many times over and in more than one church to get a revival but they have never got it. Why not? Well you see the answer is it comes from God. There are some of us who have been praying for revival for many years, and preaching, and talking about it, and urging people to pray for it.

'Why doesn't revival come?' say people. Well, you know, part of the answer may be that we are passing through a phase of judicial hardening. I say 'We'. I do not mean those who are truly evangelical but, after all, we are attached to the Christian church and it may be that in the present circumstances what God sees we need, speaking generally, is punishment, restraint, withdrawal of His blessing.

Thank God He gives us individual blessings, He can bless, and does bless individual churches. But as for a general revival we have not seen it and it is not happening at the present time, and it seems to me that this is the explanation. So it is very wrong to say, 'You do this and you must get revival'. The answer to that is, It may not be God's will to give revival at certain points but quite the opposite, to withdraw the influences of the Spirit. I am not saying this to comfort you, I am not saying this that you may sit back and say, Well there is no point in praying for revival then if this is God's determination. We do not know, my friend, and you cannot be sure of it, and in any case you do not know when the period is going to stop and revival is going to come. You read the history of the past and the history of revivals and you will find that they have often come at the end of a period of judicial blinding and hardening; so it is our business always to pray for revival. This is something entirely in the hands of God. We do not understand it but I must confess that I am comforted by this doctrine. If I felt that revival depended on us, well I would not feel justified in trying to sleep at night. I would feel that I ought to be active day and night and exhorting everybody else to be so too. But you know you can work day and night and that will not produce revival. It is God who gives revival. God hardens: God softens. God exerts the pressure of the Spirit: God withdraws the Spirit. So we are always subject to this. This is our comfort, you see, that God is always in control. And whether we understand or not our business is to go on preaching the gospel, is to go on pleading with Him to have mercy upon us.

That is always to be our position. Not to say, Do this, and that will happen. No, no! We can but cry for mercy, we can but plead with God in the name of His dear Son to have compassion and to have pity upon us.

# *Six*

*

*What then? Israel hath not obtained that which he seeketh for; but the election hath obtained it, and the rest were blinded (according as it is written, God hath given them the spirit of slumber, eyes that they should not see, and ears that they should not hear;) unto this day. And David saith, Let their table be made a snare, and a trap, and a stumblingblock, and a recompence unto them: let their eyes be darkened, that they may not see, and bow down their back alway.* Romans 11:7–10

---

We have expounded these words and indicated that there are some four great principles or lessons taught us here which we must consider. They have a relevance to the particular argument which the Apostle is deploying but over and above that to the whole state and condition of the church at the present time. What the Apostle is really showing is that, although it was true that the majority of the Jews were outside the Church and were rejecting the gospel, nevertheless God had not totally rejected His people. Having put that argument before us he sums it up in the seventh verse by saying 'What then?'. What is the position? It is this, that 'Israel hath not obtained that which he seeketh for; but the election hath obtained it, and the rest were blinded'. He then substantiates all this in his customary way by giving these quotations from the Scriptures.

The first lesson therefore that we have learned from this is the importance of seeking the Lord and His salvation in the right way. The second relates to the matter of 'judicial blindness' expressed in the words: 'God hath given them the spirit of slumber' and we have tried to show how this really happens.

The third principle or lesson which we must consider arises from Paul's quotation from Psalm 69. This is one of the Imprecatory Psalms. Imprecation is a desire expressed to God that certain evil things should happen to sinners. There are other Psalms of this kind, for example, Psalms 58, 109 and 137, and what we are going to say about Psalm 69 applies to them also.

It is important that we should look at this because this element of imprecation creates profound difficulties in the minds of many people. There are many unbelievers who rest practically the whole of their case against the Scriptures on statements like this. Also, there are many believers who, while they do not reject this, are in trouble with respect to it, and the devil uses that in order to shake their confidence and their assurance.

Now what is generally and frequently said about this statement? The common view is that here is a case of a man in a temper who is simply asking for personal vengeance. Somebody has been unkind to him and he calls upon God to punish them in this violent manner. It is just a very crude and sinful manifestation of prejudice and passion and a desire for personal vengeance. Then, what is always added is, 'How different that is from the teaching of Jesus'. Incidentally, one observes that the people who bring this sort of criticism always refer to the Lord Jesus Christ as 'Jesus'. These things go together. These clichés come from the kind of people who are obviously in trouble about the deity of our Lord and His work of atonement. But that is what they say. They contrast a statement like this with the teaching of Jesus, and with the love that He manifested. Those are the charges which are put.

So how do we approach Psalm 69 and similar statements? It seems to me the way to approach it is to face the questions which it raises. The first of these is the whole question of the character of the Old Testament. Early in the history of the Church, a heretic called Marcion more or less rejected the whole of the Old Testament. He said that the church made a mistake in attaching its new documents to it. That the Old Testament has got nothing to do with us at all is a view which appears today in modern form. There is nothing new, therefore, about saying that the Old Testament is not to be believed. It is a very old heresy.

This is elaborated and people say how shocking it is to have to read the history of a man like David, and so on. They affect a delicateness, even a purity, and say, 'Fancy asking Christian people, and especially children, to read the Old Testament with things like that in it!' 'But Psalm 69', they say, 'is even worse than that because you can excuse natural failure, but not sheer vindictiveness'. Then they add, 'but that is the Old Testament outlook, nothing to do with Christianity at all'.

The whole of the Old Testament is dismissed, therefore, because it contains statements like this.

The next question that obviously arises is the question of the inspiration of the Scriptures because the moment you make a criticism like this of any portion of Scripture you are raising, in an acute form, the question of the divine inspiration of its writers, both Old Testament and New. But, of course, these critics are in no trouble about that. They do not believe in the inspiration of any part of the Bible. They say, 'I believe the Bible is inspired, but so is Browning, so is Wordsworth'. They only believe in inspiration in the sense that a poet, an artist, a writer or a singer can be inspired. That is what they mean by inspiration. But it is not what the Bible means, which is that all Scripture is breathed out by God [*2 Tim.* 3:16], or that those who wrote it were borne along, and controlled by the Holy Ghost [*2 Pet.* 1:20–21].

Then thirdly, and this is still more serious, you cannot say a thing like this about the Old Testament, or any portion of it, without raising immediately the whole question of the Person of the Lord Jesus Christ and His authority. He is involved because He believed in the Old Testament. This applies even to the early chapters of Genesis. You may say, 'Ah, this is a pure matter of science'. It is not, you know. Our Lord is involved even there. He is involved everywhere with respect to the Scriptures. We should therefore speak with great caution when we come across a passage in the Scriptures that seems to us to be wrong.

The fourth question relates to the character of God because the whole question of punishment cannot be separated from Him. Of course, these critics say quite blatantly that they do not believe in the God of the Old Testament. One of them who was a bishop of a certain church in the United States of America put in print that he regarded the God of the Old Testament as just a 'bully'.

Now then what do we say about these? Well, let us start at the lowest level, let us start with David himself. He wrote that sixty-ninth Psalm and it is he, therefore, who is denounced as a prejudiced, vindictive person who in effect says, 'They made me suffer, let them suffer', and prays down upon them this curse from the hand of God.

It is very interesting how the answer to many difficulties is really just to know your Scriptures. What sort of a man was David, the man who wrote these words? What was his attitude towards people who dealt very harshly with him? There is only one answer and it is that

David was one of the least vindictive men that ever lived. How do I prove that? Well, we have some incidents from his life recorded in the Bible. King Saul treated David in a most abominable manner, but look how David treated him. David could have killed him several times quite easily, but he did not do so. He bore it all with extraordinary patience. He was insulted, he was cheated by Saul, Saul even tried to kill him many times, but David never showed the slightest vindictiveness, he never showed the slightest desire for vengeance. Once, when that unfortunate fellow came to him and told him that he had actually thrust a sword into Saul, David punished him and said, 'You think you are giving me good news, you are not'. He was grieved, he was sorrowful; there was never a more magnanimous man than David. This is really enough in and of itself to disprove the charge.

But then you remember he had a son, Absalom, who treated him in a most abominable manner. Absalom tried to kill him and take the kingdom from him. But what was David's attitude towards Absalom? Not only was he patient, and entirely lacking in vindictiveness, but when he sent his expert generals to deal with the rebellion which Absalom had instigated, he said,'Don't do anything to the lad; don't harm my son; spare Absalom'. He gave them specific instructions. And when Joab, one of his generals, came to him and told him what he had done, David was overwhelmed with grief that they should have put his son to death in that way. Now that is the story of David. If ever a man had a right to feel a certain amount of vindictiveness and a spirit of vengeance within him it was surely David with respect to Absalom, but the whole story is the exact opposite.

Indeed, to sum it all up there is nothing to me more wonderful about David than the way in which he was distressed by those vindictive men, Joab and his brothers. He says, 'The sons of Zeruiah be too hard for me' [*2 Sam.* 3:39]. They had murdered Amasa, who had fought against David but whom David had not only pardoned, when he confessed, but promoted. But Joab and his brothers had murdered him as they had several others, thinking that they were pleasing David. But David was distressed.

This evidence is more than enough to show that David seems to display in a most astonishing manner a complete absence of any spirit of vindictiveness. Psalm 69 cannot, therefore, be explained in terms of David's bad, evil, vindictive character. He was not that sort of person.

But secondly, with regard to the question of inspiration, we have a complete answer in Peter's quotation in Acts 1:16 which he introduces with the words, 'the Holy Ghost by the mouth of David'. So, you see, you cannot get rid of this statement as if it were just David's words because they are the words of the Holy Spirit. David was an inspired writer. When he wrote his psalms it was not merely David with a poetic gift, it was the Holy Spirit. Here is a specific statement with respect to that. And that, of course, is what we are told everywhere about all the Scriptures. So that the problem is not as easy and as simple as it appears to be. These are statements whose explanation must include the fact that they are indited and inspired by the Holy Ghost Himself.

Thirdly, we come to our Lord's attitude to the Old Testament which He entirely accepted. He quoted from it freely and clearly. Having been brought up in it, He knew it and was able to quote from it to the Pharisees and to others. In John 10:35, our Lord refers to a psalm and describes it as part of the law, saying,'The Scripture cannot be broken'. In referring to a psalm as 'law' He was describing it as a manifestation of God's character and His purpose. Different terms are applied to different parts of the Old Testament and sometimes the whole of it is summed up in the word 'law'. So it is perfectly obvious that our Lord accepted the whole of the Old Testament as the divinely inspired Word of God.

This includes, as I have just said, the early chapters of Genesis. These modern critics say, 'Ah, of course there is no difficulty at all. Jesus was a man of his time and of his age, he was ignorant and did not know certain things that we know now'. All right: are you going to say then, that He was fallible, made some mistakes, said things that were wrong? If He is wrong about some things how do you know He is right about anything? You see, you cannot pick and choose in these matters. You have got the Person of our Lord as He is, and you have got to take His attitude towards the Old Testament when you are discussing a matter like this. He describes a psalm as the 'law' and as 'the scripture' and says, 'It cannot be broken'. So you see, our Lord Himself is involved in this matter.

So the explanation of these Imprecatory Psalms is that these statements are not personal at all. David here was not speaking from a personal angle, he is not concerned about personal vengeance at all: something else is involved here. What David is talking about is not his personal sufferings but what the enemies of God are doing to him simply because he is the representative of God. In other words, he is looking at what the enemies of God were doing to God. He has a zeal for God and His glory, and for the house and cause of God. He is therefore not speaking personally, but judicially. This is a very vital and a very important distinction which we often have to make. A man in preaching has to do it quite often. What the Scriptures say and what a godly man should feel about the enemies of God is nothing personal at all. It relates to the glory of God and one's identification with Him.

There are endless examples of this. The one which always strikes me as being very graphic comes at the end of Psalm 104. The Psalmist has been giving that amazing description of nature and creation, showing its wonderful harmony, how everything works and co-ordinates so intricately, and then in the last verse he suddenly breaks out and says this:'Let the sinners be consumed out of the earth, and let the wicked be no more'. Then he turns and says,'Bless thou the Lord, O my soul. Praise ye the Lord'.

Why does he say that about the wicked? For this reason: he has been celebrating the glory of creation with all its variety and harmony – the rivers, the streams and the animals and so on – and then he looks at sinful man and he says,'Oh what a shame, that man of all God's creatures should have brought this element of disharmony and misery and unhappiness; even creation has suffered as the result of it – 'Let them be consumed out of the earth'!

Now that is not personal. That is a man filled with the Spirit, led by the Spirit, having this vision of God's glory and His perfection in the creation. Then, seeing this dark side he says,'Oh that this might be got rid of altogether, so that there should be nothing but the harmony and the perfection and the glory of God'. Now it is exactly the same thing in Psalm 69 and in the other similar psalms.

That leads me to a fifth point which is extremely important. It is the prophetic element in all of this. In quoting what David said, the Apostle is teaching not only that David was not writing about himself but also not about his own times. Under divine inspiration, David was given a preview of what was to come. In other words, as we all must have noticed in reading the Psalms ourselves, it is obvious that this Psalm is about the Lord Jesus Christ, and David is really looking forward to the world rejecting Him, and especially the Jews as they cried, 'Away with Him; crucify Him', and as they mocked and jeered at Him even as He was there suffering that agony upon the Cross.

Indeed, some of the authorities say that these statements should actually be translated by being put into the future tense rather than the imperative mood. Instead of 'Let their table be made . . . let their eyes be' it should be: 'Their table will be made a snare . . . their eyes will be darkened . . .'. In other words, David is looking forward and saying prophetically: 'When the nation in its evil comes to do that, this is what will happen to it'. And, of course, that is what Paul is concerned to say has happened to it. He has told us that in verse 8, and here he is showing us how David saw this, consumed as he was with a sense of the glory of God. So the prophetic element is tremendously important. It shows up this whole idea that David is just speaking about himself and his own desire for vengeance.

But lastly, the sixth answer raises the whole question of punishment, and that is, of course, the ultimate difficulty. I mean 'difficulty' for these people who do not accept the inspiration of the Scriptures and who put their opinion against revelation. These people have no authority except what they think about God. They say, 'Is this kind of thing compatible with the love of God?' They do not believe in the wrath of God against sin; they reject it. So there is no punishment. It is inconceivable, they say, that God should punish. That is why so many of them are what are called 'Universalists' and believe that in the end everybody is going to be saved, even the devil.

Well now what do we say to that? Punishment is taught in the whole Bible from beginning to end. You cannot take it out of the Bible and have a Bible left. It is integral to its whole message from the very beginning. Possibilities were put before man and he was told that he would be punished if he disobeyed, and so it has gone on ever since, being repeated in the Bible from Genesis to Revelation.

In addition, the particular form that punishment takes should not trouble us. People are greatly disturbed sometimes by reading not only about a desire for the death of the wicked but of little children [*Psa.* 137:9]. They say, 'Fancy praying that little children might be destroyed'. Well now, of course to us that seems terrible, but the moment you look at all this in terms of eternity, the age element does not matter at all. That somebody should die in infancy rather than become an octogenarian to us seems a tremendously important thing, but in eternity it is nothing – nothing at all. 'Our whole life is but as a vapour' says the Bible! 'Oh', we say, 'fancy dying in youth or in infancy!' But look at it in terms of eternity!

Nor should the particular form which the punishment takes trip us up, because here again is an important principle. God, in His infinite wisdom, gives His revelation in thought forms which always suit the particular age and generation in which He gives it. Now that does not change the principle; it is simply the form that changes. And so you will find the same thought put in a different form in the Old Testament and in the New. The man blessed by God in the Old Testament is a man who has generally got thousands of sheep and cattle and so on. That is not so in the New, it is more spiritual; but it is God's blessing in both. That was how they thought in those times and God, condescending to man in order that he might understand, puts it in the thought form that he can understand; so the thought forms vary. And life was more violent then than it is now. That does not mean we are better now; we are not. We sound as if we are better, but we are not. The age of the atomic bomb has no grounds to criticize David or anybody else. If you are talking about brutality, you had better stop and think before you say too much, living in this twentieth century of ours! But in any case, that is the general principle, that the form of expression varies in order to help people to understand.

But finally with regard to this whole question of punishment, I use the same argument I have already used. It is that our blessed Lord Himself not only accepted the Old Testament teaching with regard to this, He taught eternal punishment Himself in many places. He said 'Where their worm dieth not, and the fire is not quenched'. It is also taught so plainly in the Epistles – 'everlasting destruction from the presence of the Lord', says the Apostle Paul in 2 Thessalonians 1 – and also in the Book of Revelation. Were none of these men inspired? We are therefore not only concerned with the inspiration of the Old Testament here but with the inspiration of the New. In the end, nothing is inspired and you do not know anything at all. You believe what you choose to believe and your idea of God is what you think God ought to be. Oh, the tragedy that men should be talking so loosely and glibly and lightly!

In other words, look at it like this. It is a very precarious thing always to talk about God. What do we know about God? He is in heaven and we are on earth. Let our words be few. Let us be careful. Poor old Job! He came to see it at the end. He had talked so much, he had ventured to criticize God. He said,'I had heard of thee by the hearing of the ear: but now' – he puts his hand upon his mouth. And the more you think about these things the more you realize that you really are discussing the character and the Being of God. Let us be careful lest we try to intrude ourselves into matters that are too high for us.

But here is the final word on this whole question of punishment, on the wrath of God. How do you explain Calvary? Why did the Son of God have to endure and suffer? Why did He have to endure that buffeting, that cruel scourging, that agony, that thirst? Why did He ever have to offer up the cry of dereliction? Never has anyone suffered as He did. Never! Never has there been such suffering. But why? Why was He treated like this in the way that that psalm describes, the sixty-ninth psalm describes, and the twenty-second psalm describes still more in detail – why? Why did it ever happen? How did God ever allow it to happen? That is the question you have to answer, and there is only one answer to it. It was the wrath of God against sin that demanded this. There is no other way of salvation, no other way of forgiveness. If there had been, God would never have allowed His Son to suffer. There has never been such agony. His heart broke! 'My God, my God, why hast Thou forsaken me?' You cannot conceive of it. There is suffering. He suffered more in that moment than the whole universe can ever suffer.

But why did it happen? It was because of the wrath of God against sin. The Apostle has told us that in the eighteenth verse of the first chapter of this great Epistle to the Romans:'For the wrath of God from heaven is revealed (has been revealed) against all ungodliness and unrighteousness of men, who hold down the truth in unrighteousness'. The ultimate proof of the wrath of God upon sin is the death of our Lord upon the Cross on Calvary's hill. It is the greatest manifestation of the love of God. It is at the same time the greatest manifestation of the wrath of God. Many things met at Calvary.

*Did e'er such love and sorrow meet,*
*Or thorns compose so rich a crown?*

Glory and ignominy! Love and wrath! Righteousness and mercy! And you do not see the Cross truly unless you see God's holy wrath upon sin and against sin; the very thing that David felt in a measure at this moment of being taken up by the Spirit in revelation and inspiration was God's abomination of sin. He had a glimpse of it and that is why he gives expression to the desire that all who are so guilty should receive the punishment, condign punishment, that they so richly deserve. May God keep us humble and give us a measure of understanding in this whole question of the Imprecatory Psalms.

# *Seven*

*

*I say then, Have they stumbled that they should fall? God forbid: but rather through their fall salvation is come unto the Gentiles, for to provoke them to jealousy. Now if the fall of them be the riches of the world, and the diminishing of them the riches of the Gentiles; how much more their fulness?*

Romans 11:11–12

We are now beginning to look at the second section of this chapter which runs from verse 11 to verse 32. Paul has been showing that, as a nation, the Jews are patently rejected because, speaking generally, they have not believed and obeyed the gospel. So the Apostle voices the question: 'Hath God cast away His people?' In the first ten verses he was concerned to show that the rejection of Israel was not total. In this second section he is concerned to show that the rejection of Israel is not final either; not total in the first section, not final in this particular section which is one of the great sections of Scripture. Apart from anything else, it contains one of the great prophecies of the Apostle Paul, and it is very important that we should realize exactly what it is he says.

Once more the best thing is to make an analysis of the section as a whole, that is from verse 11 to verse 32. This is because it is a very closely woven argument. We will divide it into a number of sub-sections. The first sub-section is verses 11 and 12, where the Apostle states his general theme. Doing this is his invariable practice and it cannot be improved on. It is like a kind of overture to an opera or something like that in which the theme is stated. He puts before us what exactly has happened to the Jews and why, doing so in terms of their relationship to the Gentiles. That leads him not only to explain what is happening at the present to the Jews, and what that has to do with the Gentiles, but also to take it right on to the remote future. That is the theme of all these verses from verse 11 to verse 32. It is the real position of the Jews, their relationship to the Gentiles who are in the church – in the present and in the future.

The next sub-section is from verse 13 to verse 22. What he does here is to show that it is important for Gentile believers to have a right understanding of the position of the Jews and of their relationship to the Jews in the church. Right at the beginning, there was a danger of this being misunderstood by Gentiles, as there is now.

Really, there were two main misunderstandings. The first was that the Gentiles might tend to despise the Jews. There has been a great deal of this throughout the running centuries. The Jews have been persecuted in such an abominable manner by most nations because of the very thing that the Apostle is dealing with here. It was thought that God had finished with the Jews altogether because they had crucified their Messiah. That is the first misunderstanding.

But the second is that the Gentiles might say, 'If your teaching is that we are included because they have behaved wrongly and yet you are suggesting that they are going to come back, what happens to us then? Will it mean that we will be expelled?' This thinking is something that we need to consider at the present time, because there is a teaching which would have us believe that in some future age the Jews are going to be in a superior position to everybody else. We will see what this section has got to say about that. So you see there were those two immediate difficulties in the time of the Apostle and they have continued to be so ever since.

I want to divide this sub-section even further in order that we may see the steps in Paul's argument. First of all you have verses 13 and 14. This is really a personal statement which is made for pastoral reasons. The Apostle talks about the nature of his ministry and why it is what it is. It is a kind of aside, but it is germane to the argument. Having done that he sees the necessity to present his general proposition once more and that is done in verse 15. Then in verses 16 and 17 he has a most important statement with regard to the fundamental relationship of the Jew to the Gentile in the Christian church. Verses 18 to 21 are a specific warning to the Gentiles not to misunderstand this relationship, and particularly against their being too pleased with themselves and giving way to pride. Finally, he sums up in verse 22 all that he has been saying.

This brings us to the third sub-section, namely verses 23 and 24 in which he presents the possibility and the reasonableness of the restoration of the Jews. A tremendous statement follows in the fourth and last sub-section, which runs from verse 25 to verse 32, and in this he predicts the certainty of the future restoration of the Jews and their participation in the blessings of the gospel in the Christian church. That is a prophetic utterance. He describes it as a mystery which has been revealed to him and which he is making known to these Romans. It is not that it is possible that the Jews are going to be restored, nor that it is probable, but that it is absolutely certain. What is more, he tells us *when*, *how* and *why* this is going to happen.

With that general perspective in mind, we now take up the first sub-section which is verses 11 and 12. Here the Apostle presents the general theme that he is going to handle. He introduces it with the same formula that he used at the beginning of the chapter. The words 'I say then' are followed by a negative question to which the reply has also to be in the negative. Verse 11 could be translated 'They did not stumble that they should fall, did they?' to which the only possible answer is the same strong negative reply found in verse 1. But what is the point of this question?

The whole key to this, of course, lies in the difference in meaning between the two words 'stumble' and 'fall'. The Apostle has already introduced this idea of stumbling at the end of chapter 9 where he says that 'Israel, which followed after the law of righteousness, hath not attained to the law of righteousness. Wherefore? Because they sought it not by faith, but as it were by the works of the law. For they stumbled at that stumblingstone; As it is written, Behold, I lay in Sion a stumblingstone and rock of offence: and whosoever believeth on him shall not be ashamed'. The Apostle Peter says the same thing [*1 Pet.* 2:7–8].

Now what Paul is saying is that the Jews stumbled at the gospel concerning the Lord Jesus Christ. They kept on clinging to their own works and the idea that they just had to keep the law as they understood it, and that that would put them right with God. But here was a gospel being preached to them which said: 'Christ is the end of the law for righteousness'. Believe in Him; justification is by faith only; it is by the blood of Christ. They stumbled at that. They could not believe it.

Now then 'stumble' is our first important word and it explains itself. We know what it is to stumble. But Paul anticipates someone thinking that the stumble of the Jews is an irrecoverable fall; such a crash that they will never be capable of standing on their feet again, and so he frames his question in order to make the point that there is a difference between stumbling and actually falling; or not merely falling but doing so in a final and complete manner. In other words, he is asking whether the casting away of the nation of Israel in his time was something final and he, at once, answers his own question with the words 'God forbid', which means that such a thing is a sheer and an utter impossibility!

Now this is the basic point that the whole chapter is dealing with. Having shown in the first major section that all Jews have not been cast away, he goes on to say that the whole nation is not finally cast away. This is the big thing that he now sets out to prove and to explain to the Gentile Christians.

So we can put it like this: if the Jews have not been cast away finally and completely but have only stumbled, not fallen, what is he really saying about them? He gives a threefold answer to that question in the remainder of this little sub-section, verses 11 and 12. He says that what has happened to the Jews is a part of the great plan and purpose of God first for the Gentile, then for the Jew, and ultimately for the blessing of all God's people in the Christian church. We will examine each part of this threefold answer.

To the question, 'Why has this happened to the Jews?' Paul's first answer is that 'through their fall salvation [might] come unto the Gentiles'! Let us consider this. Undoubtedly, most Christians today are Gentile believers, and we are being told here how that has come to pass. The Old Testament is all about the Jews and there is nothing about the Gentiles, except insofar as they come into relationship with the Jews. How then have we ever come into the blessings of salvation? He is answering that here by saying that the stumbling of the Jews is a part of the ultimate purpose of bringing the Gentiles into the Church.

But let us look at the terms first. He says, 'but rather through their fall'. That is the Authorized Version translation and it really is a pity that the word 'fall' should have been used at this point because it has already been used to translate a different Greek word in this very same verse: 'I say then, Have they stumbled that they should fall?' There the word 'fall' is excellent but here the word which it translates means 'trespass'. 'God forbid: but rather through their trespass (or their transgression) salvation is come to the Gentiles'.

The word the Apostle used means 'a false step', that is, a trespass. It is sometimes translated as 'missing the mark'. It means that instead of going straight ahead, a man has gone astray, or has taken a false step either to one side or the other. So instead of 'fall', it should be either 'trespass' or 'transgression'. It means 'a culpable and a punishable act'. We therefore understand the statement to mean that as a result of their culpable act in rejecting their own Messiah, salvation has come to the Gentiles.

This is a staggering statement. It is made many times in the New Testament and, not only that, it had been prophesied. You will find it in the forty-ninth chapter of Isaiah, verses 4 to 6. 'Then I said, I have laboured in vain, I have spent my strength for nought, and in vain: yet surely my judgment is with the Lord, and my work with my God. And now, saith the Lord that formed me from the womb to be His servant, to bring Jacob again to Him, Though Israel be not gathered, yet shall I be glorious in the eyes of the Lord, and my God shall be my strength. And he said, It is a light thing that thou shouldest be my servant, to raise up the tribes of Jacob, and to restore the preserved of Israel: I will also give thee for a light to the Gentiles, that thou mayest be my salvation unto the end of the earth'.

In other words, this thing has happened to the Jews as a part of God's inscrutable purpose of bringing the gospel to the Gentiles.

But it was not only Isaiah who prophesied this but our Lord Himself. He spoke the parable of the householder who had a vineyard to the religious leaders of the Jews and summed up its message by saying: 'Did ye never read in the Scriptures, The stone which the builders rejected, the same is become the head of the corner: this is the Lord's doing, and it is marvellous in our eyes?' Then: 'Therefore I say unto you' – here is the prophecy – 'the kingdom of God shall be taken from you, and given to a nation bringing forth the fruits thereof'. That is it. Here is His distinct prophecy that the Jews as a nation are going to be put on one side and instead of them the Christian Church is coming in, 'a nation bringing forth the fruits thereof' [*Matt.* 21:43].

What our Lord had said when speaking to the Syrophenician woman who came to Him about the healing of her daughter is also to the point. He said to her 'I am not sent but unto the lost sheep of the house of Israel'. Even to the woman of Samaria he had said 'Salvation is of the Jews'. But at the end of His life He says, As the result of your rejection and crucifixion of Me you are going to be put aside, 'the kingdom is going to be taken from you and given to a nation bearing forth the fruits thereof'. There is the prophecy of what actually happened.

Let us review the history. Our Lord came as the Jewish Messiah and preached the kingdom of God to the Jews. If they had believed His message and had accepted Him, then something entirely different from what actually happened would have taken place. But it was known to God before the foundation of the world that that would not happen. The rejection of Jesus Christ as their King and Messiah by the Jews led to the cross on Calvary's hill. That was known to God from all eternity and not only known, but, as Peter said on the day of Pentecost at Jerusalem, it was 'according to the determinate counsel and foreknowledge of God'. The rejection of the Jews was the occasion but it was God's eternal purpose that Christ should die for our sins upon the cross.

The story continues in the book of the Acts of the Apostles. In chapter 8, following the death of Stephen, Jewish persecution was the very means which caused Christians to scatter and preach the gospel in Judea and Samaria. There is a most important statement on this matter in Acts 13:45–46. The opposition of the Jews at Antioch, in Pisidia, caused Paul to 'turn to the Gentiles'. Now, if you want to understand history, lay hold on that profound statement. It was the opposition of the Jews which caused Paul to actually become the apostle to the Gentiles. The same thing is found in Acts 28:28 where Paul speaks to the Jews in Rome and in 1 Thessalonians 2:14–16. So it was the persistent rejection of the gospel by the Jews which drove the apostles to take it to the Gentiles. This proves what Paul says here in the phrase – 'rather that through their trespass, salvation is come unto the Gentiles'.

But there is something even beyond that. Even the Jews that did become Christians were in great trouble over the gospel being preached to the Gentiles. The unbelieving Jews, of course, were furious at it but even the believing Jews were in trouble about this. It took a vision from heaven to put Peter right on this matter! There is also no doubt but that the Apostle Paul in Arabia had to go through a struggle before he saw this, although the Lord had commissioned him, not only to preach to the Jews, but also to the Gentiles. So those were the things that eventually brought the gospel to the Gentiles.

But there is something else to note. It concerns the council, held in Jerusalem, which is reported on in Acts 15. Why was that council ever held? It was because Jews who believed the gospel were in great trouble for many years about this whole matter of the admission of the Gentiles. This shows the power of tradition. They could not quite understand this. 'How can a man', they said, 'be a child of God if he has not been circumcised? Of course we agree he has to believe the gospel; that salvation is really in Christ; but surely a man must be circumcised before he is really put right'. So believing Jews were pressing for this, as is also shown in the Epistle to the Galatians. Indeed, this very Epistle was largely written in order to put people right on this very matter. The Jews all along were a hindrance to the evangelizing of the Gentiles.

Well now, what the Apostle is saying is that God has used all this. You see it was this very opposition of the so-called Judaizers that brought the decision of the council in Jerusalem, that produced the mighty Epistle to the Galatians where the doctrine of justification by faith only is stated more clearly, perhaps, than anywhere else, and it has established it once and for ever, giving this liberty and freedom to the Gentiles. So what the Apostle is putting before us is, that this 'stumbling' of the Jews is something which has been used of God to promote the salvation of the Gentiles. That is his first answer and we must never lose sight of the fact that God has not only permitted this stumbling, but inflicted this 'judicial blindness' upon them, partly so that the Gentiles might believe.

But then there is the second, most extraordinary thing. In the last phrase in verse 11 he says: 'for to provoke them to jealousy'. And the 'them' is the Jews. You see there is a sort of circle here. The rejection of the gospel by the Jews sends it to the Gentiles but the Jews, seeing the effects of the gospel in the Gentiles, are provoked to jealousy by that fact and are made to reconsider the gospel which they have already rejected. Now there is the second great lesson.

But what does he mean by 'provoke to jealousy?' The self-same phrase is used by the Apostle in the 14th verse where it reads 'If by any means I may provoke to emulation'. It is exactly the same phrase. We need not be troubled about that variation, the two things mean the same, as long as we do not give a meaning to 'jealousy' which is only negative. It may start with negative, useless jealousy, but it does not stop there; there is more than that in it. It makes people ask questions, to review and to be concerned. It first provokes to jealousy but ends in a desire to emulate. Seeing the blessings of the Gentiles it will create in the Jews a spirit which will make them say 'Well, why are we not getting this blessing?' and that will make them examine the whole question over again and eventually it will bring them back.

This had happened, of course, to certain individuals at that time. It has also been happening ever since. But the Apostle's point here is, that a day is coming when it will happen to the Jewish nation as a whole. He is not saying that they were being provoked to jealousy or to emulation there and then, except in the case of individuals. But he is already introducing the big idea that a day is coming when the nation of Israel as a whole will be provoked to jealousy and emulation when they see the blessings of the Gentiles, and that will be the means of bringing them back. So the circle is completed. The Jews reject, that sends the gospel to the Gentiles; seeing the blessings of the gospel in the Gentiles eventually brings in the Jews. That is the third answer the Apostle gives as to why the stumbling has taken place. It is that ultimately through this, God is going to bring back the bulk of the nation of Israel to salvation, to blessing, into the Christian church.

So let us summarize, to ensure that we have grasped this clearly. In these two verses the Apostle is taking up his general theme: Why has the nation of Israel stumbled? Is it a final step? No, it is only temporary. They have not fallen; they have only stumbled. But why did even that happen? It has happened in order that the gospel might go to the Gentiles; secondly, in order that the Gentiles, enriched by gospel blessings, might stimulate the Jews to jealousy, and so thirdly, that at some point in the future they will see their error and believe the gospel which they have so tragically rejected!

# *Eight*

*

*I say then, Have they stumbled that they should fall? God forbid: but rather through their fall salvation is come unto the Gentiles, for to provoke them to jealousy. Now if the fall of them be the riches of the world, and the diminishing of them the riches of the Gentiles; how much more their fulness?*

Romans 11:11–12

Having shown that God's rejection of the Jews as a nation is not a total one because he and many other Jews had believed the gospel, the Apostle Paul asserts that it is not a final one either. We have seen that he gives three reasons for that position. We have considered the first two which are that by means of Israel's rejection salvation has come to the Gentiles and that, in turn, is used by God 'to provoke the Jews to jealousy'.

We come now to the third reason which reads: 'Now if the fall of them be the riches of the world, and the diminishing of them the riches of the Gentiles; how much more their fulness?' The 'them' to whom Paul is referring is, of course, 'the bulk of the nation of Israel'. They are the people who have fallen and been diminished but through being provoked to jealousy, the nation as a whole will come in fulness to believe the gospel, and when that happens it will bring yet greater blessing to the Gentiles. Now that is the meaning of this twelfth verse which argues that if the condition of the Jews as they are has been a means of blessing to the Gentiles, how much greater will that blessing be when they are believing the gospel in great numbers.

It is not difficult to imagine why the Apostle says this. He says it, of course, because it is true. But he also has a subsidiary reason which is that the Gentiles might very well have argued like this: 'If we are included because they were rejected and our being in the church is going to provoke them to come in too, what will happen to us then? Will we be put out?' Not at all, says Paul. If as things are you have been blessed, how much greater will your blessing be when they enter in fulness?

Now let us first of all make sure that we have the argument of the Apostle clearly in our minds. He puts it in a manner that is very typical and characteristic of him: 'If this – well then, how much more that?' There are many instances of an argument from the less to the greater in this Epistle, for example, 'For if, when we were enemies, we were reconciled to God by the death of his Son, much more, being reconciled [having been reconciled] we shall be saved in his life' [5:10].

There is another feature of Paul's style to note at this point which is not only interesting but instructive. Actually, it is a defect. He starts a sentence but does not finish it. He is often guilty of that. In this twelfth verse he has a double argument and he does not complete the first half. There is no parallel in the second part of the argument to 'if the fall of them be the riches of the world'. However, the reference to 'their fulness' not only corresponds to the diminishing, but also answers to 'their fall'.

Now that is actually a defect in style but, of course, not an error. Are there errors in the Scripture? No! A defect in style is not error. It is a blemish from the purely literary standpoint. But it indicates that the writers of Scripture were not typewriters and it ought to be a great comfort to every preacher!

We have considered the word 'fall' in this verse and so we turn to examine the interesting word 'diminishing'. The commentators have a great argument about this. They are all troubled about this word, and Charles Hodge is the one who is troubled most of all. He says that the danger here is to interpret this word 'diminishing' in a numerical way. This must not be done, he says, and he presents three reasons for rejecting all idea of numbers. First, he says that the only other time that the word which is translated 'diminishing' is used in the New Testament, it has nothing whatsoever to do with numbers. Hodge is referring here to 1 Corinthians 6:7 which reads: ' Now therefore there is utterly a fault among you' and the word rendered 'fault' means 'defeat', 'failure' or 'loss'. Secondly, a numerical interpretation does not suit the context because Paul is not saying that it is the conversion of the few Jews who have become Christians which has been the occasion of good to the Gentiles but rather the rejection of the gospel by the great body of the nation. Thirdly, he says a numerical connotation does not suit the first clause of the verse at all, where the term 'fall' answers to and explains their diminishing. Hodge therefore argues that we must understand Paul to be saying that their 'diminishing' means their loss for the time being of the great blessings of God with which they were favoured. Because they have not obeyed the gospel they are reduced to a very poor condition in terms of the blessing of God.

Now I am putting this before you for a particular reason. It relates to our understanding of 'riches' and 'fulness' and we will return to this question after we have considered those words. In saying, 'If the fall of them be the riches of the world, and the diminishing of them the riches of the Gentiles', let us note that there is no distinction in meaning between 'world' and 'Gentiles'. They really mean the same thing, although 'Gentiles' would be better translated as 'nations'. But the main point is that it is because of the failure of the Jews that all the richness of the gospel has come to us.

Now this is something that we should glory in and something, therefore, in the light of which we should examine ourselves. Do we realize how enriching the gospel is? Do we realize what has come to us and what is true of us as the result of this very thing which the Apostle is here handling? What does he mean by saying that their fall and their diminishing has led to our enriching? What he means is what he is so fond of calling 'the exceeding riches of his grace', or 'the unsearchable riches of Christ'. He expounds this theme to the Corinthian believers [*1 Cor.* 6:9–11] and to the Ephesians [*Eph.* 2:11–22; 4:17–20].

Do you know this? Do you see how you have been enriched? Are you glorying in this? Listen to him in, perhaps, the greatest statement of this that he ever made. He puts it like this. He is praying at the end of the third chapter of the Epistle to the Ephesians, 'That he would grant you, according to the riches of his glory' – and you know, so many of us are living like paupers that our neighbour is not interested in Christianity. But if he saw that you were rich, if he saw that you were rejoicing, if he saw that you were living like a prince in this world he would want to find out – this spirit of emulation would be aroused in him. We must get hold of these 'riches'! So the Apostle prays, 'That he would grant you, according to the riches of his glory, to be strengthened with might by his Spirit in the inner man; That Christ may dwell in your hearts by faith; that ye being rooted and grounded in love, May be able to comprehend with all saints what is the breadth, and length, and depth, and height; And to know the love of Christ which passeth knowledge, that ye might be filled with all the fulness of God'. Are we obtaining this? Now then here is the Apostle's argument: 'If the fall of them be the riches of the world, and the diminishing of them be the enriching of the Gentiles in this glorious manner, how much more their fulness?'

We come here to another great question. What does Paul mean by this 'fulness'? Once more the emphasis of so many of the learned authorities is that we should not think of numbers. Charles Hodge is quite consistent with himself and says that as 'diminishing' is not to be regarded in terms of numbers, so it is with 'fulness'. He understands that as follows, 'If the impoverishment of them from the standpoint of blessings of God means the riches of the Gentiles, how much more their full restoration to blessedness?'.

In the light of this position, it becomes interesting to see how Hodge gets on when he comes to the twenty-fifth verse in which the word 'fulness' occurs again: 'For I would not, brethren, that ye should be ignorant of this mystery, lest ye should be wise in your own conceits; that blindness in part has happened to Israel, until the fulness of the Gentiles be come in'. What he says is: 'The blindness of Israel is to continue until something else happened. There were to be, and have been numerous conversions to Christianity from among the Jews, in every age since the advent; but their national conversion is not to occur until the heathen are converted. What, however, is definitely meant by "the fulness of the Gentiles", it is not easy to determine'.

I want to suggest that the reason for his difficulty is what he has already said about verse 12 which is: 'The question is not to be decided by the mere signification of the words'. However, that is what he did in dealing with the word 'diminishing' saying, 'This word is only used once elsewhere in the New Testament and it never has any reference to numbers'. With regard to fulness, he says: 'The fulness of the Gentiles may mean that which makes the Gentiles, as to number, full' but he rejects that and other explanations before ending like this: 'All that can be safely inferred from this language is, that the Gentiles, as a body, the mass of the Gentile world, will be converted before the restoration of the Jews, as a nation'. But in verse 12 he will not allow us to think of a body, that is the 'mass' of the Jews, yet in connection with verse 25 he says it means 'the Gentiles as a body'. So the 'mass' of the Gentile world will be converted before the restoration of the Jews as a nation. Charles Hodge's admission that he is in difficulty points in the direction of his exposition being defective.

W. G. T. Shedd, a contemporary of Charles Hodge and the author of an excellent Systematic Theology, lands himself in the same sort of difficulty when he comes to deal with this word 'fulness' in verse 12. He describes it as 'Fulness, not majority antithetic to minority, but gain antithetic to diminution or loss'. In other words, you see, he takes the same standpoint as Charles Hodge. But how does he deal with the word 'fulness' in verse 25? He says it means 'the great body of the Gentiles, not the mere supplement from the Gentiles' and 'Fulness is applied in the sense of a great majority to the Jews in verse 12'. But when talking about the fulness of the Jews in verse 12 he said 'not majority antithetic to minority, but gain antithetic to diminution'. Yet here he says, 'fulness is applied in the sense of a great majority to the Jews in verse 12'. He has forgotten what he said in verse 12 when he comes to verse 25. From the mistakes of these great expositors we need to learn when expounding the Scriptures, how important it is to look ahead before you arrive at an interpretation and to always look back when you are dealing with a word which has occurred before.

We can put it finally like this. What the Apostle is talking about here especially *is* the question of numbers, and it is because that is put out of court that expositors find themselves in such difficulties when they come to the twenty-fifth verse. But I would go further and say that the point of the argument of the *entire chapter* is to deal with the question of 'numbers'. He has already dealt with it in our first main division. He said, The rejection is not total, there are some of us who believe; quite a lot of us, in fact. Then here he says, 'Is it final?' 'No, no', he says, 'this is only temporary'. And he puts it in this particular form. But the statement in the twenty-fifth verse really is the thing that settles this once and for ever. 'The fulness of the Gentiles' means, these large numbers, most of the nations of the world. And then he goes on to say, 'And so all Israel shall be saved', and when we come to that we shall see that it means 'the bulk of the nation'. What he is dealing with in this section is the fact that now only a very small part of the nation believes, the bulk does not, but eventually it will.

Let me give you my way of explaining this word translated 'diminishing'. Charles Hodge, you notice, gives as the second reason for his argument that 'Paul is not saying that we as Gentiles have been blessed through and because only a small number of Jews have been believers' and so all thinking about numbers is to be rejected. But that is exactly where, it seems to me, Hodge went wrong in his thinking.

What the Apostle is saying can be put in this way. It is a fact that only a small number of Jews, relatively speaking, have believed the gospel and the bulk of the nation has rejected it. That is Paul's basic position. But he argues that if that reduced state of the Jewish nation as the people of God has led to our riches, how much greater will our riches be when they all come in? And that is surely a complete and a satisfactory explanation of the word. So the Authorized Version translators had the right instinct when they put down 'diminishing'. The number of true, believing Jews has been diminished, it is small now but it is going to be very great. And his argument therefore is that if this present state and condition has been a means of blessing to us, how much more when it will be the case that large numbers of them, the bulk, the mass, the body of the nation will become believers.

But how can the Apostle say that? If Gentiles have become Christians, with all the blessings of that status, through the trespass of the bulk of the Jewish nation, how can the blessing of the Gentiles be so much greater when the bulk of the Jewish nation believes? Is there not some fallacy in the argument at this point?

No, there is not, and for this reason. If the Jews *en masse* had believed the gospel at the beginning, it would have taken much longer for the message to be preached to the Gentiles. We have seen how Judaizers insisted on Gentiles being circumcised and it is likely that there would have been lengthy debates before any Gentile was told the good news. But the Jews rejected the message, persecuted those who believed it and so, in effect, drove the gospel out to the Gentiles.

But in the future, the position will be different. In the first century, the ancient world was divided up very sharply into Jews and Gentiles, and they hated one another. That the gospel was rejected by the Jews was therefore a great encouragement to the Gentiles to believe it. What the Jew liked the Gentile did not. The Greeks used to look upon the Jews, as everybody else, as 'barbarians', and the Jews looked upon everybody else as 'dogs'. But now having believed and understanding all this, Gentiles are able to take an entirely different view of these things. It would no longer upset us as Gentile believers if a large number of Jews believed and came into the church; in fact we would now rejoice in it. So you see, he is envisaging two entirely different positions. At the first the diminishing of them, their fall and diminishing, was a real help and God used it in the way we have seen. But now that we are Christian believers, and none of these prejudices remain, we look upon anyone's salvation as a most desirable event and so their coming in can lead to nothing but still greater riches and rejoicing. So there is no contradiction in the argument at all. You have to see the two entirely different positions: what happened at the beginning and what is going to happen in the future.

In conclusion, I refer you to the fact that a discussion on Religious Liberty has been going on in the Second Vatican Council and that today the Pope has announced a decision about the attitude of the Roman Catholic Church to the Jews, as a nation, and to their responsibility for the crucifixion of the Lord. We will consider these things further but meanwhile note that it is what the Apostle has said on this question that is true and foundational for an authentic Christian position on this whole matter.

# Nine

*

*I say then, Have they stumbled that they should fall? God forbid: but rather through their fall salvation is come unto the Gentiles, for to provoke them to jealousy. Now if the fall of them be the riches of the world, and the diminishing of them the riches of the Gentiles; how much more their fulness?*

Romans 11:11–12

We have seen that these verses are essential for an understanding of the teaching of this chapter. But they are basic to much more. They are a great seminal statement with regard to divine things in Scripture, in our own life and in relation to all mankind. I am going to group these truths and lessons under certain headings.

The first set of truths relates to the Jews as a nation. What are we taught here about the relationship of the Jews, as a nation, to God? The first lesson is that the condition of the Jews and their rejection of the gospel is something that had been predicted. This whole question of prophecy is a vital one and it is the greatest proof of the truth of the Christian message and of the inspiration of the Scriptures. You remember how Peter puts that so well in his Second Epistle where, having reported on what he, James and John had seen on the Mount of Transfiguration he goes on to say, 'We have also a more sure word of prophecy' – a word of prophecy made more sure – 'whereunto ye do well that ye take heed, as unto a light that shineth in a dark place, until the day dawn, and the day star arise in your hearts; Knowing this first that no prophecy of the Scripture is of any private interpretation' – the prophets were not only teachers but they received revelation from God – 'For the prophecy came not in old time by the will of man: but holy men of God spake as they were moved by the Holy Ghost' [*2 Pet.* 1:19–21]. The miracle of biblical prophecy! These things have all been anticipated, prophesied, God has revealed them and the records were there eight centuries at least before these things came to pass and in some instances longer than that.

But we can also look at it in another way. Prophecy also foresees the future of the Jews, and that is what the Apostle is doing here; he is writing as a prophet. 'The fulness of Israel is going to come in'. Remember the Apostle wrote this nineteen hundred years ago, roughly speaking. It was recorded when the situation seemed so utterly hopeless, when it seemed that Israel was finished with. But the Apostle, given the revelation, moved by the Holy Spirit, utters this great prophecy, 'The fulness of the nation of Israel is going to come in, they are going to be restored'. Prophecy is therefore a very wonderful thing. It is a miracle of course. It is something that cannot be explained in any terms except the supernatural action of God both in revealing the truth and in supervising its reliable recording.

So whatever people say we must never forget this as we are reading the Scriptures. They are trying to reduce this book to the level of all ordinary human writing. Prediction of events is a standing protest against that. This is something that you simply cannot explain except by means of the supernaturalism which is, of course, basic in the whole of the biblical teaching. That is our first point in connection with this general subject of the Jews in their relationship to God.

But secondly under this heading, in these two verses we are given the only explanation of the preservation of the Jews as a distinct nation. This, again, is one of the great standing miracles. When you consider the history of the Jews, as a nation, nothing is more remarkable than their continuance in spite of the fact that many nations have done their utmost to destroy them. They have been regarded as the outcasts of society throughout the centuries. We can always take credit that this country was one of the first countries to reverse what had been the traditional treatment of the Jews.

It is remarkable that, although they were without their country for so many centuries and nations did their utmost to destroy them completely, this nation has been preserved. The only real explanation of this is that God has not finished with them and there is a day coming when this 'fulness of Israel' is going to be brought back to salvation, back into the Christian church, and so God's ultimate promise to Abraham is going to receive a wonderful fulfilment. There can be no question but that the reason for their preservation is that God's promise might be confirmed. God has preserved them in this unique manner in order to show in the realm of history that what He has promised He is not only able to perform but also will surely bring to pass.

Thirdly, under this same heading, we are taught here what our attitude should be to Jews individually, and as a nation. The Second Vatican Council has decided to reverse the traditional attitude of the Roman Church towards the Jewish people with respect to their guilt in the matter of the crucifixion of our Lord. They have now decided to exonerate them from that particular guilt. Historically speaking, it was the attitude of the Roman Catholic Church to the Jews which very largely determined the treatment meted out to them by the nations of the world throughout the centuries. It was the decision of the Roman Church to put the entire blame upon the Jews, as a nation, for the enormity of the crucifixion which encouraged its people to repress them. My concern is to make clear that the Roman Church should never have adopted its earlier position and the fact that it did so was due to its failure to understand the teaching of these verses. If only it had understood this teaching it would never have been guilty of encouraging such an utterly indefensible attitude towards this nation and people. If it had got hold of the idea that the Gentiles were saved partly to provoke the Jews to jealousy, it could never have bolted and barred the door against them and treated them as the offscourings of the human race.

This is a good example of how failure to interpret the Scriptures accurately can lead to quite unexpected consequences. When you are dealing with a great chapter like this you should always be looking out for some practical lesson, and surely if the teaching of these verses had been grasped, nations would not have done what still remains as a blot on their history. And, as for ourselves, the lesson is surely plain and clear. We, as Gentile Christians, should be concerned about these people. We should realize that we are called to rouse them to jealousy. Far from regarding them as being rejected by God because they, as a nation, have rejected their own Messiah, we should feel a greater sense of compassion for them than perhaps for anybody else and do all we can to bring the gospel to them.

We come to a second group of remarks. I have called these two verses 'a seminal statement' because they have a great deal to teach us with regard to God's ways. If you like, you can call them a theodicy which means a defence of the ways of God with respect to man. But there is very wonderful teaching here and it is most practical. The first lesson I find here is a warning against jumping to conclusions – the very thing which has been done with regard to the Jews. Because they are rejecting the gospel and their own Messiah it seems obvious to many to conclude that God has no more interest in them, especially as He allowed the Roman Empire to sack the city of Jerusalem in A.D. 70, scattering the Jews amongst the nations. That is the end of them. There is nothing more to be said. It is so easy to jump to that sort of conclusion.

But we are reminded by the teaching of these verses that when we are dealing with the affairs of God, whether with nations or individuals, nothing is more fatal than to jump to conclusions. I could illustrate how often we do that. Christian people are taken ill and immediately they say, 'Why does God do this to me?' That is an instance of jumping to a conclusion and, similarly, all those foolish questions which generally are put in this form: 'If God is really God and is love, why then. . . . ?' Think of all the trouble that people get into and the misery that they bring upon themselves simply because they form hasty conclusions. Whatever else you may do when you are concerned about the dealings of God with you or with anybody else, never jump to a ready-made conclusion, you will almost certainly be wrong.

But let us go on. Why should you not do this? Well here is one reason. God (if I may so put it) knows what He is doing, He has a plan. He never acts in a haphazard manner or merely as the result of something that someone does. It is of the very essence of this teaching, that as a result of Jewish unbelief two apparently impossible things follow, namely that the Gentiles should hear and believe the gospel and, through that, the Jews might be made desirous of receiving it. So that is why all this happened to the Jews. But it seems all wrong to people who thought that the promises or the Word of God were of 'none effect'. But that is not so, there is a very great purpose here. God knows what He is doing. He has a plan.

But let me put this, in the third place, as follows. God's ways of working are very strange and this is, of course, where people get into difficulty and into trouble. In our ignorance we do not understand them and, because of that, we do not see how they can be God's ways. Now this is the lesson to learn. God so often works indirectly and not directly. We have all got the 'penny-in-the-slot machine' mentality, every one of us, and we always want instant solutions or short-cuts to blessings in the spiritual life. But God does not work like that. The great characteristic of His work is, rather, that He is indirect, He seems to go a long way round. Look at Him in the natural world. See the farmer ploughing the ground and breaking it up with his harrow and sowing the seed. You do not get your crop the next day, do you? You have to wait for weeks and weeks and all sorts of things happen but the harvest always comes. That is God's method of working. It is very often indirect. Indeed, I can go even further and say that sometimes He seems to be doing the exact opposite of what any sane man would expect. There are abundant instances of this and this is a classic one: His own chosen people put out as it were, in order that Gentiles may be brought in. Now that is God! We are much too clever to accept things like that, are we not? But that is how God works. That is why William Cowper, said, 'Judge not the Lord by feeble sense'. The moment you try to do that you will be wrong already. 'God moves in a mysterious way His wonders to perform'.

This is the theme of Isaiah 45. One of the most amazing things God ever did was to raise up a pagan conqueror, named Cyrus, and use him with respect to His own people. 'Though he did not know Me', says God, 'I girded him'. And then God makes these extraordinary statements, 'I form the light and create darkness: I make peace, and create evil; I the LORD do all these things', even those things which seem to be the exact opposite of everything that one would expect of God's plan. He seems to be completely contradicting His ultimate purpose with regard to these people and throwing them right out. But He is not. It is only for a while. How vital and essential it is that we should grasp the great principle, that 'all things work together for good to them that love God'.

Now God's ways are perplexing. You read the Scriptures and you find the psalmists being honest enough to say 'Lord, have you forgotten us? Have you forgotten to be gracious? Where are you? You are behaving like a traveller, acting like a stranger; look what you are permitting. You are allowing the exact opposite of what we expected you to do. You are allowing the ungodly to flourish and we are all suffering'. God acts like that repeatedly and we, with our feeble sense, think that everything has gone wrong. The answer is that it has not. God does these things in order that, 'through their fall salvation is come unto the Gentiles, for to provoke them to jealousy'.

God is over all and He sees the end from the beginning. How difficult it is for us to realize this at times. But do not say that because there are dark clouds God is against you. There is a face behind the clouds; it is a Father's face. Never forget the end. Cowper was so right:

*His purposes will ripen fast*
*Unfolding every hour;*
*The bud may have a bitter taste,*
*But sweet will be the flower.*

*Blind unbelief is sure to err,*
*And scan His work in vain;*
*God is His own interpreter,*
*And He will make it plain.*

'Blind unbelief' – Ah, that is the enemy! Unbelief is always blind. It cannot see, and especially, it cannot see afar off. But 'God is His own interpreter' and in Cowper's two verses are the key to most of the things that get us down. So even if you cannot understand what is happening now, be quite certain and sure that eventually you will. Let us never forget that God is over all and behind all and He knows what He is doing. Trust Him and keep your 'feeble sense' in its right place.

Thirdly, this prophecy casts a wonderful light on past Church history. What am I referring to? Well, God has often employed the very method that the Apostle is dealing with here which is that He has used the rejection of the gospel on the part of the Jews to promote its success among the Gentiles. We have had exactly the same thing at the time of the Protestant Reformation. There is no question at all but that the attitude of the Roman Catholic Church to the Protestant Reformers and the early Protestants was one of the things that helped above everything else to spread the gospel to the common people. That certainly happened in this country. Tyndale and others looked forward to that day when the ploughman would be reciting Scripture, and the fact that the learned authorities were so opposed to the Reformation and the giving of the Bible to the people, made them do it all the more. Read about it in the case of a man like Tyndale and old Hugh Latimer and others. They were forced underground as it were, but that only increased their zeal. There is also no doubt but that the persecution of Protestants by the Roman Catholic Church was a means under the hand of God of spreading the gospel more rapidly, especially to the common people, than would have happened otherwise. If the doctors of the Church had all accepted this new teaching which had come from Luther and others, it might very well have stopped with them and taken much longer to get through to the masses of the people. But because of the attitude of the Church of Rome it happened, as I say, the other way round. There is God doing once more this very thing that Paul tells us He did in the first century.

I am equally convinced that He did very much the same thing in connection with the Puritan movement of the seventeenth century and the great Evangelical Awakening of the eighteenth. There can be no question at all but that it was the attitude of so many of the bishops and clergy to George Whitefield and to the Wesley brothers and their other helpers, that drove them to take the gospel out into the open air and to the masses of the people. Being refused permission to preach in London churches drove Whitefield and the Wesleys to preach in church graveyards, on Kennington Common and in Moorgate and elsewhere. The opposition of the official church drove them out to the people, and so the common people were able to hear the gospel in a way that would not have been possible if the churches had been opened to these great evangelical preachers, filled and baptized with the Spirit of God as they were.

But, I want to put a question at this point. We have been looking back at history and have seen God's method of working and I cannot but feel that all this is of very great significance to us at this present time. Is this a law in connection with the spread of the gospel? Are we perhaps living in an age when God is again doing this? Is it possible, I wonder, that the official Church is the greatest obstacle to the gospel getting to the masses of the people today? I fear that there is a great deal to be said for this, and it may well be that God will again work in this way in order that people whom we tend to regard as utterly hopeless will hear the good news of salvation. You see they are to us what the Gentiles were to the Jews at the time of our Lord. The Gentiles were 'dogs', they were ignorant, they were so hopeless that there was nothing for them at all. The Jews alone were the people of God and the Messiah was to come to them, and to them alone. But it turned out to be the exact opposite and their very rejection of it was the means God used to bring it to the Gentiles.

We, Christian people, are in grave danger and so let us learn a lesson from this. Are we becoming like these Jews at the time of our Lord and at the time of the great Apostle? Is our attitude to these whom we regard as complete outsiders such that God may have to put us on one side and may even use our utter wrongness as a means of bringing the gospel to those people? There are many indications of this it seems to me today; confusion in the Church herself, the tendency of so many Christians to live a little, confined life, putting a hedge round themselves, and their attitude towards those who are outside. If the gospel cannot save those to whom we tend to react so violently, it is no gospel. Why are the masses of the people outside the church in this country today? Why do all the efforts of the church fail to touch the working people so-called? Why is Christianity becoming increasingly and almost exclusively a middle-class movement? There is something wrong. We need to examine ourselves in the light of the teaching of these two verses, this great principle that is here enunciated. So often we have seen that God has to do this very thing to the official church which He did with the nation of Israel in order to spread the gospel to those who are regarded as completely outside.

A fourth point from these verses is that we, as evangelical believers, are given very valuable teaching with respect to our attitude to formal church members and to apostate churches. The Jews, do not forget, were God's people; they are the natural seed of Abraham, the nation of Israel. What corresponds to that today, of course, is formal church members or, as I say, even apostate churches which only have the name and have lost the spirit and deny the truth rather than preach it. This is the position to which we are rapidly advancing, if we have not already reached it. What should be our attitude towards such churches or towards such individuals?

It seems to me the answer is quite plain and it is made up of two parts. The first is, of course, separation. The church, as the book of Acts teaches us, had to separate from the synagogue. They had to go out. We have dealt with that. The apostles offered the message first to the Jews. They were told to start in Jerusalem, then Samaria, and then the uttermost parts of the earth, and they invariably started with the Jews, and they went to the synagogues. But as Acts makes clear, when the Jews finally refused, the Apostle said, Very well then, as you refuse it, henceforth I go to the Gentiles, and they all did the same. And so the Jews, as such, were left. If any Jews liked to come and listen, of course they were welcome, but as a nation and as a body they no longer remained in the same position. The preachers turned to the Gentiles and, as a result, the church became chiefly a Gentile Church. Now that is what I say is the principle of separation. You cannot possibly remain in an apostate church. You must separate yourself from unbelief and from explicit denials of the gospel.

But, secondly, and this is as important as the first, although we have to separate our deepest desire should be to provoke them to jealousy and to emulation. In other words, when you feel you are compelled to leave an apostate body, do not dismiss it, as it were, in your mind and in your spirit; be concerned about it. Yes it is 'rather through their fall salvation is come unto the Gentiles, for to provoke them to jealousy' – and that should be our object. It is very difficult to do this. The danger always is to adopt a hard and a harsh attitude towards those whom you know to be wrong. But the fact that you cannot go on with them does not mean that you shut the door and say, 'Finished! No more!' No, no, we should be concerned about them and we should always have as our ultimate aim and objective to provoke them to jealousy. We should say to ourselves, 'Well now, we will show them what a true church is, we will show them what a true Christian is'.

How often have I had to say this in my pastoral duties when people come to me in this kind of situation. They say that they are the only Christian in the family, what are they to do? Sometimes they have asked whether leaving home is the answer to this problem because they have witnessed to their relatives and prayed for them, but the result seems to be more that they become even more antagonistic. What I always say on such occasions is that leaving is the last thing such people are to do. Now I am not talking about churches here but about family relationships. The thing that I always try to impress upon them is that they may be talking too much whereas the most important thing they have to do is so to live the Christian life before their relatives that they will begin to think that you have something wonderful which they do not have, and gradually they will begin to feel they would like to have it also. That is exactly what being provoked to jealousy and emulation means. I tell people not to hammer others with the gospel, still less to condemn them, but to go out of their way to win them, to be kind and helpful to them, putting them first, and even to suffer if necessary. Live your Christian life in such a way and in such a manner that they are compelled to say – Well, there is something wonderful in this after all! And that will begin to set them thinking, seeking, searching, and eventually it may lead to their salvation. Now I say we are called upon to do that with individuals, we are called upon to do that with regard to churches which we may regard as apostate. Our ultimate objective should be to win them, to provoke them to emulation by seeing the fruits of salvation in us.

This brings me to my next point which is a word of comfort and encouragement. I need not stay with this, it is obvious; but it is the most wonderful, comforting and consoling thought. What we are taught here is this, you see, that there is nothing impossible with God. Nothing and no one is hopeless where God is concerned. What could have appeared more hopeless than the case of the Jews as a nation? What can appear more hopeless than the Jews as a nation tonight? And yet we have this definite certain promise that the fulness of the nation is going to come in. 'Nothing shall be impossible with God'. Now that applies not only to nations but to individuals. You may know an individual, who may be very dear to you, who may be in the grip of some terrible sin or other and you say that they are beyond hope. Never say that again! With God nothing shall be impossible. If God can bring back in fulness the nation of Israel that rejected and crucified the Messiah, He can do it with anybody, any nation or any individual. The most wilful can be saved.

Why, look at the Gentiles how hopeless they were; look at the descriptions we are given of them in the different parts of the New Testament. Yet they have come in! Paul reminds some of the believers at Corinth that they had been fornicators, idolaters, adulterers, effeminate, abusers of themselves with mankind, thieves, covetous, drunkards, revilers and extortioners, but they were no more. That nothing is impossible with God is proclaimed as loudly as can be in these two verses that we are looking at. Indeed, I would almost go to the extent of saying that there may well be more hope for the hopeless masses outside the church today than there is for the church herself. I am rapidly coming to that conclusion, and there are times when I almost 'despair' of the church. But I know that the God who has worked among the godless, hopeless masses in past centuries can do it again. Whatever the condition of men and women in sin tonight, as Christians we must never lose hope with respect to them. As our Lord put it in His famous parable of the two sons, He said to the Pharisees, 'The publicans and the harlots go into the kingdom of God before you', and rather than you [*Matt.* 21:31]. That is how it has been throughout the centuries and it may very well be like that again.

So my final word is this: These verses call us to humility and, in particular, humility in our thinking. We must beware of the tendency to jump to conclusions because we cannot understand. Let us be humble; let us realize we know nothing, and let that drive us to consider Him Who is over all. We are in God's work, not man's. The church is not a human institution, society or organization. Thank

God it does not depend upon us and our abilities, it is God and His purpose. These purposes 'shall ripen fast' and nothing can stop them, they are sure and certain because they are God's. Therefore, let us humble ourselves in adoring wonder and admiration before Him, and let our faith be in Him, His purpose, His will, His love, and His almighty power.

# *Ten*

⁂

*For I speak to you Gentiles, inasmuch as I am the apostle of the Gentiles, I magnify mine office: if by any means I may provoke to emulation them which are my flesh, and might save some of them. For if the casting away of them be the reconciling of the world, what shall the receiving of them be, but life from the dead?* Romans 11:13–15

We come now to the second sub-section of that division of chapter 11 which runs from verse 11 to verse 32 and as we do so the question we must face is: What is its connection with what precedes and follows it? It is always good to ask such questions and I think that, in this instance, the answer is that these verses throw light in both directions. The Apostle is giving the church at Rome, which was mainly a Gentile church, the reasons for his having given so much attention to the case of the Jews but he is also introducing what he is going to say about the relationship of Jews and Gentiles to the ultimate purpose of God and with respect to the church. In the course of doing those things, he gives us a personal statement about life as a minister of the gospel of our Lord and Saviour.

This is a very interesting sub-section, small in compass but large in content. However, learned commentators are in considerable trouble over the statement contained in verses 13 and 14. This is because of the rather odd construction which the Apostle used in writing. As we have seen before, Paul was not pedantic in his style of writing and here he is guilty of what the authorities call an anacoluthon which means a statement which is not completed. Paul assumes that his readers will be able from what he has said to supply for themselves what is lacking.

The Apostle uses two words which translated separately mean 'indeed' and 'therefore' and he uses them together. Our Authorized Version translation does not bring that out, nor do most of the other translations. It is also the case that whenever the Apostle uses these words elsewhere in the New Testament he follows them up with the word 'but'. In this particular instance, however, he does not do so and that is what gives rise to the difficulty. People disagree about whether the word should be supplied or not. There are three views on this and they appear in the various translations. Some evade the problem altogether by translating in a wholly literal fashion; others take the view that 'but' should not be supplied and finally, there are, of course, those who argue that it should. In connection with all this what seems to me to be the most helpful course to follow is to ask the question, 'What can we be sure that the Apostle is saying in this statement?'

The first thing he tells us is that he is now addressing Gentiles specifically. We read 'For I speak to you Gentiles'. A better translation would be 'but I speak' because the word 'but' suggests a new element is coming into the discussion. And there is, for he is now going to speak to the Gentiles directly – a thing which he has not done before. This is an important point because it does, I think, show quite clearly that the majority of people in the church at Rome were Gentiles. In the previous two-and-a-half chapters whenever the Apostle has referred to the Jews he has done so in the third person but from here on he will refer to the Gentiles always in the second person. If it had been a mainly Jewish church he could not possibly have done that.

What is he wanting to say? He wants to explain to the Gentiles why he has been giving so much attention to the question of the Jews and to show that it has great relevance with respect to them. But secondly, he tells us why in particular he is doing this, and the reason is because he is pre-eminently the Apostle to the Gentiles. This is where the personal statement comes in. 'For I speak to you Gentiles, inasmuch as I am the apostle to the Gentiles'.

So we come to this statement about his 'magnifying his office', or 'magnifying his ministry', which is a better translation. What does he mean by this? Everybody is agreed that he is proud of the fact that he is the Apostle to the Gentiles and he wants them to know that. But it is more than that. He is very concerned that none of them should think that the fact that he has given such attention to the question of the Jews means that he is neglecting the Gentiles. He says, 'Do not draw that false deduction. I magnify my office as the one called peculiarly and specially to be the Apostle to the Gentiles. Do not misinterpret', he says, 'all I have been saying about the Jews and even my concern about them'.

How exactly does he magnify his office? This is the crux of this problem and the disagreement leads to variations in translation. Let me first put to you what he is not saying. Or, if you like it in another form, let me give you my reason for rejecting the translation of the Revised Standard Version and the New English Bible – the view which does not supply the missing 'but'. The New English Bible says 'I am a missionary to the Gentiles and as such I give all honour to the ministry when I try to stir to emulation the men of my own race'. That makes Paul say that he magnifies his office as the Apostle to the Gentiles in order to save the Jews.

It is R. C. H. Lenski, an excellent commentator, who most clearly commits himself to this view. He goes as far as to say this: 'One would expect his glorification of his ministry to lie in what, by God, he had been able to accomplish among the Gentiles'. 'But no', says Lenski, 'he looks beyond all his accomplishment among the Gentiles and he looks to the Jews'. Then here is the crowning statement: 'The full glory of Paul's apostolic ministry among the Gentiles lies in its repercussion upon the Jews'. So you see what that amounts to is this, that the Apostle is saying that he exerts himself among the Gentiles and has been preaching so indefatigably, in order that by that means he might save the Jews.

I reject that translation because it conveys a totally untenable explanation. Why do I say that? Verse 14 is reason enough in and of itself. He says, 'If by any means I may provoke to emulation them which are my flesh, and might save some of them'. All he is hoping when he writes is that some of the Jews are going to be saved. Now you do not glory in that if that is the best you can hope for. But quite apart from that, it is so inconceivable that this man who glories in the fact that he is the apostle to the Gentiles, should say that all that he is doing among them is really designed to save the Jews.

Why is that untenable? The Apostle was aware that this commission which he had to be the apostle to the Gentiles was given to him by the Lord Himself, and it was something of which he was tremendously proud; that he had been singled out, in spite of his past as a Pharisee, for this unique privilege. He regards this as something wonderful in and of itself, which is why he gives us all these quotations. He sees that the salvation of the Gentiles is as precious in the eyes of God as that of the Jews themselves. The other interpretation sees the salvation of the Gentiles as only being incidental to the salvation of the Jews. Whereas, as we shall see as we go on with the chapter, the Apostle's great case is, that God is concerned to save Jew *and* Gentile. He has been given a special commission for the Gentiles and that is why he magnifies his office.

But secondly, when he says 'I magnify my office' he means that he gives himself to it wholeheartedly, unremittingly and at great cost to himself. That is how he magnifies his office, and he does it in order to show how privileged his position is.

But thirdly, he magnifies his office not only in evangelizing the Gentiles but also in explaining to them fully the great truth of the purpose and the plan of God. That is the very thing that he is doing here. He wants Gentile believers to have a full understanding of all this and so he explains it to them. This includes dealing with the future of the Jews as a people.

Fourthly, there is another way in which he magnifies his office and it is this. He says to the Gentiles that he wants them to see that what happens to the Jews is ultimately going to be the greatest source of blessing to them. That is verse 15: 'If the casting away of them be the reconciling of the world, what shall the receiving of them be but life from the dead?'

Furthermore, he magnifies his office also by warning them against error. We shall see that one of the dangers confronting the Gentile believers was a false notion about themselves and about the Jews. Paul is going to deal with this in great detail. from verses 16 to 24 where he says, 'Boast not thyself against the branches'. He has a most solemn warning to deliver. He says, they have been cut off, you be careful lest you are too. Do not get an inflated notion about yourselves. That is the very thing the Jews said and they have been put out because of that.

At the end of the first chapter of the Epistle to the Colossians, Paul sums up all that is involved in this matter. He says, 'Whereof I am made a minister, according to the dispensation of God which is given to me for you, to fulfil the word of God; Even the mystery which hath been hid from ages and from generations but now is made manifest to his saints: To whom God would make known what is the riches of the glory of this mystery among the Gentiles; which is Christ in you, the hope of glory: Whom we preach, warning every man, and teaching every man in all wisdom; that we may present every man perfect in Christ Jesus: Whereunto also I labour, striving according to his working, which worketh in me mightily'. That is magnifying his office.

I have gone into this in detail because it seems to me to be a very special word to ministers and preachers. We do not magnify our office unless it is what you may call in the words of Spurgeon 'an all-round ministry'. The man who is called to be a minister of the gospel, must evangelize; but he does not stop at evangelism; he must also teach, warn and reprimand. The Apostle is doing all of these things here; that is how he 'magnifies' his office. He is saying in effect to these Gentiles: 'You know, if I did not put this whole question of the Jews before you I would not be doing my job properly. I would be neglecting an aspect of my ministry and of my calling. I am not sent merely to bring you into the kingdom, I am here to build you up; so I have to warn you against false notions about yourself and the Jews, I have to show you the relevance of all this to you; that means teaching'.

So he says, I am not neglecting you by telling you all this about the Jews, I am in the very centre of my commission. I am the Apostle to the Gentiles, and I am magnifying my office in seeking to present you Gentiles perfect and entire in the presence of God.

# *Eleven*

*

*For I speak to you Gentiles, inasmuch as I am the apostle of the Gentiles, I magnify mine office: if by any means I may provoke to emulation them which are my flesh, and might save some of them. For if the casting away of them be the reconciling of the world, what shall the receiving of them be, but life from the dead?* Romans 11:13–15

What the Apostle is saying here is that while he is pre-eminently the Apostle to the Gentiles he is anxious that they should be perfectly clear about an aspect of his ministry which they are liable to forget or perhaps to misunderstand. He says in effect: 'Though I am the Apostle to the Gentiles pre-eminently and magnify my office, that does not mean that I have forgotten the Jews, or that I am unconcerned about them.' There had been a time, recorded in Acts 13, when the Apostle definitely turned from the Jews and said, 'Henceforth go I unto the Gentiles'. That was an action which was being misunderstood, as is shown by the verses that follow. The Apostle has not forgotten the Jews and he is certainly not uninterested in them or unconcerned about them. Why? Well, because, as he has already told us at the end of verse 11, he is anxious to provoke them to jealousy or to emulation. His evangelizing of the Gentiles is therefore to have an indirect effect upon the Jews and he wants the Gentiles to bear this in mind constantly.

What he says at the beginning of chapters 9 and 10 makes clear how concerned he was about them. 'I say the truth in Christ, I lie not, my conscience also bearing me witness in the Holy Ghost, that I have great heaviness and continual sorrow in my heart. For I could wish that myself were accursed from Christ for my brethren, my kinsmen according to the flesh'. Now he says that, though he is spending virtually all his time in evangelising amongst the Gentiles, he still has this great burden; and he repeats that more or less in chapter 10:

'Brethren, my heart's desire and prayer to God for Israel is, that they might be saved'. He never forgot this, it was always in his mind, though he is the great Apostle to the Gentiles.

But he is also anxious that these Gentiles should be clear about this, in order that he may warn them against the danger of thinking that the Jews are utterly cast out, and therefore of despising them. He is most anxious to save them from that. There was a time when the Jews used to look upon the Gentiles as 'dogs' because they were outside the commonwealth of Israel. The danger now is that the Gentiles should do exactly the same thing to the Jews. Knowing that they are in the favour of God, seeing the Jews as a nation outside, they might despise and reject them, regarding them as entirely outside God's mercy.

Another reason he writes as he does is this: he wants them to understand God's ultimate purpose both for the Jews and for the Gentiles. He is going to open out a great panorama of history, and this is a matter about which both they and we must be clear. The ultimate purpose of God for the church is that she should include both Gentiles and Jews. And it is as wrong for the Gentiles now to exclude the Jews as it was formerly for the Jews to exclude the Gentiles. Above everything else, therefore, Gentiles must be humble.

This brings us to his next statement in verse 14, where he says that what is happening at the moment is simply this, that some of the Jews are being saved. This is part of his whole argument which is to show that the Jews have not stumbled that they should fall finally and completely. There is going to be a restoration. For the time being they have stumbled, but even now some of them are being saved. 'If by any means I may provoke to emulation them which are my flesh, and might save some of them'. As things stood at that moment, the Apostle did not expect many of them to be saved. And it is true, as we have seen many times over, that it was but a remnant that was being saved, 'a remnant according to the election of grace' although the remnant was bigger than some people might think. But the Church was predominantly Gentile and there was only a minority of converted Jews in it.

Now the Apostle understands that. He would prefer that there were more, but he understands. He has been given a view of the ultimate purpose of God. But even so there is nothing that he is not prepared to do if by any means he might save some of them. So you see he is showing them that the fact that he is the Apostle to the Gentiles, and that he magnifies his office, must never be interpreted as meaning that he has lost interest in the Jews or that he is unconcerned. Whenever a single Jew was converted it thrilled the heart of the great Apostle; it gave him tremendous joy, and that, as I have already suggested to you, should be our attitude. It should be our attitude today to sections of the Christian church that we may regard even as apostate, that we should have this concern about them. And it does give us great joy when we find such being awakened and coming to a knowledge of the truth.

The general warning to us is this, that we must be very careful that we never 'write people off' as being beyond redemption. We must denounce unbelief, we must denounce error still more, but we must never write people off. We must never say that someone 'cannot be saved'. We do not know. Indeed we should be anxious for their salvation and anxious for them to be saved. It is a question once more of drawing a careful distinction between contending for the truth and condemning individuals who are guilty of error or of apostasy. We must always draw a distinction between the sinner and his sin. We have a serious view of sin, but that does not mean that we condemn the sinner. Now that is the point the Apostle is making. The Jews should have accepted the gospel but they have not, they have stumbled. Nevertheless, the Apostle longs for their recovery and he rejoices when even one of them is converted.

Now this is the position as we come to look at verse 15. Here he says, 'If the casting away of them be the reconciling of the world, what shall the receiving of them be, but life from the dead?' This is virtually a repetition of the twelfth verse. There is very little difference between them. So why does the Apostle say it once more? Well, the answer is that it depends exactly how you divide up this sub-section. If verses 13 and 14 are regarded as a digression what he says in verse 15 is to show that he is taking up the point again and going on, and that is always a good thing to do. The whole art of teaching is repetition. You have to keep a thing in people's minds, because they constantly forget it and they miss a logical connection very easily. So the Apostle is taking up where he left off at the end of verse 12, if you like. But I think there is more to it than that. He is once more pressing home his argument. At the end of verse 11 he used an explanatory phrase, 'for to provoke them to jealousy' and expanded that a little in verses 13 and 14. He now repeats his great argument but adds significantly to the way in which he concluded it in verse 12. There he had just spoken in a general way, about 'their fulness' but in verse 15 about 'life from the dead'.

Now this last phrase is really important. But let us make a comment or two about some of the things that lead up to it. The Authorized Version here has the word 'if' at the beginning which should really be rendered 'since' because their 'casting away' is a fact not a supposition. Rendering it like that strengthens the argument which is that if the Gentiles have received this great blessing when the majority of the Jews are outside, what is it going to be like when they are brought in? Paul's answer is that it will be like 'life from the dead'.

This expression has caused great discussion and is still doing so. What exactly does it mean? There have been three main interpretations of its meaning. Some have said that the Apostle, by the phrase 'life from the dead', is referring to what will happen to the Jews when they are restored. They say he means this: 'If the casting away of them be the reconciling of the world, what shall their restoration or their receiving back again be to them (and to everybody else who sees it happening to them) but, as it were, life from the dead?' There is the bulk of the nation, the Jews, in unbelief, and from the standpoint of salvation they are dead. But suddenly they are going to accept the gospel, and when they do so, people will say, 'This is like life from the dead!' These people who have been dead for all the centuries, they have come to life. That is the first explanation that is put forward.

But we really cannot accept this for a moment, because it entirely misses the point of the Apostle's argument. What he is concerned to show here is the effect, not upon the Jews, but upon the Gentiles. From the beginning of verse 11 he has been showing that the fall of the Jews is for the benefit of the Gentiles. When he asks 'how much more their fulness?', how much more to whom? To the Gentiles. The same is true here. Of course, when a man is converted, or when a number of people are converted, it is 'life from the dead'. But what the Apostle is arguing here is the benefit that is going to come to the Gentiles. He says, 'I am speaking in particular to you Gentiles now. I want you to see that if the casting away of them has meant your reconciliation to God in Christ, then their restoration will be to you life from the dead'. So it does not refer to what will happen to the Jews so much as what is going to happen to the Gentiles.

There is a second interpretation which sounds as if it is more along the right lines. It is that at the time when the Jews, as a nation, are going to come back, the 'Gentile' church will, as a whole, have fallen into a very low spiritual state; indeed, very much as it is at the present time. And therefore, according to this argument, what the Apostle is saying is this, 'You know there is a time coming when you Gentiles, who are liable to be a bit proud of yourselves at the moment, will have fallen into backsliding and will have become lifeless. You will be more or less dead. You will still be a church, but only just alive. And then this great restoration of the Israelites, the Jews as a nation, will take place, and it will be such a blessing to you that you will be revived and lifted up to the heavens; from your dead condition you will be filled with a new life. It will mean a great revival for you'.

This is an interpretation which has to be taken seriously because it is in line with the Apostle's main argument. There is a further reason for paying attention to it and it is that Robert Haldane accepts it and it is always a serious matter to have to disagree with Robert Haldane. Hodge is not quite as clear about this and does not commit himself as definitely as Haldane. But I venture once more to disagree even with Haldane. Why? Because it seems to me in the first place to be quite gratuitous to assume this falling away of the Gentiles into backsliding and so on; but still more it seems to me that the context makes it quite impossible. Why? Well take the argument of verse 12 where he says, 'If the fall of them be the riches of the world, and the diminishing of them the riches of the Gentiles; how much more their fulness?' Paul is not comparing a dead, lifeless condition with one of blessing; he is comparing 'riches' with yet greater blessing. The contrast is not between nothing and a great deal; the contrast is between a great deal and an overwhelming superabundance. He has used the term 'riches' and done so twice over. The Apostle's argument is this. If, even as they are now, you have had such great blessings, such riches – how much more will you be blessed when they are fully restored? It does away with the 'how much more' if you take it to mean that the Gentile church will be in a dead and parlous condition. And exactly the same applies to the argument here in verse 15. It is the same argument. 'If the casting away of them be the reconciling of the world, what shall the receiving of them be, but life from the dead?'

But there is a still more powerful argument. Take what we are told in verse 25 – and it is important to look ahead, because if we arrive at an interpretation here which is wrong, we shall find ourselves in difficulty later. So it is always good to try to take in the whole argument before you arrive at a precise interpretation about particular details. Verse 25 states that 'blindness in part is happened to Israel, until the fulness of the Gentiles be come in'. The Jews are therefore going to come in after the fulness of the Gentiles and the term 'fulness' cannot possibly carry the interpretation of a lethargic and almost hopeless condition. It is the exact opposite to that. You see, it is not the case, as so many people seem to argue, that as things are now, Gentiles are being saved but when the Jews as a nation come in, then the evangelization of the Gentiles is going to eclipse everything that has ever been seen. That is the argument that is used. But to me it is impossible in the light of verse 25 which says that the fulness of the Gentiles precedes the fulness of Israel. The fulness of Israel does not produce the fulness of the Gentiles. So we have to reject this second exposition.

This brings us to the third explanation. It is that 'life from the dead' can mean nothing less than the general resurrection of the dead associated with the Second Coming of our Lord. There have been many who have adopted this view, some great expositors among them, but it seems to me that we cannot accept this for a moment. Here we are in line with Haldane and Hodge and most other expositors throughout the century. The Apostle here speaks of 'life from the dead'. In the New Testament, the resurrection is *never* referred to in that way but *always* as the 'resurrection from the dead'. The Apostle here deliberately chose the word 'life' rather than 'resurrection'. If he had meant resurrection he would have obviously said so, as he does in other places. Take, for instance, what he says in Philippians 3:11: 'If by any means I might attain unto the resurrection of the dead'. That is resurrection. It is not life. This fact is really sufficient to reject this exposition which says that what will bring in the Jews is the Second Coming of Christ and the resurrection from the dead.

But there are further reasons for rejecting this explanation. First, it is quite incompatible with the New Testament picture of the condition of the church, preceding the coming of our Lord. Our Lord Himself says, 'When the Son of man cometh, shall he find faith on the earth?' The picture that is given in the Gospels of the Second Coming of our Lord is that it is sudden, unexpected, and that He will come at a time when people will be heedless and thoughtless. That is also what you find in the Epistles of Paul. Such a state of affairs is therefore quite incompatible with what we have here. Paul says that there is going to be so much blessing when the Jews, as a nation, come in that it will really be like life from the dead.

But secondly, in the teaching of the New Testament, the resurrection always ushers in the 'end' of all things, and the last judgment.

There will therefore be no opportunity left for the great blessing indicated here which is so essential to the Apostle's argument. So, not only in terms of the Apostle's language but also the general teaching of the New Testament about the Second Coming and the general resurrection, we have to reject this exposition.

What, then, is the proper exposition? It is really quite straightforward. It is the same as we have already seen in verse 12. 'Life from the dead' is a hyperbolic statement, and it is a very powerful one. Paul's argument runs as follows, 'If the casting away of them, as it is at the present time, has meant the reconciling of the world, what shall the receiving of them be? It will be like 'life from the dead'. He is really saying that it will be so wonderful and so glorious that we cannot compare it to anything else but life from the dead itself. In other words, it is his way of expressing this exceeding great blessing – the same point as in verse 12, 'how much more their fulness?' We have riches now, but when their fulness comes in – how glorious, how wonderful it will be!

This is another example of the contrast between the church experiencing the blessing of God, with individual conversions taking place here and there, seasons of liberty in prayer and preaching, consciousness of the Lord's nearness – and revival. This has been the universal testimony of people in a time of revival. They say, We have had blessings before and have rejoiced, even with great joy, but of course it was nothing compared with this. This is so overwhelming, so transcendent, so tremendous – it is like life from the dead! That, it seems to me, is the kind of thing the Apostle is saying.

This is something to look forward to. It is a part of that glorious hope that we have as children of God. I do not mean the Second Coming. I mean something that is going to be witnessed before the Lord returns. What is it? The bulk of the nation of Israel will be converted to Christ and come into the church. What will this lead to? A confirmation of our faith! A tremendous proof of the inspiration of the Scriptures! The Scriptures have said all along that God has not abandoned His ancient people, though nearly two thousand years have passed and they are still outside. But we, as God's people, still believe this and will go on believing it. We say this is going to happen because nothing is impossible with God. All appearances may be to the contrary, but then suddenly it will happen and we will find our faith confirmed and we will be filled with a glorious sense of joy. We will then realize how right we have been in holding on to the

Scriptures in spite of all the destructive criticism of men and all the ridicule that they have poured especially upon prophecy. And over and above this we shall say, 'What a wonderful God we have. He never breaks a promise. All the promises of God are sure. He said this so long ago. There are hints of it even back in the Old Testament prophets; He said He was going to do this and He has done it!' Can you not imagine what it is going to be like when we shall see the realization of all this? The church, obviously, will be lifted up into a state of ecstasy, amazement and of glory.

Now let me use this comparison again. We all know the stimulating effect of seeing the conversion of others, and especially when it is the conversion of somebody who seemed to be a completely hopeless case. We know the exhilaration that accompanies any such event, even in one individual. There is nothing more wonderful in the life of the church than just this very thing. I have seen it many times and it is most wonderful; especially, as I say, when you get some kind of an abandoned character.

I can think of two outstanding examples of this, one an old man of seventy-seven who had lived about as riotous, evil, foul a life as a man could ever live; I distinctly remember still the thrill we all had when he even came into a meeting for the first time. But when he was converted, well, it is very difficult to describe the sense of exhilaration and of wonder and of joy that filled us all. And exactly the same with the other man who, in a sense, had sunk even lower into the mire and the filth of sin, and to see that man changed, becoming a new man in every respect. It is something that simply moves the heart of any Christian believer to its very depths. We know already that the gospel is true, but when we see some striking illustration of its truth and of its power, it lifts us up to the very heavens; and the Apostle is not exaggerating when he says, When this happens to these people of all others, and they come in as a nation, it will be nothing short of 'life from the dead'. The impossible will have happened. That is what he is saying. It cannot mean that there is going to be a great 'mass conversion' amongst the Gentiles because of that. That will have already happened before this takes place. But when the Gentiles in the church see the Jews coming in also, they shall be lifted up to the heavens of delight and glory and wonder and amazement. If, even as things are now, with just some of them, an occasional one here and there, being saved – if that has led to so much blessing for us, when they come in as a nation and as a body it will be so wonderful that we will scarcely be able to contain it, we will be lost in wonder, love and praise. The church will be glorying, she will be triumphant, she will be filled with this 'joy unspeakable and full of glory'.

# *Twelve*

*

*For if the firstfruit be holy, the lump is also holy: and if the root be holy, so are the branches. And if some of the branches be broken off, and thou, being a wild olive tree, wert graffed in among them, and with them partakest of the root and fatness of the olive tree; boast not against the branches. But if thou boast, thou bearest not the root, but the root thee. Thou wilt say then, The branches were broken off, that I might be graffed in. Well; because of unbelief they were broken off, and thou standest by faith. Be not highminded, but fear: for if God spared not the natural branches, take heed lest he also spare not thee. Behold therefore the goodness and severity of God: on them which fell, severity; but toward thee, goodness, if thou continue in his goodness: otherwise thou also shalt be cut off.* Romans 11:16–22

In these verses which constitute a further sub-section we have what is perhaps the most important statement anywhere in the Bible of the respective positions of Jew and Gentile in the Christian church. Paul presents it because he is concerned lest Gentiles should misunderstand their position with respect to the church, the Jews and to the whole question of salvation.

Here again is something that I want to sub-divide and suggest an analysis along these lines. In verses 16 and 17 he states the fundamental relationship of Jew and Gentile in the church. In verses 18 to 21 he issues a serious pastoral warning to the Gentiles not to misunderstand this relationship and give way to pride. And thirdly, in verse 22 itself he sums up the whole of this particular argument in terms of a general proposition.

In this portion, Paul gives us an extraordinary insight not only into God's plan and purpose, but into the whole question of the nature of the church and the respective places and positions of the Jews and the Gentiles in it. And what he really is going to tell us is this, that the Jews, speaking nationally, have a special place in the whole purpose of God for the Church.

We now proceed to consider this statement and begin with an analysis of it. You notice that he starts with the word 'For' but a better translation would be 'Now' or 'Since'. Take it like that. He is still speaking about the great truth that 'a fulness of the Jews' is going to come in but is now going to explain why that must be the case. So, why is that certain? His answer is given by way of two pictures. The first is: 'If the firstfruit be holy, the lump is also holy' and the second is, 'If the root be holy, so are the branches'.

Now these pictures have caused a great deal of trouble to many who have studied them, so it is important that we should try to be clear about their reference. Difficulty has often arisen because the moment people see the word 'firstfruit', they tend to go off at a tangent. They get hold of a concordance and look up the references to firstfruit and then they immediately draw various conclusions. They find that the Lord Jesus Christ is referred to as 'the firstfruits of them that slept' [*1 Cor.* 15:20], and that sends them off along that line. Then they remember that at the time of harvest, in the ancient days of the children of Israel, the firstfruit of the harvest would be gathered and offered to God. So commentators tend to have their exposition of the firstfruit controlled almost exclusively by that idea.

But that is a mistake because the Apostle is thinking about 'firstfruit' here in terms of a 'lump', and you do not speak of a lump of grain or a lump of fruit. There is, of course, in the Old Testament an exact description of the very thing to which the Apostle is referring. It is in the book of Numbers chapter 15 and verses 17 to 21: 'The Lord spake unto Moses, saying, Speak unto the children of Israel, and say unto them, When ye come into the land whither I bring you, Then it shall be, that, when ye eat of the bread of the land, ye shall offer up an heave offering unto the Lord', and here is the particular reference, 'Ye shall offer up a cake of the first of your dough for an heave offering: as ye do the heave offering of the threshingfloor, so shall ye heave it. Of the first of your dough ye shall give unto the Lord an heave offering in your generations'.

We are therefore to think of a lump of dough, a bit of which is to be taken, baked into a cake and offered to God. The point of this teaching was that the offering of that first bit out of the lump of dough to God as a holy sacrifice, means that the remainder of the lump also becomes holy. If the specimen is holy, the whole mass is holy. That was the teaching under the Old Testament dispensation and the

Apostle here takes it up and uses it as an illustration.

But then he comes to the second illustration which is much more straightforward. He says, 'If the root be holy, so are the branches'. There is no difficulty as to what he is saying here. It is that there is an essential, organic relationship between the root and the branches, so that whatever is true of the root must of necessity be true of the branches. Whatever root you plant in the ground, you will know exactly what to expect to come up. The nature of the root and the branches is one. And so he argues that if the root is holy, the branches must be too.

The word 'holy' is obviously important here and there is really no difficulty about its interpretation, as long as we realize that it does not refer so much to moral character as to something which has been consecrated or dedicated to God. Sometimes the word 'holy' does carry the meaning of purity. When we read that 'God is holy' it means He is absolutely perfect and sinless. But the word 'holy' does not always mean that. In its primary meaning, it carries this notion of something that is set apart for God. So the mount on which the Ten Commandments were given to Moses is referred to as 'the holy mount' because God had told them to set it apart and to put up fences, and the people were not allowed to approach it. In the same way, vessels in the temple are called 'holy vessels'. Or, if you want a still better example of this meaning of the word you have it in that statement in 1 Corinthians 7 where the Apostle is dealing with the position of a wife who is a Christian but has an unconverted husband, and the whole question of the children whom he describes as 'holy'. He does not of course mean that they are sinless or perfect; the same thing is said about the unbelieving father. What it means is that they are allowed to come as it were into the realm of the church. It does not mean moral purity.

So the Apostle is arguing like this: If that first bit of dough is consecrated to God in that way, then God has said that He will regard the whole lump in the same light and the nature of the root determines the nature of the branches. The question that arises for our consideration is what is being signified by these illustrations which are really saying the same thing, the second working out more clearly the point of the first.

To whom then does the term 'firstfruit' refer? To whom does the word 'root' refer? The firstfruit is to the lump exactly what the root is to the branches. So the question is, What is the meaning of the 'firstfruit' and the 'root'? Two main expositions have been put forward.

A common interpretation of these words is that the 'firstfruit' is a reference to the first Jewish Christians and so the Apostle is arguing that, since the first believers were Jews, so the great harvest is going to be of Jews also. This is quite a popular interpretation especially at the present time. Professor F. F. Bruce in his Tyndale Commentary tends to take this point of view but he puts it rather tentatively. He says, 'Here, the firstfruit most probably comprises those people of Jewish birth who had, like Paul, accepted Jesus as Messiah and Lord'. About the second picture he says, 'Changing the metaphor Paul now says that since the whole of the tree is of one character throughout, the holiness of the root sanctifies the branches. It is natural to give the root the same significance as the firstfruit, but if the "root and branch" figure stood by itself we should think of the patriarchs as constituting the root of the tree whose branches are the Israelites of the Christian era. This would be in line with Paul's later description of Israel as "beloved for the fathers' sakes" [verse 28]. Perhaps there is a transition of thought here as Paul passes from one metaphor to the other'. And then he adds another thought in a footnote: 'It is of course possible to interpret the "firstfruit" of verse 16 of the patriarchs, but this is a less likely interpretation'. Quite clearly he finds this somewhat difficult. He does not give us his reasons, but he just says that it is a less likely interpretation.

I suggest that this view is not less but much more likely, and, indeed, it is the only interpretation which is harmonious with the whole argument. The fact which should settle this point is that if the 'firstfruit' and the 'root' means believing Jews, like the Apostle Paul and others, then the branches, namely the Jews who are at present unconverted but who are to be converted, correspond to them. In other words, it has to be concluded that the unconverted Jews are the branches which come out of the Jews converted at the time of the Apostle Paul and others.

Now that seems to me to be entirely wrong because the argument of the entire chapter is to say that the bulk of the nation is outside, temporarily rejected. There is therefore no connection there. We cannot therefore say that he is arguing that these are branches that come out of that particular root. It is inconceivable that he should say so.

What then is the true exposition? The only natural interpretation here, surely, especially as we bear in mind the Apostle's whole fundamental objective, is to say that the firstfruit consists of the patriarchs: I mean by that, Abraham, Isaac, and Jacob in particular. Why? Well, because they were the beginning of the Jewish nation. They are the root of the Jewish nation. They are this 'firstfruit', the 'lump' of the great nation that came into being. There was a point when it was just Abraham alone. But then come Isaac and Jacob, and you get these constant references in the Scripture to 'the God of Abraham, Isaac, and Jacob'. There you have your 'firstfruit'. But when he comes to talk about the other picture it is in the singular: 'If the root be holy', he argues, 'so are the branches', and this, I do not hesitate to assert, is a reference to Abraham himself, to Abraham alone. Abraham is the root of the Jewish nation.

Now my argument is that the Apostle is concerned in the whole of this chapter with the Jews as a 'nation' and he is going to substantiate his statement that a day is coming when, as a whole, they will come in. So his undergirding argument is that as the first cake that was offered of the baked dough was holy; as the 'root', which is Abraham himself, was holy, so what comes out of Abraham is in the same category: it belongs to God.

My justification for this view is that Paul has, in the fourth chapter, already referred to Abraham in this very sense. He wrote: 'What shall we say then that Abraham our father, as pertaining to the flesh, hath found?' Abraham is the father of the Jewish nation, he is the root out of which they have all come. They were very proud of this and the Apostle is reminding them of it. Indeed, the prophets of the Old Testament often spoke in this way and a good example is in Isaiah chapter 51, verses 1 and 2: 'Hearken to me, ye that follow after righteousness, ye that seek the Lord: look unto the rock whence ye are hewn, and to the hole of the pit whence ye are digged. Look unto Abraham your father, and unto Sarah that bare you: for I called him alone, and blessed him, and increased him'. That is it! Abraham is the father, he is the 'pit' out of which the rock of the nation has been hewn.

Now where does all that lead us to? Before we can arrive at a definite conclusion we have to consider the statement of verse 17, 'If some of the branches be broken off, and thou, being a wild olive tree, wert grafted in among them, and with them partakest of the root and fatness of the olive tree.' We do not need to consider all that detailed argument for the moment but only the words 'the root and fatness of the olive tree'.

The Apostle puts a picture before us. He says, Here is a good olive tree and here is a wild one. Because some of the branches of the good olive tree are not bearing fruit they are cut off and thrown away, and some branches are taken from that wild olive tree and grafted into the good olive tree. The meaning of the phrase 'graffed in among them' really is 'grafted in in their place'.

Now where does the difficulty arise? Well it is almost amusing to read the commentators on this important verse. Large numbers of them immediately begin to say something like this: that the Apostle is showing very clearly here that he knew nothing at all about horticulture, that he was mainly a townsman and that the foolish thing which he does is typical of preachers who use an illustration when they do not know enough about the subject to which it relates. They say, 'The Apostle Paul is telling us that the picture of a bit of a wild olive tree, which is very poor in the matter of fruit production, grafted into a good olive tree, depicts the relationship of the Gentile to the Jew in the Church.' Well, they say, any man who knows anything at all about horticulture knows that that is something which is just never done. What is done is the exact opposite. You always graft a good branch into one that is not as good, and the result is you will then get a greater crop out of this grafted-in branch. It makes use of the life and the sap that is in the other, but you never do it the other way round. They say this is quite elementary, and it is merely indicative of the Apostle's ignorance of this matter.

But they begin to do research work and then they find that sometimes that is actually done after all! It is not common practice, but certain scholars, Sir William Ramsay in particular, who was a great archaeologist and interested in these matters, discovered that this was sometimes done. If you had a good olive tree which was becoming rather lethargic, it was not a bad thing to graft into it a bit of a wild olive tree, and this new graft would provide a kind of stimulus to the old tree and make it produce better fruit and even fairly good fruit on the graft itself. And so they feel that after all the Apostle Paul knew more about this business of horticulture than some of his critics tend to imagine!

Now all that seems to me to be completely irrelevant, and it shows the danger of going off at tangents because of some supposed special knowledge. I could easily elaborate on this point. I know people who say, We now understand things in the Bible which we did not before, because of our recent knowledge. The moment you say that you have already gone wrong, because obviously the Apostle uses illustrations which could be understood two thousand years ago; and if you can only understand an illustration in terms of modern scientific knowledge you are wrong. That knowledge was not available then, so the Apostle's illustration would have been of no value.

But all that is quite worthless to us for this reason, that the Apostle himself tells us in verse 24 that he is referring to something that is not according to nature. 'For if thou wert cut out of the olive tree which is wild by nature, and wert graffed contrary to nature into a good olive tree'. You see this is the tremendous point being made here and I included the earlier discussion in order to highlight it. The Apostle says, God has done something that is quite unusual, indeed He has done something that is miraculous: God has done something to enable even a wild olive tree to produce good olives. This is regeneration, if you like. God does not act according to nature in the matter of salvation. It takes a miracle to save a man, it takes a miracle to save the Gentiles. God does something contrary to nature, something supernatural. He tells us that. So we need not waste any of our time in recondite discoveries and try somehow or another to justify the great Apostle. He tells us that this is a most amazing thing. Who would ever have imagined that there was any hope for people like the Gentiles? But God, because He is God and because of the miraculous element of His grace, God is able to do this tremendous thing. And Paul says that that is exactly and precisely what God has done!

# *Thirteen*

*

*And if some of the branches be broken off, and thou, being a wild olive tree, wert graffed in among them, and with them partakest of the root and fatness of the olive tree;* Romans 11:17

This is a tremendous statement on a most important subject. From the standpoint of the future of the Christian church, and the future of the Jews as a nation, nothing is more important than this. There has been a good deal of discussion with respect to it and once again we are confronted by a number of interpretations. Having dealt with the technicalities of these verses, we now face up to the important question: What then does the Apostle mean by the olive tree?

I am going to confine attention to two main views. There are those who say that the olive tree is the Jewish nation. Abraham is the root, the tree is the Jewish nation. It is interesting to notice that Robert Haldane belongs to this company. Haldane says quite specifically, 'The Jewish nation was God's olive tree'. Professor F. F. Bruce appears, like Haldane, to believe this too.

I suggest to you that that is a wrong interpretation and I want to give you the reasons which lead me to say that. Incidentally I find myself in agreement with the vast majority of the older commentators, Calvin, and Hodge and others, who reject that idea. What are the reasons? Well here are some of them. If the olive tree is the Jewish nation, Gentile believers in Christ who are grafted on to that tree automatically become Jews. That seems to me sufficient in and of itself to refute that interpretation once and for ever.

But there does also seem to me to be a contradiction in the case of those who seem to espouse this view. Take, for instance, the following statement by Professor Bruce. He says, 'In such an unusual grafting, the old stock is reinvigorated by the new graft, and the new graft, in turn fed by the sap of the old stock, is able to bear such fruit as the wild olive could never produce'. But if the olive tree itself is the Jewish nation, what that tells us is that the coming in of the Gentiles has 'reinvigorated' it, whereas the Apostle's whole argument is that the Jews as a nation have been cast out. Far from being invigorated by the coming in of the Gentile believers, they have gone out that the Gentile believers may come in. In other words this view is a flat contradiction of the whole of the argument of the Apostle in this particular section and the whole chapter.

But we come to a third objection. We shall find that the Apostle refers to the nation of the Jews as 'branches'; not as the tree. You see he has a picture of a tree with branches, some cut off and others put in. There is therefore a difference between the tree and the branches. That again, it seems to me, is a most important argument against the identification of the olive tree with the Jewish nation.

And then fourthly, he says that we, as Gentile believers, have been grafted in 'and with them partake of the root and fatness of the olive tree'. But the Jewish nation is not 'the root and fatness' of which we receive, not in any sense at all. The Jewish nation is something that has stumbled, has failed, and has been cast out for that reason. We therefore receive no nutriment from the Jewish nation. The Jewish nation obviously therefore cannot be described as 'the root and the fatness'.

And I conclude, in the fifth place, that this is an entirely wrong interpretation of the meaning of the olive tree for this further reason: that the remainder of the argument does not fit in with that exposition at all. We must therefore seek a different one.

But how has this confusion arisen? Well it seems to me that it is because of the difficulty which relates to any analogy. It is almost impossible to get an analogy, an illustration, which really does perfectly convey the meaning that you want to convey. So what the Apostle, like every preacher, has to do is to use an illustration for one particular reason or purpose. You see the danger is to look at these two olive trees, one good and the other wild, and to proceed from that, saying, Well of course this is the contrast between the Jewish nation and the Gentiles. But that is not what the Apostle is saying at all. His meaning, it seems to me, is quite clear as long as we do not mechanically apply all the details of the illustration.

What then do I suggest the olive tree is? And my answer is, the olive tree means *the people of God*. They are given many names in Scripture. They are called the covenant people, the redeemed, God's nation and in Galatians 6, 'the Israel of God'. But the best term to use, it seems to me, is 'the people of God'.

The key to the understanding of the olive tree, as I see it, is really given to us in the ninth chapter of this Epistle in that famous sixth verse. I remember saying many times over that that sixth verse of the ninth chapter is the key to the understanding of the whole of these three chapters: 'Not as though the word of God hath taken none effect'. Why? Here is the answer: 'For they are not all Israel, which are of Israel'.

In other words, as we were taught there and as, indeed, the whole of the Bible in a sense reminds us, two nations came out of Abraham as the father and the root. Abraham leads to two nations; one of them is a natural nation and people, the other is a spiritual 'nation' and people. You remember that he goes on there in the ninth chapter and says, 'Neither, because they are the seed of Abraham, are they all children: but, in Isaac shall thy seed be called'.

Ishmael was a child of Abraham as Isaac was, and yet you see there is this vital difference of the spiritual seed: 'That is, They which are the children of the flesh, these are not the children of God' – these are not God's people – 'but the children of the promise are counted for the seed'. These are the people of God all along. And you remember how he went on working out that analogy and illustration. You get it in exactly the same way in the children of Isaac, in Jacob and Esau. Both are natural children but only Jacob is the spiritual child. He therefore constitutes the seed.

Now the whole difficulty arises when people forget that vital distinction. It is very easy to slip into this because all do come out of Abraham, and some of the promises which were made to Abraham were material or physical. There are indeed points at which the physical and the spiritual coalesce and seem to be one, hence the confusion. That of course was the ultimate reason why the Jews rejected our Lord and Saviour, and that is why they continue in trouble, and it is why many people today, concerned about prophetic questions, get into trouble. They forget this vital distinction between the two 'nations' if you like that came out of Abraham, and the fact, which complicates it still more, that at certain points they are both one.

Now I am putting it to you that the olive tree here is nothing but the spiritual nation. That is what I mean by 'the people of God'. Not the natural nation, but the spiritual nation that came out of Abraham.

These two, as I say, are related and yet it is vital that we should realize that they are separate. Now in Abraham, of course, they were one. He is the father of both the material nation, and that which is purely spiritual. And in general, this is true also of all the descendants of Isaac and of Jacob. But you notice that in every one of these instances there is also a division. One of the sons of Isaac is natural only, the other one is spiritual – spiritual and natural. And so it goes on as you follow out the working of this principle. You remember that Jacob was actually called 'Israel' himself, and it is through his twelve sons that you really see the nation of Israel, as it were, fully grown, and you are able to look at this developed nation.

Now the nation of Israel is regarded in the Old Testament as 'God's people'. In that sense they were the church of that time. Or as Paul puts it here they were certainly the 'natural branches' in this olive tree. They were the first to appear and so you often find them addressed as such. God addresses the whole of the nation of Israel as His people. You remember how, in the book of Exodus, in connection with the giving of the law, you have the great account of this at the beginning of the nineteenth chapter, where God addresses the whole nation. He turns to them and reminds them that He is their God, and He makes certain promises to them. 'Ye have seen what I did unto the Egyptians, and how I bare you on eagles' wings', and so on; and, 'If ye will obey my voice indeed, and keep my covenant, then ye shall be a peculiar treasure unto me above all people: for all the earth is mine'. And so God addresses them as His people and as His nation, and makes certain promises to them.

You will find that He speaks to them in the same way in many other places. There is an example in Deuteronomy chapter 7 and verse 6. And you remember how Stephen in his great address, recorded in the seventh chapter of the Acts of the Apostles, refers to the nation of Israel in general as 'the church in the wilderness'. So you are entitled to look upon the children of Israel as the 'church' under the old dispensation. God is there, as it were, looking at the whole nation as His people; but you must never forget the distinction that while they are all 'of Israel', they are not all Israel.

The olive tree, then, the true people of God, are those to whom the Apostle is really referring. There are others who seem to belong to it for a while, but they do not really do so. The olive tree constitutes only these true spiritual people of God. With them you always have these others, and at times you cannot tell the difference between them. But all is known unto God, 'The Lord knoweth them that are his'.

Now then what is the Apostle's teaching? Well we can put it like this. The unbelieving Jews, though they are Abraham's seed, and though in a sense they are the natural branches upon this olive tree, are cut off because of their unbelief and do not really belong to the olive tree. But on the other hand, he says, the believing Gentiles are grafted in. They have come from the outside, they did not belong to the nation of Israel, and therefore in a sense you can call them a wild olive tree. But the only point of importance is that they do not belong to the visible nation of Israel. But, says the Apostle, because they have believed they have been brought in and grafted in. They have not been grafted into the Jewish nation but into the people of God. Now that is the point. And that is why, I say, you must insist upon saying that the olive tree is the people of God.

The Apostle tells us in many places that when Gentiles believe in the Lord Jesus Christ they are not only grafted into this olive tree, into the people of God, but because of that they become 'Abraham's children' and they begin to share in all the blessings of this covenant people who trace their origin and their root back to him. There is a particularly clear statement of this which is to be found in the Epistle to the Galatians, in chapter 3 and verse 29: 'Now if ye be Christ's, then are ye Abraham's seed, and heirs according to the promise'. Paul is writing to Gentile believers who are not only Christ's, but also Abraham's seed. They are in this olive tree, in this covenant people of God that come out of Abraham and so are heirs according to the promise.

But let us go on to draw the conclusions or the lessons that arise inevitably from all this. I would divide them into two sections. First of all, there are certain conclusions about the Christian church because that is what the Apostle is dealing with here. We start with that. The second section will be about the Jews in particular.

Now there are some very important things to be learned here about the Christian church. The first is that it is not something entirely new. Many people make that false statement. They say, the church is something absolutely new. There was no such thing at all until you come to the New Testament times. Here I think we are shown very plainly that that is quite wrong. It is true that the distinctively and specifically 'Christian' church did come into being then but we must not say that the 'church' did. I have already quoted you Stephen's statement in which he refers to the 'church' in the wilderness, the children of Israel. We must get hold of this idea of 'the people of God'. That is the fundamental thing in the Bible. The people of God under the old dispensation were mainly, almost exclusively, the children of Israel; under the New Testament, they were almost exclusively Gentile, with but a few Jews, this 'remnant according to the election of grace' about which the Apostle has been speaking. But the church is not something new which only starts in the New Testament.

Secondly, I would say that God's people are always one. They are one in the Old Testament and in the New Testament. Now the Apostle proves that very clearly by this analogy of the olive tree. The olive tree did not come into being in the New Testament. It has been there since Abraham. So it has been going since then. You must not say that the people of God, the redeemed, 'start' after Calvary or after our Lord's ascension, or after Pentecost. The people of God are in the Old Testament as well as in the New. It is the whole point of this illustration. The Apostle's entire argument is going to depend upon this great statement. There is only one olive tree. Some branches are removed, some branches come in, but the tree remains one, and there is only one. So the church, God's people, is one always.

Although it is true that there are certain differences between the redeemed in the Old and the New, they are not fundamental. They are differences in the degree of blessing and of understanding as well as circumstantial detail but we must not conclude from these that we have finished with one thing in the Old Testament, and start with something absolutely different in the New.

This has often troubled the Christian Church. Quite early on there was a heresy which rejected the whole of the Old Testament and there are many people today who tend to do that. One sometimes hears even evangelical Christians speak as if they were more or less dismissing the Old Testament. They do not see why we need it any longer. They have never seen the continuity of the people of God, and that the people of God in both Testaments are one. But this is a vital part of the teaching here. We have misunderstood the olive tree completely unless we are clear about this.

Then I go on to say that there is only one way of salvation and it has always been the same. Now we have seen this at great length in this Epistle. The Apostle proves that in chapter 4 where he makes clear that Abraham was justified by faith. There has never been a way of salvation except 'by faith'. Never! And here of course he puts it in the picture of the olive tree. It is only our relationship to this that saves us. It does not matter who we are, it is always by faith, it is always by God's supernatural action. What saves anybody is to be put into the olive tree, nothing else can save at all. What saves us is that we are brought into relationship with 'the root and fatness' of this olive tree. This is eternal life, the life that God gives; and He gave it in the Old Testament as well as in the New. Abraham, remember, is our father; we are his children.

Some people do not realize this; they think these Old Testament saints were not saved. But they were. They were in the kingdom. They are the children of God as much as we are, and we are the children of Abraham because we are the children of faith. They received of 'the root and the fatness of the olive tree' and that is precisely what we receive. We are only Christians, and we are only saved, because we are born again, because we have all the results of being born again. We have this 'life', this root and fatness of the olive tree. Now you know there are people who say that in some future time the Jews are going to be saved by keeping the law. That is an absolute denial of the meaning of this picture. There is only one way of salvation, there is only one olive tree, and it is being in this that saves, and nothing else.

So our fourth lesson is that nationality and natural birth is in no sense the deciding factor. There is only one deciding factor and that is our faith relationship in Abraham. In this olive tree you may be a Jew by nature, you may be a Gentile by nature, it does not matter. The Jews tended to say that they alone were saved. The Gentiles, as the Apostle is going on to tell them here, were in danger of saying the same. But nationality does not come into it at all. 'There is neither Greek nor Jew, . . . Barbarian, Scythian, bond nor free' [*Col.* 3:11]. It does not matter at all. The only thing that does matter is, Are you engrafted into this olive tree, or are you not? So you see he cuts the ground from people who tend to rely upon their nationality or any of these things that are true of us by nature. That is all brought out in this wonderful picture of the olive tree.

And then I make my fifth point, which is this: the blessings which all who belong to the olive tree receive are always the same blessings. It is the same for the natural branches, it is the same for these other branches that are grafted in 'contrary to nature'. It is all the same, they receive exactly the same blessings.

Now this is, of course, the great point that is made by the Apostle in Ephesians, chapter 2. He is writing to these Gentile Ephesians and he says: 'Remember, that you in time past were Gentiles in the flesh, you were called Uncircumcision by that which is called the Circumcision in the flesh made by hands'. But 'remember', he says, 'that at that time you were without Christ'. Outside Christ! Well, what was true of them as such? Well, he says, 'You were then aliens from the commonwealth of Israel, and strangers from the covenants of promise, having no hope and without God in the world'. He says, 'You, as Gentiles, had nothing to do with God's commonwealth'. You were strangers from the covenants of promise that God had made with His covenant people. But immediately he adds, 'but now in Christ Jesus you who sometimes were far off are made nigh by the blood of Christ'. In what sense are they 'made nigh'? In the next verses he goes on to show how they have been made nigh by our Lord's work upon the Cross, where He has 'broken down the middle wall of partition, and has reconciled them by the blood of his Cross, and has made of twain one new man, has preached peace to you which were afar off, and to them that were nigh, to Gentiles and to Jews'. Now then, he says, in the nineteenth verse, Because you have become believers you 'are no more strangers and foreigners, but fellow-citizens with the saints, and are of the household of God'.

In other words, You were outside the olive tree, but now you are in it. Before, all these wonderful covenant promises had nothing to do with you. They now have everything to do with you. You are included, you belong to the olive tree, and now therefore you are 'heirs of the promises', you are 'heirs' of all the blessings of salvation that God has promised to His covenant people. This is also emphasized in the third chapter of Ephesians. As I say, this is not something absolutely new. What has happened to us is that we are allowed to share in what had been received and experienced by the people of God through the centuries of the Old Testament dispensation. It is no longer one nation, it is now many nations, it is now the Church, but essentially it is the same thing. And all the blessings that we enjoy are those blessings which had been promised to Abraham's seed of old, which until this point only the Jews had received.

But in the second place, there are conclusions to be drawn from this great teaching which concern the Jews. While it is true that it does not matter whether you are a Jew or a Gentile in the matter of salvation, at the same time the Apostle is concerned to teach that there is something special and unique about the Jews' position. Now we must not lose sight of this. The danger is to make either too much or too little of the position of the Jews. I am now dealing with the danger of making too little of it.

What then is special about the Jews' relationship to the whole purpose of God with respect to His people? First: the Jews have a special position because, after all, they were the first or the natural branches. At first the olive tree consisted of them and of them alone, Abraham and his own natural progeny. The Gentiles were right outside. But I hasten to add, in the second place, they are in that special position not because of who they were but only because of God's choice of them and His promises to them, and because of what He did in them and through them. God did not choose them because they were better than anybody else. He tells them that repeatedly in the Old Testament. But they are in a special position because God did choose them. They were the first that He chose, and He chose them in general as the natural progeny and seed of Abraham.

But while I say they have a 'special' position I assert equally strongly that they do not have a 'separate' position. Special but not separate. Let me expound that. The Jews are only branches in the olive tree exactly like the Gentiles. They are no more. They belong to the same olive tree as the Gentiles, but they are not the olive tree itself. They do not have a separate, or different, or special salvation in God's kingdom. This notion that the Jews, in some future age, are going to come back and have some special position – some carrying it even to the ridiculous extreme of saying that the Jewish portion of the church will remain always on earth, and the Gentile one will be in heaven – is a flat contradiction of this teaching. They are to be grafted into this same olive tree that contains the Gentiles; nothing more is going to happen to them. There is a great promise here; this is the Apostle's argument, that in a national sense they are going to be converted. Yes, but they will need to be converted like everybody else, and they will be grafted into the same olive tree as Gentiles and all others who are believers, simply because of the grace of God.

In other words there never will be two churches. There will never even be two divisions in the Christian church. The Christian church is one and one only. It takes the same grace of God to convert a Jew as a Gentile, and the Gentile as a Jew, and they will share the same blessings, they are all joint-heirs of exactly the same promises and of the same blessed hope.

# *Fourteen*

⁂

*Boast not against the branches. But if thou boast, thou bearest not the root, but the root thee. Thou wilt say then, The branches were broken off, that I might be graffed in. Well; because of unbelief they were broken off, and thou standest by faith. Be not highminded, but fear: for if God spared not the natural branches, take heed lest he also spare not thee. Behold therefore the goodness and severity of God: on them which fell, severity; but toward thee, goodness, if thou continue in his goodness: otherwise thou also shalt be cut off.* Romans 11:18–22

In verses 16 and 17 of Romans chapter eleven, the Apostle is very concerned to put clearly to these Gentile believers the position of both Jew and Gentile in the Christian Church. He is dealing with this great and extraordinary phenomenon, that the Jews, who had been the people of God throughout the centuries, are in the main outside the Christian church, whereas the Gentiles, who had no knowledge of the only true God, but were steeped in paganism and all that accompanies it, had come into the church.

That provides the context for the Apostle's treatment of the subject of the Jew and Gentile in the Christian church and their relationship to each other. Nowhere else in the New Testament is there such a full exposition of this theme. The Apostle presents it in terms of his picture of the 'olive tree' which represents 'the people of God', starting with Abraham, but going back beyond him to Noah, Abel and others, and even Adam and Eve.

This is made particularly clear with the call of Abraham, and that is why Abraham is described so constantly in the Scripture as 'the father of the faithful', and that is why we as Gentile Christian believers are described at the end of Galatians 3 as the children of Abraham.

The Apostle turns aside, for a moment. Having laid that down

Paul addresses an exhortation to the Gentiles. He has explained their position to them but now he is particularly anxious that they should be aware of a certain danger that confronted them. This is what we have in verses 18 to 22 before the Apostle returns to his main theme, which is to expound yet further the position of the Jews in relation to this olive tree which is the people of God.

We turn therefore to verses 18 to 22 which are a clear indication of the fact that the great Apostle was always first and foremost a pastor and a teacher. Although he is handling the profoundest doctrine conceivable he is no dry-as-dust lecturer who would go on speaking if there were nobody listening to him. That is not the Apostle Paul. He is concerned that people should understand the truth, and is equally concerned that they should obey it.

How shall we deal with this little sub-section? Well, I have divided it for your consideration under four main headings. First of all, of course, we have to engage in actual exposition. We must have clearly in our minds exactly what the Apostle is saying.

Secondly, we have got to extract from that the teaching of the Apostle. In other words it is never enough merely to give an alternative translation or a kind of paraphrase. We start with that but we do not stop with it. We ask, 'What is taught here; what are the principles enunciated; what is the doctrine that the Apostle is anxious to convey?'.

And then thirdly, in considering the teaching we shall find ourselves confronted with a problem. A problem is raised here, not by the Apostle, but as we relate what he teaches here to what he has taught elsewhere about the final perseverance of the saints and assurance of salvation. So there is a problem implicit in his teaching and we have got to look at that.

And then fourthly, I hope to be able to take the whole of this teaching, having dealt with that problem, and show its relevance and its application to the very situation that is confronting us as Christian people at the present time. We are members of the Christian church and there is great confusion in the world today with regard to the nature of the church. Indeed, the teaching presented by the Ecumenical Movement seems to me to be suffering from a failure to understand the essential teaching of the Apostle at this very point.

Let us start, then, with exposition. What is he talking about here? Well, as is his custom, he states his theme straight away. At the beginning of verse 18 he says, 'Boast not against the branches'. This is where the context is helpful. The branches are the bulk of the Jewish nation that is now outside the Christian church. They had been the people of God. They were 'the natural branches' in this olive tree, but they have been plucked away and broken off. Having described it like that he says, 'Now, do not you make the mistake of boasting against those branches'. He is addressing Gentile Christians who have been grafted into the olive tree in the place of those natural branches, the Jews.

Now that is the point: he realizes that there is a danger that the Gentiles who have been brought into the church somewhat unexpectedly, will succumb to the danger of pride in their own position and begin to despise the Jews. That is what is in his mind when he writes, 'Boast not against the branches'. You Gentiles, he says, must not boast in yourselves as over against the Jews, you must not despise them.

Now how were they in danger of doing this? First, they just took it for granted that they were better than the Jews. They say, We are the majority in the church and so it is obvious that we are better than the Jews and the church is ours. Now the Apostle immediately answers that in the second part of the eighteenth verse. He makes clear to Gentiles that they are only branches in the tree and not the root. Their boasting is quite ridiculous and preposterous. He is reminding them, in other words, that they are not the tree but that from outside they have been grafted into it, and they are what they are because they have been enabled to 'partake of the root and fatness of the olive tree'. That is his whole case. That is what makes people Christians, they are put into Christ, put into the church, and receive this 'life' that is in Him. So his immediate reply to them is that they have no grounds for boasting at all – nor does anyone.

Secondly, they pointed to the fact that natural branches had been broken off so that Gentiles might be grafted in and claimed that this must indicate some superiority on the part of Gentiles. To be told by Paul that the natural branches had a priority and a special dignity did not to them seem to take account of the fact that they had not only been removed but also replaced.

The Apostle deemed that to be a very serious matter and so he deals fully and firmly with it. He is taking no risks at all about this point and he wants them to see how any such thinking on their part is really a betrayal of the fact that they have not thoroughly understood the whole question of the way of salvation. He deals with it like this. First of all he gives them a direct answer. This is the first part of the twentieth verse. Watch his method. 'Thou wilt say then, The branches were broken off, that I might be graffed in. Well;' says the Apostle, 'because of unbelief they were broken off, and thou standest by faith'. What does this mean? The Apostle says: I of course accept the fact that the Jews as a nation and as a people are no longer in the olive tree, they are not in the church but are outside. That is what he has been saying at great length from the beginning of chapter 9. Your facts, he says, are perfectly right, but the deduction that you have drawn from them is altogether and entirely wrong. Of course, he says, the Jews have been broken off, but they have not been broken off for the reason that you are assuming.

What he is saying is this: If you think that the Jews have been broken off and that you Gentiles have been put in because Gentiles are inherently superior to the Jews, you have fallen into precisely the same error as the Jews themselves fell into and you have completely misunderstood the way of salvation. Salvation is never a matter of nationality or of merit. By saying we are in because we are superior you are falling back on nationality, you are saying Gentiles are better than Jews. Yes but you see, says the Apostle, that is the very mistake of the Jews. They thought they were the people of God, were superior to everybody and alone were to be saved, simply because they were Jews. You are repeating their own error which is to think that what decides whether you are a saved person, a Christian, or not, is your nationality. The moment you begin to think that you are already wrong. If you think you are saved by your nationality or by your own inherent goodness or any merit that belongs to you, you are denying the whole of the Christian teaching with regard to salvation. Why? Well, because, as he puts it – 'Well; because of unbelief they were broken off, and thou standest by faith'.

You see the thing that determines and controls salvation is not nationality or upbringing or inherent goodness or anything you have done; it is one thing only. Faith! Belief! The Jews are cast off solely because of their unbelief. And why are you Gentiles in? Not because you are a wonderful people, simply because you have exercised faith. Nothing else at all!

I must draw your attention briefly to the word 'standest'. It has a crucial place in Romans 5:2. It means having a standing before God through faith in the Lord Jesus Christ. It is the opposite of what will happen to the wicked in Psalm 1. They will not 'stand in the congregation of the righteous' but will be blown away like chaff. This is a tremendous notion that we must never lose sight of. The Christian is not someone who either grovels or lounges before God. Realizing the way of salvation, he 'stands'. He is neither uncertain nor hesitant. 'There is therefore now no condemnation to them who are in Christ Jesus.' Once a man realizes the way of salvation he 'stands'.

But he does not leave the matter there. He starts by correcting them but continues with a warning, 'Be not high-minded, but fear'. Now he is reprimanding them and they deserve it. How arrogant of anyone to claim he is in the Christian church because of what and who he is. This is not only wrong, it is terribly dangerous. To have a more exalted view of oneself than is warranted is a grave danger. The antidote to that, he tells them, is 'fear'. This is the same as 'Take heed' in verse 21. 'If God spared not the natural branches, take heed lest he also spare not thee'. So you see, having put them right with his direct answer on the pure matter of doctrine, he issues this terrific warning – 'Beware of being high-minded'. This is a great theme running right through the whole of the Bible as we shall see.

So the third thing he does, having corrected and reproved them, is to produce an unanswerable argument which is going to put this matter right once and for ever. He says, verse 21: 'If God spared not the natural branches, take heed lest he also spare not thee'. Now why do I say that this is unanswerable? Well, I will go further, I will say that at this point the Apostle simply demolishes this foolish case put up by the Gentiles in their ignorance. How does he do so? By taking up his favourite formula which is an argument from greater to less. This is pure logic, of course, and the Apostle was a master at logic.

He begins with what is greater which is that God has taken out of this olive tree the Jews, who were the natural branches, His own people, because of their arrogant pride and cast them aside. He then goes on to what is less which is that no one should be surprised if He does that with people who are not His own original people and were brought in in an unnatural manner.

Let me put it to you like this. Charles Hodge, I think, deals with this in a most excellent manner. It is an argument, if you like, in this way. Imagine a man who has a son to whom he looked to carry on his business and his tradition. The father lavished his love on the son and did everything he could for his well-being. But unfortunately this son turns out to be a poor character, insults his father, does everything contrary to his father's will. The father can see the whole of his purpose going astray, and he feels this to such an extent that he puts his son on one side and he takes, if you like, a servant or somebody else's son with whom he is acquainted, and he adopts this other man and puts him into the position of his son. Now this is the Apostle's argument: he says if the father is such a righteous man and has got such a view of his own purpose that he even puts his own natural son on one side, you be very careful as the adopted son. If he will put his natural son on one side because of his ill behaviour, how much more so is he likely to do it with you.

Now that is the argument and it is an unanswerable argument. He here demolishes the case of the Gentiles once and for ever. 'Look here', says Paul, 'it was because of their arrogant pride in themselves that God has put aside the Jews, the people whom He prepared for Himself. If He has done that with them, how much more so will He do that with people like you Gentiles who have come in from the outside and have been grafted in in this (as it were) unnatural manner. Now that is the argument I say from the greater to the less. It is the argument from what God has already done to what He will inevitably do with others who are in a like situation and position.

And then fourthly, in verse 22 he goes on to draw a great deduction from all this with regard to the character of God and God's ways with respect to man. Now here it is: 'Behold therefore the goodness and severity of God: on them which fell, severity; but toward thee, goodness, if thou continue in his goodness: otherwise thou also shalt be cut off'. Now here is of course a great general statement and, as I say, it is a kind of deduction. That is why he starts by saying, 'Behold therefore . . .' In the light of what God has actually done this is the only conclusion to which we can come.

In other words, he lifts up the whole argument to this position. Men become boastful and proud and despise others in the kingdom of God for one reason only, and that is, that they fail to realize the truth about God Himself. That is what it all ultimately comes to. This is the root cause of nearly all our troubles. How has it become possible, how is it conceivable that anybody should boast in the presence of God, whether Jew or Gentile? And there is only one answer – it is that they have failed to understand the truth about God, about His nature, about His character, about His attributes; and therefore he says nothing is more important than that you should be clear about this. God has revealed the truth concerning

Himself and for this particular object we are dealing with here He has revealed not only His goodness but also His severity. And men and women get into trouble always because instead of taking the revelation of the character of God and His ways with respect to men as we have it revealed in the Bible, they substitute their own ideas for that, or they take a part of the teaching of the Bible and they reject the remainder.

You can see immediately how this is so applicable at this present time. We are living in an age when people even justify the fact that they never attend a place of worship at all on the grounds that 'God is Love'. They justify immorality in the same way, 'God is Love'. There is no such thing as the wrath of God, there is no justice, there is no severity. That is the very thing that is happening at the present time; men and women who believe in God. So they say they do not believe in God as He has revealed Himself. They have got partial notions; they pick and choose. They accept what they like, they reject what they do not like. In other words they do not worship God at all, they worship an image which they themselves have erected. And there are others, of course, who go still further, who instead of taking the biblical revelation in any sense discard it completely and in terms of philosophy and so on construct a 'god' after their own image and say that this is God, and obviously, therefore, they are wrong in the whole of their thinking and become wrong likewise in their behaviour and in their conduct.

This is the exposition of what the Apostle says about this whole matter. Paul is dealing with the Gentiles who, like the Jews before them, were imagining that they were included simply because they were such good people, because they are superior to others and so on. He is therefore speaking to people who think they are Christians because of their own worth. He is dealing with people who think they are Christians because they were christened or baptized or born in a 'Christian' country. He is dealing with people who think they are Christians because of the good life they have lived. He is dealing with people who are boasting about anything at all. And you notice what he says. He says this is all due to the fact that you have misunderstood that salvation is by faith alone, this basic principle. It is a denial of that; still more it is a failure to realize the truth about God, and that the only thing that matters is our relationship to God, and that that is always a matter of faith only.

# *Fifteen*

*

*Boast not against the branches. But if thou boast, thou bearest not the root, but the root thee. Thou wilt say then, The branches were broken off, that I might be graffed in. Well; because of unbelief they were broken off, and thou standest by faith. Be not highminded, but fear: for if God spared not the natural branches, take heed lest he also spare not thee. Behold therefore the goodness and severity of God: on them which fell, severity; but toward thee, goodness, if thou continue in his goodness: otherwise thou also shalt be cut off.* Romans 11:18–22

Having developed our exposition of these verses, we come to the teaching we find in this statement. Now what is it? Well there is a general point to note and it is that our troubles do not come to an end when we become Christians. The impression is sometimes given that once you come to Christ your troubles are ended, and that to be a Christian means you have no difficulties, everything is clear to you. This passage we are looking at, if we had no other, is enough in and of itself to tell us that that just is not true. The moment we are born again and become Christian we immediately need teaching, we need instruction, we need warnings, reproofs, reprimands – all the things which the Apostle lists in what he says about the Scriptures, you remember, in 2 Timothy 3:16. The mere fact that we have become Christians does not mean we are perfect in behaviour. We need a tremendous amount of instruction and guidance. Here, you see, we are reminded of all that. The Gentiles have been brought into the church but they are in trouble, in danger even, and the Apostle has to address this very serious and solemn exhortation to them. Very well, there is the first lesson and a very important lesson it is. I think that I, like most other pastors, have seen more people get into trouble at this point, perhaps, than at any other, this kind of magical notion of the Christian life – that you take it all by faith and you do not need instruction, and you do not need teaching: but nothing is more dangerous than that. But that is a general point.

But what is the particular teaching? Well the first thing we find here is this, that our greatest danger always in this life, before we became Christians, and since, is our pride. Pride is the greatest enemy of man in all his states and conditions. Now you notice how the Apostle puts it – 'Boast not'. 'Do not boast against the branches' he says to these Gentiles. Or he puts it in other terms in the twentieth verse: 'Be not high-minded'. How often is boasting, high-mindedness, dealt with in the Scripture! This is not surprising because pride was the cause of the original fall of man. Indeed it was the cause of the fall of the devil before that. Here is the root cause of all our evils and all our troubles – pride. And, of course, the great Apostle knew this in his own personal experience. Here is the man who had been a proud self-righteous Pharisee, and, knowing all about this, he was constantly very watchful. In his epistles how often did he have to deal with it!

Look at the whole problem in the church at Corinth; it was all really due to pride, showing itself in different forms. Even the disputes over Paul, Apollos, and Cephas were ultimately to be traced to this. Boasting in men instead of boasting in the Lord only. It was also present in the disputes over food offered to idols and over spiritual gifts. The Epistle to the Philippians also concentrates attention on it, indeed it can be found running right through the pages of the New Testament Epistles. It is such a pernicious thing, so utterly contradictory of the spirit of the gospel. Indeed, I am concerned lest I give you only a head knowledge of this great Epistle.

How does this tendency to boasting and to pride show itself? Well, we can divide this into positive and negative. How does it show itself positively? In various forms. First, there is pride of nationality. What havoc that has wrought, not only outside but even inside the church. Throughout the centuries it has led to trouble, and though we have become Christian we are not immune to the pride of 'nationality' and boasting in connection with it. Then there is pride in one's ancestry! Sometimes one's forefathers may have been great or important religious people and important in the church. Boasting of that, resting on that, feeling it gives you some place of superiority. Oh I could illustrate that to you at great length. Many a famous minister has fallen into that trap and has sometimes been instrumental in putting his own son into his own succession in a pastorate when the son was not fit to be there. You can think of endless illustrations of this.

Then sometimes it takes the form, as it did mainly here with these Gentiles, of pride in one's own worth, feeling, 'Of course we are Christians because we are good people and so on, there is something good about us.' Pride in one's works, moral outlook or intellectual ability and understanding. 'Knowledge puffeth up,' says Paul, whereas charity builds up. Knowledge always has this terrible tendency. It is not at all surprising. The intellect is God's greatest gift to man, and therefore the devil knows that, so he presses us on this and leads us astray.

And then, of course, pride in various other gifts. I do not only mean the spiritual gifts but even pride in natural gifts which can be of use and of service in the kingdom of God. Pride in speech, pride in singing and so on has been a curse in the church so often, has led to quarrels, disputes and difficulties. What a horrible thing it is!

And how does pride show itself negatively? I can sum up its manifestations by saying that it means 'despising others'. Now that is what these Gentiles were guilty of. The Jews in the main were outside the church; they had been excluded. God, as it were, had put them on one side, they had 'stumbled' as the Apostle has been putting it, and the Gentiles began to look down upon them and to despise them. And as we have already seen there has been this terrible danger amongst Gentiles ever since to despise the Jews, and not only to despise them but even to persecute them and to handle them in a shameful and entirely indefensible manner. Despising is but the reflex of pride. You elevate yourself, you demote others.

What does the Apostle mean to point out on this matter? He makes it quite clear that the moment you begin to boast of yourself or despise anyone, what you are really doing is showing very clearly that you are thinking in terms of justification by works instead of justification by faith only. And it simply is that and nothing else at all. That was the whole trouble with the Jews. 'We are the people of God. We keep the law. We are Abraham's seed. That justifies us.' That is what they were resting on – and here are Gentiles who have come into the church on the terms of justification by faith only; they have seen what the Jews could not see. But now having seen this, they have slipped, in their minds, back to justification by works. The devil will always try to get us back on to works. And there is nothing that shows that more plainly or clearly than this tendency to 'boast' and to glory in self in any shape or form.

So the Apostle gives us the answer to all that, he answers it now, and he answers it by saying this. Salvation is always and entirely by grace through faith. Now he puts that here, of course, in terms of his own illustration, this illustration of the tree and the branches. 'If some of the branches be broken off, and thou, being a wild olive tree, wert graffed in among them' – they did not graft themselves in, they have been grafted in – 'and with them partakest of the root and fatness of the olive tree'. They were a wild olive tree, nothing at all. It is only their position and their condition in which they are now receiving of the root and fatness of this olive tree that makes them what they are. 'Do not boast', he says. 'If thou boast, thou bearest not the root, but the root thee' – and on he goes to put it in terms of this great faith principle. 'Because of unbelief they were broken off, and thou standest by faith' – nothing else. 'Be not high-minded, but fear', and so on.

The same truth can be put in another form which is that there is no such thing as inherent worth in anybody. Now this is absolutely fundamental and Paul has emphasised it repeatedly and nowhere more clearly than in the third chapter of this Epistle where he says, 'Now we know that what things soever the law saith, it saith to them who are under the law' – Why? Well – 'that every mouth may be stopped' – not some mouths, but 'every mouth shall be stopped' – 'and all the world' – Gentile, Jew – everybody, 'all the world may become guilty before God'. 'Therefore by the deeds of the law there shall no flesh be justified in his sight: for by the law is the knowledge of sin.' 'But now the righteousness of God without the law is manifested, being witnessed by the law and the prophets; even the righteousness of God which is by faith of Jesus Christ unto all and upon all them that believe: for there is no difference: for all have sinned, and come short of the glory of God'. All! There is no exception. 'Being justified freely by his grace, through the redemption that is in Christ Jesus', and the emphasis is on the 'freely' and 'grace' [*Rom.* 3:19–24]. Very well, I am simply putting that to you in this form, that there is no such thing as inherent worth in anybody. Not in any nation, not in any individual – 'the whole world lieth guilty before God.' 'There is none righteous, no, not one'. Anyone who boasts in any respect is denying this central primary principle and doctrine of justification by faith only.

Or let me put it still more plainly and strongly. All spiritual difference amongst men is the result of God's grace only. You can divide the world into Christians and non-Christians. What makes the difference? There is only one answer. It is not because you belong to a certain country or have had certain parents. What makes the spiritual difference that you see amongst men is nothing but God's grace. Nothing else at all. And you must never allow anything else to insinuate itself.

So I go on to say this: The Christian life starts by faith, it continues by faith and ends by faith. It is all of faith. There is no other basis for a relationship between man and God at any time. Now we saw in the fourth chapter of this great Epistle that the Apostle there surely has established this once and for ever when he takes up the case of Abraham and of David. The Jews got muddled over this. Paul says, Look here, God has always dealt with our forefathers, with us, with everybody, solely on the basis of faith. That is the method always. Or as he has put it in the fourth chapter, you remember, in that tremendous statement in verses 16 and 17: 'Therefore it is of faith, that it might be by grace; to the end that the promise might be sure to all the seed; not to that only which is of the law, but to that also which is of the faith of Abraham; who is the father of us all'. It is of faith, not nationality, or gifts; do not bring anything because it is all useless; it does not count in the currency of heaven, it is not accepted. Nothing matters, nothing counts save 'faith'.

But we must go on to state this principle: man is responsible for his damnation but he is in no sense responsible for his salvation. Now you remember how we saw that several times in the ninth chapter and we followed the Apostle as he worked out this argument. It is what we call an antinomy. It seems to be contradictory. You cannot encompass it in your mind, you cannot understand it. Well thank God we are not meant to understand it, but here it is plainly stated in the Scriptures. Man is responsible for his damnation, but he is in no sense responsible for his salvation.

Now where do I find that? Well here it is. 'If some of the branches be broken off, and thou, being a wild olive tree, wert graffed in among them, and with them partakest of the root and fatness of the olive tree; boast not against the branches' – you have done nothing. 'If thou boast, thou bearest not the root, but the root thee'. You have not saved yourselves, this is the action of God. It is God Who grafts anybody in; nobody can graft himself in. Nobody wants to. We were 'dead in trespasses and sins', and, you see, in terms of this picture, we were the wild olive tree. No good! No value at all! No fruit! Worthless! And it cannot graft itself in. It is God!

But there is this other side, that a man is responsible for his damnation because of unbelief. They were broken off. That is the cause of their being broken off, their unbelief. They are responsible for damnation but not for salvation, and he is warning them to be careful.

And then you see he is going to say later on: 'If they abide not still in unbelief, they shall be grafted in: for God is able to graft them in again. For if thou wert cut out of the olive tree which is wild by nature, and wert grafted contrary to nature' – this miracle of redemption – 'into a good olive tree: how much more shall these, which be the natural branches, be grafted into their own olive tree'. And then he goes on to say that he knows that this is going to take place, and gives the reason for it.

Now the principle that we are involved with at this point is that unbelief, for which we are responsible, is always the cause of damnation. So that man is always responsible to God. The gospel is preached. You remember we saw it in chapter 10, where he says 'How shall they preach unless they be sent' and so on; and here is the gospel preached, 'How beautiful are the feet of them that preach the gospel of peace, and bring glad tidings of good things'. Then suddenly, 'But they have not all obeyed the gospel'. They have been called to obey it; the proclamation, the announcement has been made, the offer has been given, and they should obey it. If they do not they are damned and they are held responsible. Man is always responsible. The doctrine of election does not say that man is not responsible, it says he is responsible. Man is responsible for his damnation. Unbelief is the cause of damnation, and a man is saved by faith. Where does his faith come from? It is entirely of grace. 'By grace are ye saved through faith; and that not of yourselves, it is the gift of God'. It is God Who quickens the dead by His Spirit. The dead are lifeless. 'The natural man receiveth not the things of the Spirit of God: for they are foolishness unto him: neither can he, because they are spiritually discerned'. No, no, salvation is altogether and entirely of God. Everybody who is a Christian, is a Christian not because of nationality, or ancestry, or morality or because you chose to believe . . . No, no! You are what you are by the grace of God.

But remember that the Apostle preaches and inculcates the constant need of humility, of godly fear, and of watchfulness. Look at it in verses 20 and 21: 'Well; because of unbelief they were broken off, and thou standest by faith. Be not high-minded, but fear.' 'What?' you say, 'Is it part of the gospel of Christ to tell people to be afraid, to fear?' It is. Not the popular gospel of today perhaps, but it is the New Testament gospel. Fear! 'Be not high-minded, but fear'. 'For if God spared not the natural branches, take heed lest he also spare not thee.' You watch the 'take heeds' of the New Testament in the Epistles. 'Take heed!' 'Watch!' 'Fear!' 'Be careful!'

1 Corinthians 10 is a great instance of this. The Apostle has been giving the Corinthians the story of the children of Israel in the wilderness and he says: 'Now all these things happened unto them for ensamples: and they are written for our admonition, upon whom the ends of the world are come' [*1 Cor.* 10:11].'Wherefore' – here is the message – 'let him that thinketh he standeth take heed lest he fall' [verse 11]. There it is, once and for ever. He also states it in the Epistle to the Philippians, chapter 2. Having exhorted them to be humble, to have the mind of Christ in them, you remember he puts it like this: 'Wherefore, my beloved, as ye have always obeyed, not as in my presence only, but now much more in my absence, work out your own salvation with fear and trembling' [*Phil.* 2:12]. 'Fear and trembling!' That is New Testament teaching. How much have we heard of that teaching this century? Is that the popular holiness, sanctification teaching? No, it is not.

And then take the great passages in Hebrews. The Epistle to the Hebrews has more of this kind of thing than any other section of Scripture, but listen to the writer. He has given this tremendous introduction in chapter 1 showing the pre-eminence of Christ and immediately says, 'Therefore we ought to give the more earnest heed to the things which we have heard'. This is addressed to Christians, to believers, to church members – 'We ought to give the more earnest heed to the things which we have heard, lest at any time we should let them slip. But if the word spoken by angels was steadfast, and every transgression and disobedience received a just recompence of reward; how shall we escape if we neglect so great salvation; which at the first began to be spoken by the Lord, and was confirmed unto us by them that heard him' [*Heb.* 2:1–3].

Very well, all the great warnings of Scripture are based upon the very argument that the Apostle is using here. It is addressed to people who are liable to boast, and who say, 'We are in the church because we are what we are and not like those other people who are outside'. The moment you say that, there is only one thing to say about you. You are speaking and thinking like a Pharisee, not a Christian. Any pride, any tendency to boast, any sense of superiority in any sense at all . . . I am what I am because I am such a learned man, because I have read so much, because I have got so many books, because I am so moral, I am unlike that other man, that 'publican' especially. . . That is the antithesis of Christianity. 'Boast not against the branches'. Do not boast at all. You have nothing to boast of – nothing. The Christian is a man who says, 'I am what I am by the grace of God'.

# *Sixteen*

⁂

*Boast not against the branches. But if thou boast, thou bearest not the root, but the root thee. Thou wilt say then, The branches were broken off, that I might be graffed in. Well; because of unbelief they were broken off, and thou standest by faith. Be not highminded, but fear: for if God spared not the natural branches, take heed lest he also spare not thee. Behold therefore the goodness and severity of God: on them which fell, severity; but toward thee, goodness, if thou continue in his goodness: otherwise thou also shalt be cut off.* Romans 11:18–22

This is one of those great, crucial statements which are found in the pages of Holy Writ. Having examined it in detail, we have begun to consider its teaching which I suggested could be divided into four sections: exposition; teaching; the problem raised; and general application, especially at this present time.

Looking at the teaching we have seen that our greatest danger always, as long as we are in this world, even as Christian people, is our pride. Secondly we have seen that the Apostle emphasises the constant need of humility, of watchfulness and even fear. He says, 'Be not high-minded, but fear'.

We come now to the third strand in the teaching which the Apostle gives us at this point and I will put it like this. He tells us that the best corrective against pride and all that accompanies it is to know God, His character and the truth about Him. That is the message of this twenty-second verse which begins with the words 'Behold therefore'. This is the antidote to boasting and this is the way to do so – 'Behold therefore the goodness and the severity of God'.

Our greatest need, therefore, is to know God as He has revealed Himself to us in the Scriptures, and if we have that knowledge it will save us from most of our troubles. That is what he is laying down here as a proposition. Put negatively, it means that our greatest lack as

Christian people always is the lack of a knowledge of God. Now that sounds almost incredible, does it not? But it is the truth, it is the very thing the Apostle is saying here. These Gentiles were falling into this temptation to boast against the branches simply because they were ignorant of God, and this is the main cause of most of our troubles and problems. The greater the extent of our knowledge of God, the freer we shall be in our thinking and practice, from problems and troubles, failures and sin, and final tragedy.

It is this emphasis which makes this passage such a crucial one. Thank God that the great Apostle, with his pastoral heart, turned aside from the mere statement of prophetic truth if you like, to apply it to the Gentiles, for we need it above everything else. Let me show you first of all some of the ways in which our failure to realize the truth about God manifests itself in us.

The first thing it does is that it manifests itself even with respect to our doctrine. If this knowledge of the truth about God is not over-arching everything we do and are as Christian people, the first respect in which it is likely to show itself is in the realm of doctrine.

Now this again may come as a surprise to some of you. You may say, 'Well I am a Christian and therefore my doctrine is all right'. That does not follow at all. If that were true there would be no Epistle to the Romans or any other epistle. The idea that the moment you believe on the Lord Jesus Christ you have got perfect doctrine and you are immune from error, is, of course, the most dangerous of all the fallacies. The New Testament is proof positive that because we start the Christian life as 'babes' and as 'children' we are always liable, as Paul puts it to the Ephesians, to be 'carried about by every wind of doctrine', we are liable to go astray, and there is even a phrase which talks about making 'shipwreck' of the faith, as well as this tremendous warning here, 'goodness toward thee, if thou continue in his goodness: otherwise thou also shalt be cut off'.

How then does this manifest itself in the matter of doctrine? The first way in which it shows itself is by a tendency to ignore God altogether. 'But', you say, 'surely that is impossible; that is impossible in a Christian'. Is it? Is it not the case that many Christian people today never seem to think nor to speak of God the Father? They talk only about the Lord Jesus Christ, and they pray to Him. You rarely hear some Christian people mentioning God the Father. It is an amazing thing but it is true. That is one of the ways, then, in which it manifests itself, that He is really forgotten. If you ask them if they believe in God, of course they will say they do, but I am saying that in their normal thinking they never think about God at all. The doctrine of the Trinity has been a stumblingblock to Christian people from the beginning. All sorts of heresies have arisen with respect to this, and this is quite common – a kind of 'Jesus-olatry' which excludes the Father altogether from its thinking. This is a most terrible thing.

Or secondly, it may manifest itself like this, and this again is so common, that people's view of God is not in accord with the Bible's teaching. There are people who tell us repeatedly that 'God is love'. Nothing else, only 'love'. They really have constructed a 'god' of their own. That is idolatry, the very thing against which God through His servant Moses warned the children of Israel who had had such signal manifestations of God and His power and His glory – the thing that Moses has to warn them of above everything else is the danger of falling into idolatry. And it is a constant danger. People do not take the God Who has revealed Himself in the Scriptures but they have their ideas about Him. They say, 'I cannot believe in a God who does this or that'. That is idolatry and it is most common.

A third way in which our thinking is affected if we do not start with God and if He does not control the whole of our thinking, is that we will have a false view of sin, and of man in sin. Now what is your definition of sin? I think you will find that very often we tend to think of sin simply as something wrong which we do, and that is all; something which makes us unhappy afterwards and leads to remorse and so on; or sin as a man letting himself down by failing to live up to his own moral code; or sin as a sort of sickness and almost a disease. But that is to think of sin entirely in terms of man, whereas, obviously, in the Bible sin is always defined in terms of 'God'. Sin is transgression of the law, sin is disobedience to God. But if you do not start with God your view of sin is necessarily going to be wrong. And that in turn leads on to a view of man in sin which is also false and defective.

Now this is true, speaking generally, of the Christian church at the present time. People do not like the whole notion of sin. They say they can explain it away psychologically, and man in sin, we are told, must not be thought of as evil. It is a terrible thing, we are told, to say that, because man just needs a little education or encouragement. The whole view of man in sin is involved. The Bible's view of man as a lost, condemned, hopeless sinner is not common today, and this is simply due to the fact that we have not started with God.

In the same way, of course, it leads to a false view of the atonement. All these things hang together. That is the extraordinary thing about biblical truth. It is a complete whole, and if you are seriously wrong at one point it will affect all the rest; and if you are wrong at this first point, this fundamental postulate, you are going to be wrong right throughout. The result is that ideas of the atonement today are tragically far removed from what is in the Bible. People dislike this notion of sacrifice. The popular idea today of the atonement is this, that what is happening on the cross is that the Lord Jesus Christ is saying there, 'Though you do this to Me I still love you; though you are even putting Me to death I still love you'. Or they sometimes put it like this, that what God the Father is saying is this: 'Though you are murdering My only begotten Son, I still love you'. That is the popular view of the atonement today, of the meaning of the death of our Lord upon the cross. Indeed there is no atonement there, but that is what they call it and they say once we realize this it will break our hearts and we will just thank God for His love.

Going along with this wrong idea of God, sin and the cross, there is no need of regeneration. You just accept forgiveness and you go on eventually to heaven and all is well. People do not realize that because God is who He is no man can possibly enjoy heaven unless he has been born again and has a new nature within him. The same thing can be said with respect to wrong teachings about holiness and sanctification. You will find that such teaching just concentrates on how a person can be delivered from falling into a particular sin, or how I can be given power to overcome a particular temptation. It is all directed to man; it is all designed to help 'me' to overcome and to be victorious. It is never put in the context of God and my relationship to Him; and so it is not the biblical teaching of holiness and sanctification. There is nothing that is more vital than that we should start where the Bible starts, with the doctrine of God. Always, in everything, God and the truth concerning Him must be the controlling factor.

But to come to the realm of practice, here again we find that this failure to start with God leads to certain inevitable consequences. Look at it for instance in the matter of evangelism. Here is the first great activity of the Christian church – evangelism; preaching the gospel of salvation to men; calling them to repentance and to faith in the Lord Jesus Christ. How is evangelism to be conducted? Well, if you do not start with the knowledge of God your evangelism will show it in a kind of general bonhomie, jokes and laughter, and entertainment. That is what inevitably happens. All that is thought of is that you are going to do something for people and you want to get them to do certain things for themselves. But you have not started with God. And so the atmosphere may at times resemble a music-hall much more than a Christian service. Or the whole emphasis is upon man's needs – a need for friendship, happiness, peace, purpose, healing and so on.

The answer to all that is this: man's only need ultimately is to be reconciled to God. Nothing else. You see if you start with man and man's needs you will find there are a large number of people who are not interested in your evangelism. They say, 'But I never do that, I have never been guilty of that sin'. Highly moral, intellectual people, living a good life and trying to help others, sitting in their self-contained homes – they do not see any need of coming to Christ. There is only one explanation; they know nothing about God. There is only one way to show that everybody needs Christ, and that is to hold them face to face with God. Then – 'all the world becomes guilty before God'. 'There is none righteous, no, not one.' 'All have sinned, and come short of the glory of God'. You see how it affects, of necessity, our whole approach to the unbeliever, the whole matter of evangelism. And so you get wrong appeals. You actually get evangelists sometimes saying, 'Come! God needs you'. Have you not heard that? It is quite common. Or it is put in the form of the benefits of salvation. 'How foolish you are. Come! If only you came this is what you would get' – and so the things are put before them. And of course when you get to the point of pressure being brought to bear upon people to take an immediate decision, it is still further wrong.

No, no, this is not New Testament evangelism; you do not find things like that in the New Testament. The one thing that matters is our relationship to God and our need to be reconciled to Him. That is why I have always said that true evangelism is not interested in particular sins. It does not matter what the sin is, everybody is a sinner, and we must not particularize about these things. It puts the emphasis in the wrong place, it creates a false interest. No, no, what we have got to realize according to the Bible is this – God and man – any man – and the need of reconciliation.

But on this practical point let me take up something else which results from an emphasis on man. It is a wrong emphasis placed upon experiences. You see if you start with man and think of salvation only in terms of something for man, well then our hearers are only interested in having a particular experience. But, you see, that is not the object of the preaching of the gospel, it is not the object of the whole message of the Bible. It is to bring us to a knowledge of God. The Apostle Peter puts it in a memorable phrase. He says that our Lord died in order to bring us to God, to this knowledge of God [*1 Pet.* 3:18].

Do not misunderstand me; thank God for every experience, whatever form it takes. But you know the primary business of the gospel is not to give us experiences. It is to put us right with God.

And then, as I say, these false ideas of holiness tend to come in, and they come in in practice also, and we think of holiness in terms of deliverance from particular sins, but that is not its object. The object of holiness is to bring us into fellowship with God, that we may enjoy this fellowship; it is to prepare us for heaven. It must all be thought of always in terms of this fundamental relationship to God and not of some feeling you are going to get. No, no; but to give you this deep knowledge, and to lead to a communion that goes on ever deepening so that eventually you shall have the vision of God: 'Blessed are the pure in heart, for they shall see God'. That is the object of holiness. Of course, it includes deliverance from sins and so on, but you do not stop at that because that is negative, you are always looking back. You look forward. The Vision of God! That is the motive for holiness and there is to be no other.

And then, failure to start at the right place leads, as the Apostle is emphasising here in particular, to all sorts and forms of pride. Pride in our own activities. Oh, of course, how clever and subtle we are. We say, 'I am not advertising, I am reporting this for the glory of God. Of course I am not doing it that you may know what a wonderful preacher I am, or what a great worker I am. No, no, I am doing it all to the glory of God'. All right: 'we are not ignorant of his devices'. So you get men boasting of their activities, boasting of their holiness even, boasting of their experiences, calling attention always to themselves in some shape or form and not to God. This is how it works out in practice.

Let me say finally that every failure to realize the truth of Romans 11:22 leads to a lack of godliness, a lack of 'the fear of the Lord'. It leads to a lightness, a glibness, a superficiality, a self-contentment, and finally, this ugly boastfulness. We do not even use the word 'godliness' as our fathers used to use it. How often do you hear people talking about 'the fear of the Lord'? But, you see, those are the terms that are used in the Bible. Take for instance in that most lyrical book, the Book of the Acts of the Apostles; I read this in chapter 9 and verse 31: 'Then had the churches rest throughout all Judaea and Galilee and Samaria, and were edified; and walking in the fear of the Lord, and the comfort of the Holy Ghost, were multiplied'. Why is this so true of us today, that there is not much evidence of 'the fear of the Lord'? We all must be bright and breezy, back slapping and happy. That is not in the Bible! 'The fear of the Lord'. You start with God. Godliness! These terms have gone out and I suggest to you that they have gone out because our thinking has gone wrong. We have forgotten this verse; we have forgotten the fundamental message of the whole of the Bible. We are so subjective and so interested in what we can get and become. The approach is so man-centred that it leads inevitably to these consequences.

Let us therefore consider the answer to all this as given here by the Apostle. The way in which he puts it is by saying 'Behold therefore'. Do not forget this word 'therefore'. It means that the doctrine which he is going to put before them is obviously the conclusion they ought to arrive at. 'Behold therefore the goodness and severity of God'. The answer to all our troubles is to know the truth about God, to believe it, and to be subjected to and pervaded by it.

Well, what is this and how do we obtain it? The answer is we obtain it only through God's own revelation. You have got to start with that. You must not start by saying, 'Now I cannot believe that God can . . .' The moment you say that, you have left the Bible, you have rejected revelation, you are thinking of yourself and are making your own 'god'. You are guilty of idolatry.

Very well, we start with this revelation, but – and this is the thing that the Apostle emphasises here and which we must emphasise – you must not only submit yourself utterly, absolutely to the revelation which God has so graciously given of Himself and recorded in the Bible, you must take it as it is.

What do I mean? Well I mean that you must take to heart the word '*and*' in the expression 'the goodness and severity of God'. 'What do you mean?' asks someone. What I mean is that 'Behold therefore the goodness of God' is the modern cry. Only goodness! Not goodness and severity. And it is because the modern world and the modern church is leaving out this 'and' that things are as they are, and I see no hope of restoration until we have restored it. I do not see any hope of revival until people have got hold of this, then they will be humble. We have got to take the revelation as it is. If you pick and choose with revelation you might as well be a philosopher, because you are acting as if you were one. The philosopher as such is not interested in the Bible at all. He starts with his own thoughts and works it out. You say, 'Ah no! No, no, I believe the Bible'. But *do* you believe the Bible? If you say you do, then believe it as it is. Do not take one aspect only; do not say 'I believe in the goodness of God'. No, you have got to believe also in the severity of God. Goodness and severity.

How much do we know about the severity of God? How much time have we given to a consideration of the severity of God? What do the terms mean? Well, goodness means, of course, 'kindness and compassion'. What does severity mean? It means 'severe and exact justice'. It is exactly what the Apostle has already told us in the eighteenth verse of the first chapter of this great Epistle. 'For the wrath of God has already been revealed from heaven against all ungodliness and unrighteousness of men, who hold down the truth in unrighteousness'. That is what severity means, the 'wrath of God'. He repeats it here. It is everywhere. It is, of course, the message of the whole Bible. But this is the thing that men neglect, and, alas, many men who say they believe the Bible. Indeed it seems to me this is creeping even into Evangelicalism. Only one side is represented – the goodness, the love of God, the mercy, the kindness and the compassion, and we are hearing less and less and less about the severity, the justice, the righteousness, the wrath of God upon sin. That is where all our troubles come from. That is why the church is as she is.

Now I would put this point in this way, that we have got to realize, says the Apostle here, that when God acts, the whole of God acts. God does not act in parts. God acts always in the light of all His attributes and they are all in operation at exactly the same time. All the attributes of God are always displayed together – 'the goodness "and" the severity' of God. And we must never isolate any one of the attributes of God – that is the modern heresy – the love of God has been isolated from all the others. And it is a form of idolatry, it is a form of unbelief, it is a form of philosophy and speculation. We must not only not isolate any one of the attributes of God, still less must we ever 'play' one of the attributes against the others. That is equally bad. Often men have done that – they have set the righteousness of God against the mercy of God, and the mercy of God against the righteousness of God. In this same way goodness has been opposed to severity and vice versa. You must not set them against one another. Not only do not isolate them, do not play them against one another. God is everything that He is, always. He is goodness, severity, love, holiness and light. All these things are always true of God and they are always true at the same time. Goodness and severity; justice and mercy; righteousness and peace; holiness and love – and so on. And this is of course the very special point that the Apostle is making here and is emphasising. He says, You know if you begin to extract certain things, as it were, out of the character of God you will soon be in trouble, you will soon go astray, and it will happen to you as it has happened to these Jews against whom you are now boasting; but you are travelling the same road. That is exactly the mistake they made, they say 'Ah, God has chosen us, and because God has chosen us we are all right'. They had forgotten the justice and the righteousness of God, they had forgotten what God had said to them through Moses, recorded there in the Book of Deuteronomy – 'I am leading you into this land; do not trust in yourselves and say, "We are all right for ever". If you do not keep on, then . . .' That is God!

Then to drive his argument right home the Apostle puts in the word 'therefore'. 'Behold therefore'. He says, in effect, 'Is it possible that there is anybody who is not clear about this, that God is all these things and always all these things together, at one and the same time?' He says that this is so obvious because of what had happened to the Jews. He argues as follows in verse 21. If Christians think that because God is good and they have been chosen by Him, they can live as they please, then they need to remember what happened to the Jews. 'If God spared not the natural branches, take heed lest He also spare not thee'. This is a great demonstration in history of the character of God. It is one of the most amazing manifestations of God's justice and righteousness and of compassion – the way in which He has handled the Jews. You see it in the Old Testament. They thought that because they were His people they could do what they liked. He soon showed them that they could not. He would raise up enemies to attack them, God would actually do that. He caused them to be carried away into captivity – it was God who did all that. He punishes His own people, though they are His own people, and He puts it in very strong and striking language at times in order to enforce this particular lesson. An example of this is what He said to them through the prophet Ezekiel during the captivity of Babylon. In Ezekiel 14:14, we read: 'Though these three men, Noah, Daniel, and Job, were in it, they should deliver but their own souls by their righteousness, saith the Lord God'. Verse 20 says the same thing. The Jews were always falling back on Abraham, Isaac, and Jacob – 'Noah, Daniel, Job' and so on, as if that was going to . . . No, no! not with a righteous and a holy God. God cannot do that sort of thing. 'God cannot lie'. God cannot contradict His own nature and He has given this amazing demonstration of this in the history of the world in the handling of His own people. Though they are His own people, He punished them. And here at this point He has actually, as it were, cast them off temporarily, plucked them off the tree, thrown them aside as branches that are useless and worthless.

But that is not the most striking illustration in history of this principle. There is something that rises even above God's dealings with the Jews in the Old and New Testament times. If you really want to see the 'goodness "and" severity of God' being manifested together, do you know where you find it? – at the cross on Calvary's hill. And there, of course, the Apostle has already been putting it before us. You remember the great statement in the third chapter, verses 25 and 26: 'Whom God hath set forth to be a propitiation through faith in his blood' – it is God Who hath set it forth, it is God Who put Him there – 'to declare his righteousness for the remission of sins that are past, through the forbearance of God: To declare, I say, at this time his righteousness: (listen!) that he might be just and the justifier of him which believeth in Jesus'. 'Goodness *and* severity'. He must always be just even when He is forgiving. Justice and holiness are always there and they must always act together, and they always do act together. That is why there is only one doctrine of the atonement, not only in the Bible, but which is true to the biblical revelation concerning the character of God. God's love, let us never forget, is a holy love. I say it to the glory of God – that God cannot forgive anybody by just saying, 'I am going to forgive'. He cannot. There was only one way in which

God could forgive; it was by putting our sins on His Son and by punishing them in Him. He poured out the vials of His wrath against sin on His own son. He has 'set Him forth as a propitiation'. God has done it. That is His severity working with His goodness – the two together. It is a holy love. It is a righteous forgiveness. God must always be just and He is never more just than when He justifies him who believes in Jesus.

Let us never, never try to separate the goodness and the severity of God. They both exist and operate together at the same time. On any other view of the atonement you cannot understand the sacrificial teaching of the Old Testament, or what John the Baptist meant when he said, 'Behold, the Lamb of God that taketh away the sin of the world', or why Jesus 'set his face stedfastly to go to Jerusalem', or why He said, 'I have come for this hour. I am not going to say "Save me from this hour"'. You do not understand what He meant when He said, 'The Son of man is not come to be ministered unto but to minister, and to give his life a ransom for many', or why He was baptized; or anything in connection with Him. Oh, He came into the world only because of 'the goodness and severity' of God. It is because sin must be punished that the incarnation and all that followed had to take place. 'Goodness *and* severity'! Not one without the other. Do not separate them. Do not even put your emphasis on the severity alone without the goodness, otherwise you are putting yourself in hell. In your reaction against the glibness and the lightness of today beware lest you go to the opposite extreme and say that God is only severe. Do not forget His goodness, do not forget His grace and mercy – they are all there together at the same time. Believe the revelation as it is.

Let us try and bring this aspect of the teaching to a conclusion by putting it like this. The object of salvation always is to bring us to God and to a knowledge of Him. The ultimate object of salvation is the glory of God, not primarily anything in man. The way of salvation is God's way of salvation, not man's, and whether man understands it or not it is God's – and that is what it is. The object of salvation is not just to give us forgiveness but to make us holy, to make us righteous. 'Who gave Himself for us', says Paul to Titus in chapter 2 verse 14 – 'that he might purify unto himself a peculiar people, zealous of good works'. That is the object of forgiveness. It is not an end in itself. And therefore in the light of this we must never presume on the love of God or on the forgiveness that we have received. If you presume on the fact that you are a Christian and a child of God – oh! I tremble for you and what may happen to you. Complacency or self-satisfaction in the Christian life should be impossible, and it is impossible if you realize this. Whatever a man may have had by way of forgiveness, whatever experiences he may have had, whatever God may have enabled him to do, when he puts himself in the sight of God who is he, what is he? Complacency, self-satisfaction, still less pride, is unthinkable; and this is the great antidote to such tendencies. Carelessness, thoughtlessness, glibness and lightness are impossible in the light of this reminder of the goodness 'and' severity of God. 'On them which fell, severity; but toward thee goodness, if thou continue in his goodness; otherwise thou also shalt be cut off'. 'Work out your own salvation with fear and trembling'. That is it! 'For it is God that worketh in you both to will and to do of his good pleasure'. Work it out 'with fear and trembling'. Do not think of salvation in terms of yourself and your subjective states and conditions or your benefits; think of it in terms of your relationship to Him, and remember His goodness *and* severity. Never presume. But walk circumspectly, walk 'with reverence and godly fear; for our God is a consuming fire'. As we are tempted of the devil along these lines the word of the Apostle to us all is this: 'Behold therefore'. 'Behold therefore the goodness and the severity of God'.

# *Seventeen*

*

*Thou wilt say then, The branches were broken off, that I might be graffed in. Well; because of unbelief they were broken off, and thou standest by faith. Be not highminded, but fear: for if God spared not the natural branches, take heed lest he also spare not thee. Behold therefore the goodness and severity of God: on them which fell, severity; but toward thee, goodness, if thou continue in his goodness: otherwise thou also shalt be cut off.*

Romans 11:18–22

We come now to the problem which is raised by these verses. It arises because the Apostle makes a statement of sheer historical fact, namely that the Jews, speaking generally, were not in the Christian church. These people of God of whom we read so much in the Old Testament, who were looking forward to the coming of the Messiah were not only outside the church but had been 'broken off', as branches from that olive tree which is the people of God. That in itself raises a problem but over and above the actual event is the explicit statement which we have in the latter part of verse 22 which reads,'On them which fell, severity; but toward thee, goodness if thou continue in his goodness: otherwise thou also shalt be cut off'.

Very well then, what is the problem? We can describe it as being a kind of double problem, but essentially, of course, it is only one. But it comes before us here in a double manner. First of all, is not the Apostle suggesting in this paragraph that it is our faith and belief after all that saves us? Now he appears to be saying that, does he not? He says, 'Thou wilt say then, The branches were broken off, that I might be grafted in. Well; because of unbelief they were broken off, and thou standest by faith'. There the suggestion seems to be that after all the thing that really counts and matters is our faith. They fell because they did not believe; we are in because we do believe. He seems therefore to be suggesting that our faith and belief are a kind of 'work' and that this is the thing that determines whether we are saved or not.

And secondly, is he not suggesting also in this teaching that it is our faith that also keeps us in salvation? Or if you prefer it, is he not teaching that we can fall from grace and that there is no such doctrine as the doctrine of the final perseverance of the saints? These are his words; he says, 'toward thee, goodness, if thou continue in his goodness: otherwise thou also shalt be cut off'. If you do not continue in His goodness you shall be cut off. So, if you are not cut off it is because you have continued in His goodness. And 'to continue in his goodness' means this: that you recognize it and continue to believe it. So he seems to be saying, that what really determines our continuance and persistence in the faith and our final perseverance and preservation is our own continuing, our act of belief, our act of faith.

Now there is the problem which, I say, can be divided up in that way into two aspects: What is it that brings us in? What is it that keeps us in? And the Apostle seems to be suggesting on the surface that it is 'our faith' in both instances. And then, of course, the problem posed for us is this: Is the Apostle therefore not flatly contradicting here what he has taught so plainly in other parts of this Epistle whose whole object is to establish the doctrine of justification by faith only? Does this statement not contradict what the Apostle has been teaching about election, about assurance and about the final perseverance of the saints?

You have only to read a number of commentaries on this passage by different people to see at once that they are divided into two groups with regard to this matter. Some are pleased to find what they think is a contradiction in the Apostle because that supports their view that he was no more divinely inspired than any other and only presents his own opinion. They find in it what they consider a great argument against the whole doctrine of inspiration.

Others use this passage just to show that they are right after all. But we will approach this question with the aim of helping those who find this a genuine difficulty. God forbid that we should approach this doctrine in any kind of partisan or prejudiced spirit, but with one desire only, and that is to understand the teaching of the Scriptures so that we may glorify God, and in order that our souls may be strengthened in the faith.

How then do we approach a problem like this? The first thing I would suggest is that we start with the facts, historical facts. In what is before us in this chapter we have the fact of what happened to the

Jews. That is plain and clear and it just has to be accepted. Secondly, we must consider other biblical statements about the same fact, or set of facts.

What our Lord said in Matthew 8:11–12 and Luke 13:28 is most relevant. Our Lord says, 'I say unto you, That many shall come from the east and west, and shall sit down with Abraham and Isaac, and Jacob, in the kingdom of heaven. But the children of the kingdom shall be cast out into outer darkness: there shall be weeping and gnashing of teeth'. You notice the emphasis is that these people are going to come from all parts of the world, are going to come from the east and the west, but the children of the kingdom are going to be cast into outer darkness where there shall be weeping and gnashing of teeth.

Then take Luke 13:28 – where our Lord again is dealing with the same point, He says, 'There shall be weeping and gnashing of teeth, when ye shall see Abraham, and Isaac, and Jacob, and all the prophets in the kingdom of God, and you yourselves thrust out. And they shall come from the east, and from the west, and from the north, and from the south, and shall sit down in the kingdom of God. And, behold, there are last which shall be first, and there are first which shall be last'. So it is clear that our Lord prophesied the very thing that happened to the Jews which the Apostle Paul is acknowledging.

The next step in our consideration is to look for other statements in the Scripture which seem to be teaching the same thing. John 15:6 is most relevant. 'If a man abide not in me, he is cast forth as a branch, and is withered; and men gather them, and cast them into the fire, and they are burned'. So is 1 Corinthians 10 where Paul reminds the Corinthian believers of the Israelites who perished in the wilderness and says: 'All these things happened unto them for ensamples, and they are written for our admonition upon whom the ends of the world are come'. There Paul is invoking this history and applying it to them, in exactly the same way as he does here in Romans 11. The same is seen in Hebrews 3:7–4:13 and in that passage the emphasis on faith and fear is explicit, 'Let us therefore fear, lest a promise being left us of entering into his rest, any of you should seem to come short of it. For unto us was the gospel preached, as well as unto them: but the word preached did not profit them, not being mixed with faith in them that heard it'. So you see the emphasis seems to be upon the fact that it is our 'faith' that matters. The gospel can be preached but if we do not exercise this faith, well then it is of no value to us. The Lord said in Mark 13:13, 'He that shall endure to the end, the same shall be saved'.

Well, there is the main evidence. It is made up of facts and explicit teaching. Now the question before us is, how can all this be reconciled with that other teaching which has already been put before us so plainly and clearly? Well, I suggest to you that this is the method of procedure. We lay down first of all a general rule, or principle of interpretation which is this: Never base a doctrine on an individual passage. We are all aware that we must compare Scripture with Scripture because Scripture is a whole.

Then secondly, you can lay down as a general principle that the Scripture does not contradict itself. The Scripture is the Word of God – not words of man but the Word of God. In the Old Testament, 'Holy men of God spake as they were moved by the Holy Ghost'. 'All Scripture is given by inspiration of God'. It is all 'God-breathed'. He breathes it out; all of it. It is foundational that it can never contradict itself.

Thirdly, we must proceed from the known to the unknown. We must begin with those statements whose meaning is clear, about which there is no difficulty at all concerning the matters which are being examined.

Whenever you find yourselves confronted by a difficulty in the Scripture, something about which you do not have exact knowledge, the principle is, to start with something about which you are certain and approach your difficulty from an already established position. This is comparable to taking a run-up if you want to jump over a hurdle. Do not stand too close to your problem if it is difficult, go back to certain general positions and move forward from there. You will be able to jump your hurdle or solve your difficulty. This is especially true with regard to the doctrines of election and the final perseverance of the saints.

Now the moment you do that, you find that this very chapter in which your difficulty arises, in and of itself has something to say which helps you. You remember how the Apostle began the chapter, and I am taking particularly the second verse now. He says, 'God hath not cast away his people which he foreknew'. That is the great principle, 'his people whom he foreknew'. And then in verse 5 we saw it: 'Even so then at this present time also there is a remnant according to the election of grace'. The apostasy of the Jewish nation was not total. The Apostle reminds them that he was a believer, and there were others, and this he describes as a remnant – yes, but 'a remnant according to the election of grace'.

As he goes forward the Apostle is still continuing this same idea. 'What then?' he says in verse 7, 'Israel hath not obtained that which he seeketh for; but the election hath obtained it' – and it has obtained it because it is the election – 'the rest were blinded'. So that our whole chapter in and of itself helps us if we ask ourselves, What are the basic principles taught in the chapter? At once you are reminded that it is this great doctrine of election. And that, of course, then reminds you that the Apostle has been expounding that in detail and at length especially in the ninth chapter, where we worked it out in detail – where he puts it, of course, so clearly: 'The children being not yet born, neither having done any good or evil, that the purpose of God according to election might stand, not of works, but of him that calleth' [9:11].

Now the Apostle has gone out of his way to show that the only manner in which you can understand the history of the Jews and the whole of the way of salvation, is to see that it is 'according to the election of grace'. There is no other explanation; and he has given us positive and negative arguments, he has put it in such a clear manner that when an objector comes forward he says to him, 'Nay but, O man, who art thou that repliest against God?'

There is therefore this explicit statement with regard to this doctrine of election, that that is the only way of understanding why some are saved and some are not saved, the only way of understanding why anybody is saved, for it is clear that, were it not for God's election, there would be nobody saved at all, for we are 'all dead in trespasses and sins', have 'the natural mind which is enmity against God', and are those to whom 'the things of the Spirit of God are foolishness'. We cannot understand them, it is impossible. We need to be quickened. That is the only explanation of how any single soul has ever been saved.

And it is exactly the same, of course, with the doctrine of assurance and of the final perseverance of the saints. We saw this in dealing with the basic and glorious certainty at the end of chapter 8. The Apostle at verse 28 starts this great statement, 'We know that all things work together for good to them that love God, to them who are the called according to his purpose' and he ends it with the words: 'I am persuaded that neither death, nor life, nor angels, nor principalities, nor powers, nor things present, nor things to come, nor height, nor depth, nor any other creature, shall be able to separate us from the love of God which is in Christ Jesus our Lord'. Now that is what I call explicit, clear, unmistakable teaching: nothing could be clearer.

There are also other strong statements which are relevant, for example, the Lord's own words, 'And I give unto them eternal life; and they shall never perish, neither shall any man pluck them out of my hand. My Father, which gave them me, is greater than all; and no man is able to pluck them out of my Father's hand' [*John* 10:28–29]. The same truth comes out so clearly in the high-priestly prayer of our Lord in John 17:12. The Apostle Peter is equally emphatic on this point in 1 Peter 1:4–5.

We now move on and our next step it seems to me is to say that if our ultimate salvation, our ultimate arrival in glory, depended on our faithfulness, the credit would ultimately have to be given to us. If it is our faith and our persistence that brings us eventually into the glory everlasting, it is no longer the goodness of God that does it, it is us. You may say the goodness of God gave you a chance or a start, but after all the thing that decides whether a man arrives in heaven or not is what he does, so it puts it back ultimately to man, and the credit and the glory to that extent must go to man.

But there is no need even to think that. Is it not perfectly plain and clear that if our perseverance were to depend upon us and our efforts that not one of us would ever arrive in heaven, that none would ever be glorified? Is there anyone who would like to claim that he or she is in a given position as a Christian this moment because of what they have done? The moment you examine it from the standpoint of experience we all must recognize it at once. All the regenerate fail, all go astray, all fall into sin, and not one of them would have any hope of arriving in glory if it depended upon them.

But it seems to me always that the most powerful argument of all is this. If this ultimate arrival in glory, put at its very lowest, depended upon us, getting there would be a very precarious matter. Actually, as I have said, nobody would arrive there. But putting it at its very highest and best and thinking of the most that anyone could do, it would be a most precarious matter. And you see what is involved in that is the ultimate triumph of the devil, and our Lord came into this world in order to make the success of God's way of salvation certain and sure. There can be no failure. God made the first man Adam perfect and set him in Paradise. He fell. The devil triumphed. Is it conceivable that God would send His own Son into this world and in the likeness of sinful flesh and as a man – is it conceivable that God would send Him into the world on an errand which could fail? No, no, the whole glory of the plan and purpose of salvation in Christ Jesus is that it cannot fail. That is why the son of God has come. that is why you did not have another Adam created. That is why you have the man from heaven, the second Man, the last Adam. He is the man from heaven. He is the Lord from heaven. Salvation therefore cannot fail and will not fail. It is certain, it is absolutely sure.

In other words, in order that it may be certain and sure, it is not dependent upon us at any point, otherwise it would fail. It is dependent upon the Lord Jesus Christ. It is the election of grace.

Now the Apostle has already told us all this in the fourth chapter of this Epistle and particularly in verse 16. Winding up his great argument on justification by faith only, he says, 'Therefore it is of faith, that it might be by grace; to the end the promise might be sure to all the seed'. That is the point. That is why it is 'of faith' – that it might be of grace – 'to the end' – this is the object – 'that the promise might be sure to all the seed'. Not one will fall, not one will be left behind. All the elect shall be saved. It is one of the greatest and most glorious statements of the final perseverance of the saints. But as I say, the whole doctrine of salvation makes this an absolute necessity, otherwise the devil would still be the victor, and God would have failed even in His own Son. No, no, our salvation does not depend upon us at any point, it is entirely in Him and of Him. Very well.

But what of the question as to how all this relates to what is explicitly stated in the verse we are considering – and other similar statements? I suggest to you that the answer can be put as follows. All these passages which seem to be putting the onus on us and suspending our ultimate glorification upon our faithfulness and persistence, all these passages are invariably addressed only to the visible church, the equivalent of 'national' Israel.

Now then, let me expound that. What is the whole central argument of this chapter? The leading theme of this chapter is the two Israels. We have had to deal with that in expounding the teaching concerning the olive tree and so on. That is the point that has stood out, is it not – that there is an external Israel, and there is a kind of inner Israel. Our controlling text after all is still Romans 9:6. – 'For they are not all Israel, which are of Israel'. There are two Israels. There is an external, physical Israel; there is a spiritual, inner Israel. It is all this old difference, after all, between the two sons of Abraham and the two sons of Isaac – Jacob and Esau. It is Israel after the flesh and Israel after the Spirit. Now that is still the big broad distinction which the Apostle is holding in his mind, and what he is dealing with in this chapter, as we have seen so many times, is external Israel; Israel in general as a nation. He is not talking primarily about the elect, he is talking about those who stumble temporarily and who, he is telling us, and will tell us yet more explicitly, are going to be brought back at some future point. That is what he is dealing with. The promise is to the invisible Israel.

The same principle applies to the Gentiles whom he is addressing. He is not dealing now with the elect Gentiles but with the Gentiles in general. He says to those who have, by profession, come into the church and who are constituting its majority, 'Israel, in general, is out, you Gentiles, in general, are in; do not make the mistake that they made'. That is precisely the argument. So this passage is not really dealing specifically with the general position of those who are in the Christian church. He says to the Gentiles that Israel was included in the same way as they now are, but she is now excluded. That has got nothing to do with the elect because, though Israel in general is out, the remnant according to the election of grace is in. Paul was in and there were others in with him; there is the elect. The elect have not been cut out. It is those who belong en masse to the nation who are cut out, not the elect.

These remarks, in other words, apply, as I say, only to the visible church. When our Lord said to His listeners, 'But the children of the kingdom shall be cast into outer darkness' [*Matt.* 8:12] that simply means Israel after the flesh; that is not the elect. It is only true of them. It is not the true spiritual seed of Abraham. His whole argument is that they are always in. It is the same with Luke 13:28 and so on. There is no statement anywhere in the Scripture that the elect can fall, or that the elect will ever be cast out. No! The whole argument here must be thought of in terms of the general position, as regards Jews and Gentiles.

Very well, what about the passages in Mark 13:13 and Hebrews 6:4–6 and 10:26–30? Once more these only deal again with the realm of profession; they deal with people who appear to be

Christian. There have always been people like that in the church, there still are, they appear to be Christians. They may later give evidence that they have never been Christian at all. People may come forward as the result of an appeal, sign a form, join a church, they may use the right language, you may think they are perfect Christians. You find later that they are not, and the fact is they never have been, they have never been regenerate. There is not a word said in Hebrews 6 to the effect that those people were truly born again. You can have wonderful experiences and still not be born again. You may have wonderful experiences and still you may have no life within you.

What about John 15:6? This statement really deals with the realm of service. It is a parable on fruitfulness and on service. It does not deal with the question of salvation but it does very definitely deal with service, and what he is teaching is this, that a man, though he is a Christian, who loses this living contact with his Lord, will be useless from the standpoint of service. And how often, alas, has that been demonstrated in the lives of many individuals and also of groups of churches. I hope to deal with that later.

Why then is the Apostle writing as he does in the verses from Romans 11 which are before us? I will summarize my answer: He does so to warn the elect and to keep them from the subtlety of the devil, from presumption, from carelessness, and above all from pride. 'Boast not against the branches'. Or if you prefer it in another form, these passages are ways in which God actually secures the perseverance of His saints and people. Now there is a wonderful statement of this in the book of the prophet Jeremiah, Jeremiah 32:40. 'And I will make an everlasting covenant with them, that I will not turn away from them, to do them good: but I will put my fear in their hearts, that they shall not depart from me.' Now that is a statement not about the children of Israel externally or in general, this is the elect and it is true of the elect Gentiles. God puts a fear of Him into people's hearts. What the Apostle is doing here is putting the fear of God into these Gentiles so that they will never depart from Him. It is God's way of securing the perseverance of His chosen people.

So I end with this – and about this there is no question whatsoever. The only people who are ever frightened by a statement such as this are true Christian people. Nobody else. The whole trouble with these others who think they are Christians – temporary believers, temporary professors, call them what you like – the trouble with them is that they are always self-satisfied, they are perfectly happy, nothing ever disturbs them at all, and they can read through the warnings of the Scripture, without anything troubling them. Show me a man who is disturbed and somewhat alarmed by these statements and I will show you a Christian. Or let me put it as I often have to put it in my vestry, and as every minister often has to put it – When a man comes to me and tells me that he thinks he is guilty of the blasphemy or the sin against the Holy Ghost I always tell such a person, Well, if there is one man in the world of whom I am absolutely certain that he is not guilty of that it is you. If you are worried that you are guilty of that sin against the Holy Ghost you are giving me proof that you are not guilty of it. The characteristic of the people who are guilty of that is that they are perfectly satisfied; they dismiss Christ, they ridicule His death upon the Cross and the blood, they do not need Him, they are all right as they are. That is what Hebrews 6 deals with; that is what 1 John 5:16–17 deal with. That is what our Lord has in mind. It was to the Pharisees that He uttered those words about that sin that is never forgiven either in this world or in the next, the blasphemy against the Holy Ghost. That was the essential sin of the Pharisees. They were charging Him with being Beelzebub and doing His miracles in the power of Beelzebub, they did not see their need of Him. That is the spirit of the people who are under condemnation. But a man who is frightened and terrified and alarmed by these warnings, and who is afraid that he has already fallen off, or has already been cut off, and is troubled because of it, that man is giving proof that he is very much in the olive tree, and that he is in no danger at all.

In other words, experience demonstrates the truth of the contention that it is through passages similar to this that God ensures and secures the perseverance of His own people. It is only to His own people He says, 'Work out your own salvation with fear and trembling'. He does not say that to an unbeliever, He only says that to His own people, and they are the only people who listen to it, and they are the only people who know anything about 'fear and trembling'. One of the best tests of assurance is that we know something about fear and trembling. 'Knowing the terror of the Lord, we persuade men'. This is God's way, then, of securing the final perseverance and the ultimate glorification of His people.

# *Eighteen*

⁂

*Thou wilt say then, The branches were broken off, that I might be graffed in. Well; because of unbelief they were broken off, and thou standest by faith. Be not highminded, but fear: for if God spared not the natural branches, take heed lest he also spare not thee. Behold therefore the goodness and severity of God: on them which fell, severity; but toward thee, goodness, if thou continue in his goodness: otherwise thou also shalt be cut off.*

Romans 11:18–22

We come now to the fourth division of our consideration of these verses. This is by way of application of all this to us and our present situation. We should always apply the truth. The Bible and its teaching are never to be approached in a detached or a theoretical manner, which is the besetting sin of commentators. They are interested in the words and meanings and shades of meanings and arguments and disputations, and they tend to leave it at that. I know that a case can be made for the commentator as such, but that is all that he is called upon to do and we do not look to him so much for application.

Exactly the same is true about historians. It is a very interesting and peculiar thing, and something against which we should all guard ourselves. I have noticed throughout the years that, speaking generally, historians seem to have a strange capacity, or propensity, almost, to be entirely uninfluenced by the very history about which they write and to which they give their lives in study. For example, I have known many men, and some of them I have known very well indeed, who have been particularly interested in the eighteenth century, and I can say about some of them quite truthfully that I have never known men who are further removed from the Methodist Fathers of the eighteenth century in whom they are so interested. They merely have a kind of antiquarian interest.

Now it is a terrible thing, it seems to me, that we should approach truth either in the form of didactic teaching or in the form of history, or in any other form, without realizing that it is meant to speak to us, to do something for us. There is nothing against which we should guard ourselves so much as a detached academic and theoretical interest. We should always have a living interest, and that is why it is especially the part of the preacher always to be applying the truth. I have never called myself a Bible lecturer for that reason. The Bible is to be preached, it is always to be applied.

Now the Apostle, you see, leads us to say this very thing. He is dealing primarily with an actual fact of history that the Jews had rejected the gospel and were outside the church, outside the kingdom; whereas the Gentiles had come in. But the Apostle cannot merely handle this as a fact of history, he is concerned with its meaning, with its relevance, with what it has to say to the Gentile Christians who are in the church. There is a great deal of history in the Bible, but the history that is in the Bible is not just history. That is the important point.

Why not? Why is it that the history of the Bible must never be regarded merely as history? The answer is, that the Bible history is always illustrative of great spiritual principles; and that is undoubtedly why it has been given to us. The purpose of the history is to illustrate the great teaching, the fundamental and eternal principle of God's plan of salvation. It is not meant to be something in and of itself which you can therefore either take or leave. Now there are many people who do this. There are many Christian people who ignore the historical portions of the Bible and they do not see much value in them. It is still worse when you get a Christian who dismisses the whole of the Old Testament and feels that it is no longer relevant to him. We must remember, therefore, that the history in the Bible is simply one of the ways in which the great principles are taught. That is one great lesson.

But here is another. We must pay attention to the history in the Bible because the principles that are taught, partly through history, are always permanent and eternal principles. This is why the Bible never becomes out of date or, putting it the other way round, that is why the Bible is always contemporary. Now you read here of what God did for the children of Israel thousands of years ago, but the fact that it happened so long ago does not mean that it has got nothing to say to us. It has, for this reason – that it is the same God who dealt with them who deals with us and He does not change. So the principles which are taught in the history of things which happened so long ago are as applicable and as relevant and as true today as they have ever been.

We must never read the history of the Israelites or the Jews in the Bible as we would read that of the Greeks or Romans in secular history. People have often said, 'I cannot understand why we have all this in the Gospels about the wrangling that took place between the Pharisees and our Lord; what has that got to do with us? What we want is the positive teaching of Jesus. They wish they did not have all this historical information about what happened nearly two thousand years ago. Now that, I say, is an attitude which we must avoid at all costs, and it applies to this passage that is before us. Here were the Jews and here were the Gentiles: the whole thing was new, it was a live issue – but why spend all this time on something that was very relevant so long ago but surely is of no interest today?

Now I want to show you how terribly wrong that is. When you read about the history of the Jews in the Old Testament you should always read it in this way; you should say, 'I am the Jews'. When you read about the Pharisees and Scribes you do not read it as if you are reading a book of history, you say, 'But I am the Pharisees and the Scribes, this is speaking to me; what our Lord said to them He is speaking to me.' Now that is the only profitable way in which you read the Bible. If you detach yourself and just regard it in a purely academic way, you are missing the whole point; you are turning the Bible into a textbook of history or into the account of some ancient philosophy. But the Bible is always contemporary because God remains the same and man remains the same, and the relationships between God and man remain the same. So the principles taught in terms of this 'old' history are as alive and up to date today as they have ever been.

Now the Scripture itself puts that in these words: 'These things are written for our admonition . . . upon whom the ends of the world are come' [*1 Cor.* 10:11]. That statement is a most important one which we must never forget. We are meant to learn from this history. What are the relevant, the urgent lessons?

Let us therefore look at some general points. Here is the first: There seems to be always a tendency in the church or if you like among God's people to decline and to fall away from the truth. This, of course, is because we are not yet perfect, because sanctification is a process, and because we are dull and slow of hearing. I will show you the great illustrations of this in history in a moment; but here it is, of course, in the case of the Jews.

I want to quote a sentence to you from a man who was about as far removed from being an Evangelical Christian as anyone could be, but he was a great thinker and an acute observer – the late Dean Inge. He had produced a little book on Protestantism; it was one of a series. I will never forget the first sentence in that book, it was so true. He put it all in one phrase; he said: 'Every institution tends to produce its opposite'. Now that is a very profound remark. It is a very perfect summary of the very thing I am trying to say here. He was writing on Protestantism, and what he was able to show so cleverly, and which I want to repeat is this: that by today Protestantism has become almost the exact opposite of what it was at its beginning in the sixteenth century.

Why does such a thing happen? It occurs as a result of the struggle between the spirit and the form. I do not think that there is a greater struggle than this. The spirit must have a form and that is why you have such a thing as the Christian church. An idea must always take form if it is to be of any value. But there is always a tension between these two. Certain dangers arise, and the biggest danger of all is that the form tends to cripple the spirit. I do not think you can begin to understand church history, you cannot understand the Bible, unless you have got clear in your mind this struggle and tension between form and spirit.

What happens is that you must have form. There must be a minimum of organization otherwise you cannot do anything. You can be a vague dreamer but you will not help anybody. Every idea has got to take form in some sense or other, but the moment you give it a form and you have an organization, you have to encounter the problem of how to prevent the organization from throttling the spirit. That is the trouble.

I will never forget being in America in 1937 at the General Assembly of the Presbyterian Church. A man gave an address in which he told us we were going to be informed about some marvellous movement of the Spirit which had been taking place. He took Ezekiel 1:20–21 as his text, which refers to the spirit in the wheels. There was an expectation of something tremendous, but all we were told was that an office had been obtained and what the furniture had cost. Nothing but sheer organization. In other words, it was all wheels and no spirit, and there was no movement. Now that is the danger, all wheels and no spirit. You must have the wheels, but God forbid that the wheels should put an end to the spirit.

Now this is the thing that is so clear. The whole story of the children of Israel illustrates this institutionalizing, this organization which ultimately destroys the spirit altogether. This is a very subtle process and it is sometimes a very slow one. It is almost imperceptible, and that is why the tragedy takes place so often in the history of the church. People only wake up to the fact that it has happened when it is too late to do anything about it. Of course this happens in secular history as well; it happened in Germany just before the last war. There were many good things about Hitler, and that is why many Christian people were entirely persuaded by him, and they only realized what he was when it was too late.

Now perhaps one of the clearest illustrations of all this is the way in which the so-called Higher Critical movement came in, in the nineteenth century. There was the church; she was orthodox; perhaps not as alive as she should have been but at any rate she was fairly orthodox up until about 1830. But this teaching gradually came in from Germany and it began to insinuate its way into theological colleges in this country. People began to notice but instead of dealing with it they thought that these new ideas would gradually pass. It went on and by now it has become dominant and the truth is having to fight for its life. That is the sort of thing to which I am referring – all this tendency of the false and that which cripples the spirit to come in in a very subtle and often in a slow and imperceptible manner.

Our Lord Himself, of course, used the action of a moth or rust as an illustration of this very process. That is why you used to have those disasters on railways in the nineteenth century. You have heard and read the accounts of an express train going over a bridge and suddenly the bridge collapses. They did not know about rust and stress then. It happens imperceptibly, there is nothing to be seen but something is taking place, and suddenly the bridge collapses. But this is something that you see so clearly in the Bible and you see it, still more clearly, in the subsequent history of the Christian church.

A second cause of this decline is forgetting original principles. That is always the cause of trouble. This Epistle to the Romans shows more clearly perhaps than any other single epistle that you stand by faith and by faith alone. It is the great statement of this epistle. Justification is by faith only, and it has always been 'by faith only'. It is all, 'We are saved by grace through faith; that not of yourself'. In other words, that is the fundamental, controlling principle. And things went wrong with the Jews and with the church because of forgetfulness of that first principle.

This is an astounding thing but it is nevertheless a fact that all the greatest problems in the world today are due to forgetfulness of first principles, not some complicated involved outworking of them. Is not that the whole problem of humanity today? You get all these commissions of enquiry and this and that proposal, but the whole trouble is due to ignorance of the fact that man is a sinner, and because he is a sinner he will go on behaving as he does. New institutions can be brought in and resources provided but the problem will remain. And it is exactly the same with the church. All the troubles in the church ultimately are due to the fact that we fall away from justification by faith only and also that man is wholly sinful.

And then the third general principle that I find here is this: that those who do fall away from first principles are always the ones who persecute most bitterly those who still hold to them. It was the Jews who put the Messiah to death. It was the Pharisees who were the ringleaders in that with the Sadducees. The history of the church shows a constant repetition of this, that it is those who belong to the visible church who are always the most bitter persecutors of the true Israel. It is as true today as it has always been.

But secondly, these lessons are given by way of illustrations in the Bible. That is what your Bible is. It is a great book of doctrine, illustrated by means of individuals and nations. The Jewish nation is the supreme illustration. It stands out so clearly. It should be unmistakeable. But alas it is not. We tend to look at the Jews, condemn them, without seeing that we are guilty of exactly the same thing so often. They are the people who crucified their own Messiah. 'He came unto his own, and his own received him not' [*John* 1:11]. We are guilty too.

This selfsame thing has been repeated many times in the history of the church. There was at one time a number of great churches in Asia, at Ephesus, Laodicea, and elsewhere so privileged with the preaching of the great Apostle Paul and others, and John. Where are they now? They have gone, they have disappeared. What happened to the Jews happened to them. Or take the case of North Africa where there were great and mighty churches at one time. Never forget that the great St Augustine was the Bishop of Hippo in North Africa. Where are they now? They have vanished and for the same reason. This is also the explanation of how the church of the New Testament became the Roman Catholic Church of the Middle Ages. In order to commend Christian teaching in the Graeco-Roman world, an attempt was made to show that it was not all that different from the best of Greek philosophy. In doing this, the first principle of justification by faith alone was forgotten and also that 'the wisdom of this world is foolishness with God'. The result was that many Christian apologists became humanists themselves and a downward process was begun which was accelerated when Constantine brought the Roman Empire into the church. Dean Inge's maxim became true. Think of the church of the New Testament. It had no buildings. Contrast all that with all the pomp and ceremony and the ornate buildings of great cathedrals – St Peter's in Rome or St Paul's Cathedral in London, or places like that, and Westminster Chapel in a sense. You see everybody was imitating all that last century and they have gone astray. It is not primitive Christianity. It is all a forgetting of this fundamental original principle. And it has happened in almost every conceivable section of the Christian church. Think of Anglicanism at its beginning in the sixteenth century, its clear view about Rome and so on. Look at the present Anglican church and its tendency, going back on almost everything that was done then, but still claiming to be the same thing. And it happens very slowly and in a very subtle manner throughout the centuries.

It is equally true of Nonconformity. Take Independency; it started out on that great principle. Now there is a proposal to do away with the Congregational Union and to form what will be called the Congregational Church of Great Britain. It is the exact opposite of what was started in the seventeenth century. 'Every institution tends to produce its opposite'. And we are seeing it happening before our very eyes. You can see it equally clearly in Methodism. One wonders what John Wesley would think and do if he could come back to modern Methodism. They are denying almost everything he stood for, except the circuit system; almost everything else they have long since thrown overboard.

You can see it in all the great divisions of the church; every one of them turns itself, or is turned unconsciously, into the exact opposite of what it was at the beginning. And all this is but, I say, further illustration of what we see so clearly in the Bible. Look at the prophets how they remind Israel of what she once was. 'When you were young,' says the prophet, 'oh, how I led you with the cords of a man' and so on, and 'how ready you were to be led – how you were a young virgin as it were, but you have become just a prostitute'. Is not that what the prophets are saying? How beautiful Israel was, how wonderful at the beginning, but what she has become! This is the terrible thing.

I have known this happen even in the case of places. Read of Geneva in the sixteenth century and go and visit Geneva today. You will find it very difficult to get an evangelical sermon in Geneva today. I could name you villages in Wales, for example Trevecca and Talgarth in the days of Howell Harris, or Llangeitho where Daniel Rowland preached. Go there now, I do not know of any more derelict districts in a spiritual sense. What happened? Well it is the same thing you see. The form was retained, and in pride, and the spirit was lost.

Another thing which seems to me to be shown here very clearly by the history is what I would call 'the principle of delay'. We all seem to have a notion that the moment people do anything wrong or begin to go astray God will immediately deal with them. But He does not do that. There is a principle of delay.

Now let me give you some examples of the fact that God does not always act immediately. Our Lord told two parables which teach this. The first is the Parable of the Vineyard found in Luke 13:4–9: 'A certain man had a fig tree planted in his vineyard; and he came and sought fruit thereon, and found none. Then said he unto the dresser of his vineyard, Behold, these three years I come seeking fruit on this fig tree, and find none: cut it down; why cumbereth it the ground? And he answering said unto him, Lord, let it alone this year also, till I shall dig about it, and dung it: and if it bear fruit, well: and if not, then after that thou shalt cut it down.'

Now there is the great principle. He does not cut it down at once, he gives it another trial, waits three years, is ready to listen to an argument brought forward, 'Let me try this.' That is God's way, the principle of delay.

Secondly, there is the Parable of the Wicked Husbandmen in Matthew 21:33–46. Our Lord is there giving a complete summary of practically the whole of the Old Testament. The wicked husbandmen are the Jews and they have God's vineyard, He has given it to them to look after for Him. And then He sends His servants to get the fruit and they beat them and kill them. And He goes on sending more, He does not immediately destroy them. No, He sends more than He had sent before; they do the same to them. Oh, the patience of God, running through all the Old Testament. He does not at once put an end to them, He is very patient. And at last He sends His son and they do the same to Him; and it is then, and only then, that He takes it from them. And so our Lord sums it up by saying, 'Therefore I say unto you, The Kingdom of God shall be taken from you, and given to a nation bringing forth the fruits thereof'. That is the Christian church, consisting mainly of Gentiles.

But then there is, perhaps, a still more striking statement of this principle at the end of Matthew 23:34–36. Our Lord says, 'Wherefore, behold, I send you prophets, and wise men, and scribes: and some of them ye shall kill and crucify; and some of them shall ye scourge in your synagogues, and persecute them from city to city: (Listen!) that upon you may come all the righteous blood shed upon the earth, from the blood of righteous Abel unto the blood of Zacharias son of Barachias, whom ye slew between the temple and the altar. Verily I say unto you, All these things shall come upon this generation'. God had been patiently waiting for these people, sending His messengers, giving them opportunities; He does not strike at once. But at last He does, and all comes as it were upon one particular generation.

This can also be seen in the case of an individual, for example our Lord's patient treatment of Judas. He knew all about him and his scheme, but He addresses him as 'Friend' even to the very end. He keeps on waiting patiently in this way. It can also be observed in the realm of history. Is there anything more astonishing than God's patience with the Roman Catholic Church of the Middle Ages, how He tolerated it even for centuries; and it was only at the Protestant Reformation that God acted, putting them on one side and producing again His own true church in a visible form. It is the same principle.

I come now to the particular application of all this to us at the present time. What is it? Well it seems to me that the modern ecumenical movement is an example of this thing and nothing else.

What do I mean? Well, just as the Jews in our Lord's time said, We are the people of God, we are the lineal descendants of Abraham, to whom all the great promises were made, therefore we are saved, we are the people of God, we are all right as we are. Who is this fellow that seems to suggest there is anything wrong with us? So today what is called Christendom is assumed to be the Christian church, simply because it is 'the lineal descendant' in an unbroken tradition of the church of the past. That is true of Roman Catholicism which traces itself back to the original Christian church, it is true of Protestantism tracing itself back to the Reformers and so on – it is true of all the denominations. They are assuming that because they belong to this same organization, to this one unbroken tradition, they are of necessity Christians. The external organization is regarded as the church. The tradition is regarded as a guarantee that we are all right. There is no concern about the church's purity, about its message or practice. Because a man is a dignitary in the Church, it is assumed that he must be a Christian; though he tells you in his sermons and in his books quite plainly that he is not, it is still argued that he must be because he belongs to the church and it is very terrible to say that he is not a Christian.

In other words, what makes a man a Christian is that he belongs to the church, not what he believes. You see we have left the principle of justification by faith only. You can deny the deity of Christ, you can deny the miracles, you can deny the atoning sacrifice, you can deny the literal resurrection, you can deny all these things, and the rebirth and justification by faith only – but still you are regarded as a Christian. Why? Well, because you are a member of the church, and every member of the church is a Christian. The organization has taken the place of the spirit; tradition has taken the place of truth. Men are no longer concerned about the truth which is believed or about a life which corresponds with it. The original basis of what makes a church a church is entirely forgotten. And the assumption behind the ecumenical movement is that, because of the historical and external continuity of the organization, it is of necessity the church. I say that that was precisely the error and the sin of the nation of the Jews when they rejected their Messiah and which caused God to pluck them out of the olive tree. And of course they are proving the analogy still further today by persecuting those who are still holding to the original principle.

Let me give you one other thought. Here also the whole question of children brought up in the church is acutely involved, because they of all people are encouraged to assume that they are Christians because they were baptized when they were infants or because they have always been brought to church. I am not saying that they are not Christians, so many of them are, thank God. All I am saying is that the danger of assuming that because you belong to the organization you are of necessity a Christian, the danger of forgetting the vital principle which is justification by faith only, individual experience of God and of the rebirth, is greater in them than in anybody else.

As to what the future holds, no man can prophesy because of this principle of delay that I have been showing you. All I know is this, that there is a day coming when the apostate church, however big and powerful she may be, will be rejected by God. You get the account of that in the Book of Revelation, chapters 17 and 18. The great world church that we are hearing so much about is going to be 'spewed out' as the apostate vile thing that it is, and the sons of God will stand out in the brightness of their glory. I do not know when. These tendencies may go on and on but there is this comfort, there is this hope: something great and tremendous is going to happen amongst the Jews before that happens. And it will happen.

Very well, my last word is this: What is the way of safety for us in the light of all these things? My first answer is, Never forget Romans 11:22. It is the best advice I can give. What does it mean? It means the need of constant self-examination. 'Let him that thinketh he standeth take heed lest he fall'. Do not rely upon the fact that you are sound in doctrine *now*. That is no guarantee that you will be in a year's time. Be careful lest in your correctness of doctrine you may become hard in your spirit and make your doctrine of no value to you. Thank God for any gifts He has given you, but do not begin to rely upon them, because if you do what applies to you is 1 Corinthians 13: 'Though I speak with the tongues of men and of angels, and have not charity . . . Though I have all faith so that I could remove mountains' and so on, 'though I understand all mysteries, it is no good, you are sounding brass, a tinkling cymbal'. All your knowledge is of no value to you. You see how subtle this thing is. Self-examination! Fear! 'Be not highminded, but fear'. Always realize this danger, always check yourself by the original principle lest you should, in a very subtle and slow manner, be drifting away.

The next thing I say is this: You and I are responsible only for ourselves and for our age. We are responsible for today, but we cannot legislate for the future. When I say things like this to some people they say, 'All right we agree with you, but if we do what you are saying, is it any guarantee that things will be all right in a hundred years' time?' The answer is, No. But I am not responsible for what my grandchildren may do, neither are you for yours. But we are responsible for what we do: 'Every man shall bear his own burden'. You cannot legislate for the future, but our business is to see always that the church is pure – pure in her doctrine, pure in her practice, whatever the costs. We cannot guarantee that it is going to continue so. The church has been so pure many times, but always this other principle seems to come in; they fall away from the original. But we are responsible for our own day and generation.

And lastly, it seems to me quite inevitable that we have nothing to do with a church which is guilty of repeating the fatal error and sin of the Jewish nation. We have nothing to do with a church that is apostate, with a church that puts organization before the truth, tradition before the truth, which has forgotten the very principle that brought it into being and made it what it is. A church which has departed from that is no longer a church, and for us to be associated with such a body is to partake of its sin and to be partly responsible for its apostasy.

# Nineteen

*

*And they also, if they abide not still in unbelief, shall be graffed in: for God is able to graff them in again. For if thou wert cut out of the olive tree which is wild by nature, and wert graffed contrary to nature into a good olive tree: how much more shall these, which be the natural branches, be graffed into their own olive tree?*

*For I would not, brethren, that ye should be ignorant of this mystery, lest ye should be wise in your own conceits; that blindness in part is happened to Israel, until the fulness of the Gentiles be come in. And so all Israel shall be saved: as it is written, There shall come out of Sion the Deliverer, and shall turn away ungodliness from Jacob: for this is my covenant unto them, when I shall take away their sins. As concerning the gospel, they are enemies for your sakes: but as touching the election, they are beloved for the fathers' sakes. For the gifts and calling of God are without repentance. For as ye in times past have not believed God, yet have now obtained mercy through their unbelief: even so have these also now not believed, that through your mercy they also may obtain mercy. For God hath concluded them all in unbelief, that he might have mercy upon all.* Romans 11:23–32

Verses 23 and 24 are a new sub-section in that part of this chapter which runs from verse 11 to verse 32. As we begin to consider it we ought to recall our analysis of the whole chapter and its main theme. While we must pay attention to details, we must keep on reminding ourselves of the whole picture. Indeed, a grasp of the whole is essential for an understanding of the parts. The object of the chapter is to tell us that God has not finished with the Jews as a nation although their condition in Paul's day strongly suggested that He had. The bulk of them were outside the Christian church and many had come to that conclusion – especially Gentile believers. Now there are two main sections in Paul's statement. The first section is from verse 1 to verse 10 where the Apostle demonstrates that the rejection of Israel was not total. Then from verse 11 to verse 32 he shows that it is not a final rejection, it is only a temporary one. Remember that the Apostle states the main proposition of this major division in verses 11 and 12. 'I say then, Have they stumbled that they should fall?' Is this a real, final falling away? His answer is in the word 'stumble'. They have not fallen but only stumbled. 'God forbid', he says: 'but rather through their fall salvation is come unto the Gentiles, for to provoke them (the Jews) to jealousy. Now if the fall of them be the riches of the world, and the diminishing of them the riches of the Gentiles; how much more their fulness?' That is his case and it is there he throws out his first hint that there is going to be a restoration of the Jews as a people and they are going to believe the gospel.

In verses 13 and 14 he has a little digression explaining why he is taking the trouble to say all this to Gentiles. He does so because he is the apostle to the Gentiles and he magnifies his office; he wants them to understand these things.

Then in verse 15 he states his big case again: 'If the casting away of them be the reconciling of the world, what shall the receiving of them be, but life from the dead?' There is the great proposition which he has to suggest and so he has got to establish this, his grounds for saying that they are going to be received back again, and in verse 16 he throws out an argument: 'If the firstfruit be holy, the lump is also holy: if the root be holy, so are the branches'. That, you remember, was an historical reference to the origin of this nation in Abraham and Isaac and Jacob, the patriarchs.

Then from verse 17 to verse 22 he has another digression where again his great pastoral heart comes out and his concern about these people is most prominent. He delivers an exhortation to the Gentiles, warning them against a great danger, and he exhorts them to humility.

But in verse 23, to which we now turn, he goes back again to the main argument which is the restoration of the Jews. Having hinted at it in verses twelve and fifteen, he now deals with it fully, right to the end of the thirty-second verse.

Now how do we approach this most important sub-section? There are two ways in which we can deal with it. The first is by way of a kind of mechanical division. We have adopted that method several times so far and of course it is a very good one. In many ways it is the first that one should always use in exposition. I suggest the following. In verses 23 and 24 he shows the possibility and the reasonableness and indeed even the probability of the restoration of the Jews as a nation, but from verse 25 to verse 27 he makes a tremendous statement where he speaks, not of the possibility or the probability of the restoration of the Jews as a nation but of its absolute certainty. This, he says, is something that has been revealed to him, so he makes one of his great prophetic utterances, and as is his custom he points out that, though in a sense it is new and surprising, it actually is not new, it had been prophesied in the Old Testament. He always clinches everything he says by an Old Testament quotation and here we will find there are two main ones. In verses 28 to 32 he recapitulates what he has been saying all the way from verse 11.

But there is a second way in which we can look at this, and that is in terms of the way in which this sub-section advances the great argument that the Apostle is deploying.

So let us look for a moment at the wonderful way in which the Apostle handles his matter. Let us pick out the argument and we will see the way in which he builds it up and ends on a great climax. What he is setting out to do, I say, is to show that God has not finished with the Jews. Now then here are his arguments: The first argument he uses to prove that God has not finished with the Jews is at the very beginning of the chapter where he says that he himself is a proof that this is not so. 'I myself also am an Israelite, of the seed of Abraham, of the tribe of Benjamin'. If he were the only one who had become a Christian it would be enough. You could not say that God had finished with the Jews when this man of all men, this prominent apostle himself, was a Jew who had believed the gospel.

Then the second argument was 'the remnant according to the election of grace'. He says that there are others beside himself. Then the third argument is in verse 16, the argument about the firstfruit'. 'If the firstfruit be holy, the lump is also holy'. Or as he puts it in terms of the root: 'If the root be holy, so are the branches'. The nature of the root will determine the nature of the branches. In other words, the argument is that because of what was true of the fathers of Israel, certain things must be true of those who have descended from them. That is the third argument, and it is a very powerful argument.

Then in the twenty-third verse he moves on to his fourth argument, which is based upon the power of God. 'God is able'! In verse 24 we have his fifth main argument: That in the light of what God has already done in the case of the Gentiles it is plainly not impossible for Him to restore the Jews also. He argues again from the greater to the less.

So these are the arguments: (1) His own case. (2) The remnant according to the election of grace. (3) The argument about the constitution of the nation of Israel. (4) God's power and ability. (5) What God has already done in the case of the Gentiles proves His ability to do it also in the case of the Jews.

Having come to the end of argumentation, he now makes this tremendous dogmatic and prophetic pronouncement in verse 25. He asserts that God has revealed something to him which puts the matter beyond any doubt or question whatsoever. Finally, from verses 33 to the end, he is himself so filled with amazement that he can burst out in that great exclamation: 'O the depth of the riches both of the wisdom and knowledge of God!'

Let us examine verse 23 where Paul is dealing with the possibility of the restoration of the Jews. He says, 'They also . . .' which is a reference to the Jews and it continues what he has just said at the end of verse 22, 'Behold therefore the goodness and severity of God: on them which fell' – there is the bulk of the Jews – 'severity; but toward thee, goodness, if thou continue in his goodness: otherwise thou also shalt be cut off. And they also' – back again to the Jews – 'if they abide not still in unbelief, shall be graffed in: for God is able to graff them in again'.

Now here is an interesting and an important statement. He says that there is a possibility with regard to the unbelieving Jews, but that there is a condition with respect to it which is 'if they abide not still in unbelief'. Now the Apostle here is going to reassert his great principle with regard to the way of salvation or of entry into the kingdom of God. What is it? This is the thing that he has been hammering all along, and back he comes to it again. What is this principle?

Negatively – and this is the thing he wants to say – it is not a question of nationality, it is not a question of works. What is it then? Well, it is always a matter of faith only, 'if they abide not still in unbelief'. There is only one thing that admits anybody into the church of God and that is 'faith'. Or putting it negatively, the only hindrance and obstacle is 'unbelief'. There is only one principle which God ever uses in His dealings with men and He has never used another, it has always been faith from the very beginning. There never will be any other way whatsoever. Salvation is always by faith, and by faith only. This is the cardinal doctrine of justification by faith only.

Now it is interesting to notice that the Apostle puts this negatively, not positively. 'They also, if they abide not still in unbelief, shall be graffed in'. Is there significance in this? Well, I think there is, because again he is safeguarding a very important and a very vital truth which is that of man's responsibility. Man is responsible for his damnation, but he is never responsible for his salvation. Now you may say to me 'How can you reconcile those?' It is not for us to reconcile them; that is what is called an antinomy. It is what is plainly taught in the Scripture. The doctrine of election must never be supposed to teach that man is not responsible. Man is responsible. And everywhere we have seen so plainly and so clearly that if a man ends in damnation it is his fault and his responsibility. But it is equally clear that it is God who saves, and that no man saves himself. That is why the Apostle puts the negative here rather than the positive.

In order to support this let us notice that he does not say that they are able to graft themselves in again. Oh no! It is God Who is able to graft them in again; '. . . they shall be graffed in'. You do not graft yourself into this olive tree, that is something that man cannot do. 'With men, it is impossible' [*Matt.* 19:26]. In other words, the emphasis here is on God's power. 'God is able to graff them in again'.

Now let us again recall the position with which the Apostle was dealing, and of course it is in a sense equally true today. As you and I as Christian people look out upon the whole scene we might very well come to the conclusion that the people who are in the most hopeless position as regards salvation are the Jews, because they had rejected all that their privileges pointed to. The Gentiles were tending to come to the conclusion that nothing could ever be done with them and that God had finally cast them out. Now the Apostle says it is not so, because of God's power. 'God is able to graff them in again'.

Now the word translated 'able' is an interesting and an important word. It carries in it the implication of a great difficulty to be encountered. And that is the whole point of this argument. It is a very difficult thing this, but God can do it. In other words the restoration of the Jews is possible for one reason only and that is, that it is the miraculous action of God that is going to do it. Nothing short of the power of God could possibly bring this to pass. The subsequent argumentation right until the end of verse 32 is virtually saying just that. This is the first statement and he is going to work it out more and more. This is the basis of everything, God's power, God's ability.

Another point we must notice here in this same verse is the identity of the 'them' of whom he is speaking. Who are they? And what about this word 'again'? 'They also, if they abide not still in unbelief, shall be graffed in: for God is able to graff them' – this 'them'; 'they' and 'them', the same people – 'in again'. We must be careful about this because we might come to the superficial conclusion that the people who are to be grafted in again are the same ones who have already been taken out. It looks like that on the surface does it not? But of course it cannot possibly mean that because of the passage of time. Here was the Apostle writing more than nineteen hundred years ago about something that is going to happen, which has not happened even yet. So, it is obvious he is not referring to the Jews who were alive in the first century and who had rejected our Lord and who were persecuting the Apostle Paul and other Christians. No; what he means by the 'they' and the 'them' is the Jews regarded racially or nationally. It can mean nothing else. As I have been at pains to point out to you all along, what the Apostle is dealing with in this chapter is not individual salvation. He is dealing here with the question of the bulk of the Jews. In the earlier chapters of this Epistle he has been dealing with the individual, but here he is dealing specifically with the Jews as a people. And so when he talks about 'they' and 'them' he is not referring to contemporaries of himself and of the Lord who were outside, but to the race of the Jews in some future time.

Why do I take the trouble to emphasise that particular point? Well, my reason for doing so is this – that if you read this verse superficially you might very well conclude that the Apostle is teaching quite plainly that there is such a thing as falling away from grace. He is saying that here is someone who once was in the church, who because of sin and unbelief is taken out of the church, but he can come back again. Now there are people who teach that kind of thing. They preach a falling away from grace and then a restoration. There is a type of superficial evangelism and teaching which almost gives this impression, that a man can take a decision, become a Christian, receive life from God, but he can lose it all by sinning; then if he repents he can get it back again. So that at one time you are not born again, then you are, but then you are not, and again you can be grafted in. So you can go in and out of the olive tree.

Now that is very common teaching today. It is a very superficial teaching, because it is something that is just impossible. That is why it is so important we should have an exact and a correct interpretation of what the Apostle is saying in this verse. The 'they' and the 'them' are not the same individuals whom he has referred to as already 'cast out'. It is a reference only to the Jews as a race. At this time the Jews as a race were outside. He is saying there is a day to come when they will be brought in again. So that there is nothing here to teach that a man can be saved, then lost, then saved again. Such a thing is taught nowhere in the Scriptures. There is only one reason why people ever teach anything like that and that is that they forget the doctrine of regeneration. They put so much emphasis on a man's decision.

Let me put it like this: that kind of teaching is not only wrong but impossible for this reason – it is God who does the grafting, it is God who produces regeneration. And when God puts this life of His in the soul it is put there and it remains there. It is inconceivable that you can have this life and lose it and have it again. Indeed, it implies a failure on the part of God, and there is no failure on the part of God. It is God who is able to put anybody into this olive tree, and when God does that he remains in it.

In verse 24 he really is just carrying on this same point, as is shown by the word 'For'. Here is his fifth argument, which supports the fourth argument and makes it still more obvious. It is that God has already done something which inherently is more difficult than bringing in the Jews. What is that? It is bringing in the Gentiles. 'If thou wert cut out of the olive tree which is wild by nature, and wert graffed contrary to nature into the good olive tree: how much more shall these, which be the natural branches, be graffed into their own olive tree?' Now you see, that is carrying on what he says in verse 23. God has done – if we may say so – the most impossible thing of all, and that is the bringing in of the Gentiles. This is something, he says, which is contrary to nature. We saw how that was so even in the illustration he employed. In horticulture you do not put a bad graft into a good stock, you do the exact opposite; you put the good graft into a bad stock. But here something quite different is happening, a bad graft is put into the good stock and it begins to receive of the root and fatness of the good stock. That is one meaning, then, of 'contrary to nature.'

But it has a second meaning. The Gentiles were entirely outside the covenant of God, they did not belong to God's people. You remember what we are told about the Jews in chapter 9, verses 4 and 5: 'Who are Israelites; to whom pertaineth the adoption, and the glory, and the covenants, and the giving of the law, and the service of God, and the promises; whose are the fathers, and of whom as concerning the flesh Christ came, who is over all, God blessed for ever'.

That is true of Jews; it is not true of Gentiles. They are un-natural, they are outside, they belong to a wild olive tree; they were without God, without hope; they are 'in the world', they are enemies and aliens. Peter says, 'You were not a people'. Paul describes the Gentiles as 'a foolish nation' [10:19–20].

Well now, what he is saying is this: if God has been able to bring in people like that, who are so absolutely remote in every sense from the people of God, how much easier is it for Him to bring in Jews who by nature belong to this tradition. In other words, the case of the Jews far from being more difficult than any other is nothing like as difficult as the case of the Gentiles, for the Jews after all can be described as 'the natural branches'. Israel, all these descendants of Abraham, in an external sense belonged to the olive tree, they were the first branches. And the argument is simply this: If God can bring in those who were completely outside, the 'wild' olive tree, and graft them in, well, how much easier will it be to bring in those who 'by nature', as it were, belong to this olive tree? How much easier ought it to be for a Jew to become a Christian, if you like, than a Gentile? It is not so of course, because it is God who brings in both, as he is going to tell us in verse 32; but looking at it generally and from the human standpoint it appears to be much easier. All their teaching in the Old Testament was preparing them for this, all the promises, all the ceremonial of the temple, the burnt offerings and sacrifices, even the furniture – everything was pointing to this deliverer, this Messiah. And then He comes! How easy it should have been. 'The law was our schoolmaster to bring us to Christ', how natural that it should end in Christianity. That is all he is saying. So it is an argument from the greater to the less. 'How much more then!' If God can do it in the case of Gentiles, who never have belonged to the olive tree at all in any sense, how much easier would it be for God to bring those who in an external and a natural sense do and always have belonged to this olive tree that was started by God in Abraham and the patriarchs.

The Apostle has brought us, then, up to this particular point. No-one must say that the Jews are entirely outside, finished, God has rejected them, or that it is impossible to bring them back because of their antagonism. No, no, says Paul, God can do it. And he has given proof of the fact that He can do it by doing something still more impossible. If God can save a Gentile, how much more can He save a Jew!

# *Twenty*

⁂

*For I would not, brethren, that ye should be ignorant of this mystery, lest ye should be wise in your own conceits; that blindness in part is happened to Israel, until the fulness of the Gentiles be come in. And so all Israel shall be saved: as it is written, There shall come out of Sion the Deliverer, and shall turn away ungodliness from Jacob: For this is my covenant unto them, when I shall take away their sins.* Romans 11:25–27

This is one of the most remarkable prophecies of the Bible. It is certainly one of the great prophecies of the Apostle Paul.

Now let us again remind ourselves of the context and how the Apostle ever came to say this. He is working out an argument in this chapter which is part of the great argument he has been presenting from the beginning of the ninth chapter. It is this whole question of the Jews and their relationship to the kingdom of God and to that particular form of it called the Christian church. The position he has to deal with is this – that the Gentiles were being tempted to say that God has entirely finished with His ancient people and that they – the Gentiles – were being called in because there was some inherent superiority in them.

In answer to the view that the Jews are excluded Paul presents five arguments. First, he says that the fact he is a Christian and an apostle proves that it is incorrect. Secondly, he says that there is a remnant of Jews in the church. Thirdly, the Jews are the descendants of the patriarchs who had certain promises made to them by God and, in the fourth place, there is no difficulty about their being brought back into God's favour and that is because God has the power to do so. The fifth argument reinforces the fourth and is that God has already done something much more difficult than that, and that is, He has brought in the Gentiles. What he said in the first section of the chapter is, that the rejection of Israel is not total; and in this second section he has been pointing out that it is not final, it is only temporary. And that is the way in which he has been working out that great argument.

Now then having done that he leaves argumentation and moves to the realm of direct assertion. All he has shown so far is, that the restoration of the Jews is possible, he has even shown that it is probable; but now he is going on to say that it is an absolute certainty – and that is what we are dealing with in these verses 25, 26, and 27.

Now it is again most important that we should bear in mind that what the Apostle is dealing with in all these statements is the Jews considered nationally. He is not dealing with the case of individuals, he is dealing with this whole position of the Jewish nation.

Now a perfectly reasonable question may occur to someone at this point. 'If the Apostle all along was aware of what he is now going to declare in verse 25, why then did he bother with his five arguments?' Now I wonder whether that has occurred to any of you. If the Apostle has known all along, as he did, that it was in the plan and the purpose of God to bring the Jews, nationally considered, into the church and back again into His favour, why has he bothered to take all this time, in the first twenty-four verses of this chapter, in arguing about it in the way that we have been considering? Now I think this is a very important point. Are we to say that the five arguments are superfluous? And the answer is of course a decided 'No'. But why?

The first answer is, that it is always right to use one's reason in these matters. You see, the Apostle is confronted by the suggestion that the Jews are finished with; they have crucified their Messiah, they are therefore rejected of God, and God has no further interest in them. His way of dealing with that is not to say, Listen to me, I am an apostle and I tell you it has been revealed to me, I make a prophecy, they are going to be brought back – and leave it at that. He does not do that. Why not? Well, because you meet a statement like that, first of all on its own grounds, by way of reasoning. That is where you start, as the Apostle starts here, and it is always right to do that.

But not only that, secondly, the Apostle is anxious to instruct these Gentiles and to show them that what has happened is not in any way inconsistent with the Old Testament teaching. They seemed to be dismissing the whole of the Old Testament and there are still uninstructed Christian people who tend to say that. But the Apostle will not have that, he wants to instruct people, so he does not just leave it at his prophetic utterance. He says, let us work this out together and so he demonstrates that this very thing that has happened has been prophesied by the Old Testament prophets. Consequently, they should neither be surprised nor misunderstand it, because the Old Testament prophets have already dealt with this matter.

Then thirdly, he is most anxious that the Gentiles should be clear in the principles of the teaching. Now this is a point that is of great importance. There are people who always want some direct and immediate statement. There are some people who claim to be unusually spiritual who are only interested in some direct prophetic utterance, as it were, and they tend to exclude everything else. Such thinking is refuted completely by the Apostle's method in this very chapter. He not only gives them a prophetic utterance, but he reasons on the basis of the Scriptures and with his own understanding, almost his own common sense, pointing out facts to them and showing how the position they have taken up is quite incongruous with the whole of the teaching of the Old Testament and also with the Christian teaching. In other words, he really does want these Gentiles to understand this matter thoroughly so that they will know exactly how wrong they have been in what they have been tending to say, and in order that they may be prepared for what he is now going to tell them. Very well.

The final reason which I would adduce for the Apostle's method is this: that it is never enough for us only to know the truth positively, we must also have a negative understanding of it. We must not only be in a position of saying, This is what has been revealed; we must be able to expose error also; otherwise we really will not be able to help people who are in difficulties. If you have somebody who is in difficulty about a matter and you just make some highly spiritual statement to them without meeting their position, you are not likely to help them. But if you can reason it through with them, and point out the error and where they have gone astray, they will see it and they will be saved from not only that error but from similar errors. You will have introduced them to a method which they can apply in various other cases.

Having done this he puts before them this great prophecy with regard to the future of the Jews considered in a national sense. Again, let us ask him a question – Why does he do this? Why does he tell them this prophecy? He answers such a question explicitly and says: 'I would not, brethren, that ye should be ignorant of this mystery', adding a second reason – 'lest ye should be wise in your own conceits'. Now there he gives us two reasons. The first is, that he does not want them to be ignorant. Paul is employing a figure of speech here which is called 'litotes' which means that you make a strong assertion in a negative manner. (Romans 1:16 is a good example of this.) In saying, 'I do not want you to be ignorant', what he really means is, 'I really want you to know all about this, in order that you will never go wrong in this matter again'. That is undoubtedly what this expression means.

But then his second reason is, and this is perhaps still more significant – 'lest ye should be wise in your own conceits'. This is what he has been saying to them from verse 18 to verse 21: 'Boast not against the branches. But if thou boast, thou bearest not the root, but the root thee. Thou wilt say then, The branches were broken off, that I might be grafted in. Well; because of unbelief they were broken off, and thou standest by faith' and 'Be not highminded, but fear: For if God spared not the natural branches, take heed lest he also spare not thee'. Here he is repeating all that but in a blunt and more direct manner. 'I am telling you this', he says, 'lest ye be wise in your own conceits'.

Now the terms that he uses here are interesting. The word that he uses for 'wise' is the word that is generally used for 'false wisdom' which is often accompanied by pride. He is concerned lest they should deceive themselves.

Now in what respects is he trying to save them from being 'wise in their own conceits'? First of all, he obviously wants to disabuse their minds. They thought that they understood this whole question of the position of the Jews and their own position in the Christian church. Paul had learned what they had been saying and so he takes up the whole subject. He was aware that they thought they understood the whole question of the present position of the Jews, but they were wrong and he wants to show them that.

But I think it has a second meaning also. They thought that it was because they had a superior understanding that they were in the church and the Jews were outside. After all, they had been able to see the truth of the gospel, whereas the Jews had not. The Apostle wants to show them how terribly wrong that is. He has already done so in detail in verses 16 and onwards. They were boasting as over against the Jews but they had nothing to boast about at all – and anyone who thinks that he is a Christian because of any superiority in himself comes under this castigation of the Apostle here. The Apostle is going to drive this home in a powerful statement in verse 32: 'For God hath concluded them all in unbelief, that he might have mercy upon all'.

And thirdly, therefore, he wants to deliver them from being 'wise in their own conceits' because he does not want them to be put to shame when the great reality actually takes place. He knows what is going to happen, so he says, I am going to tell you now, because if I do not, you and your descendants will go on saying that you are in the church because you have such great understanding and high morals. You will then be made to look ridiculous because it will be, when you see the Jews being brought in as a nation, evident to all that you have been wrong throughout the centuries. He wants to save them from all that. So you see it is not merely a question of delivering them from their ignorance, he has this great pastoral care for them. We can put it like this, he wants to bring an end to their making fools of themselves by saying something that is completely wrong and priding themselves on their rights. Very well, that is why he is going to give them this information.

The next point which we come to is this, that he tells them that this information that he is going to give them is a mystery. Here again is a most important term and it is interesting for many reasons. You will find in the Epistles of this great Apostle that he uses this word 'mystery' very frequently. Why did he do so? Well, I accept the verdict of the authorities on this matter – that he did so because it was a term that was very much in current use at that time. It is a well-known fact that in that ancient world, and especially amongst the Gentiles, there were what were called 'mystery religions'. They are referred to in the Epistle to the Colossians. They were a strange concoction of philosophy, ritual and asceticism. They were very common and current in the Roman Empire and had come from the East. The Apostle very often takes up the terms that were in current use in those circles and uses them in order to show through them the Christian teaching.

Here, again, is something that we can learn from the great Apostle. It is essential always that our teaching and preaching should be in terms that people can understand. It is difficult but it has got to be done, we should always make that effort. If there is therefore something that is in current usage which we can use in order to bring out an aspect of the truth, it is right to do so. But you will notice at once that the Apostle gives the term that he uses an entirely different connotation. When he says that he is going to put before them a mystery, he does not mean some wonderful secret that was only known to the initiated. Such thinking was a way of building up pride because the secret was known only to the select few. That was the great characteristic of these mystery religions.

Now the Apostle uses their term but shows them what a different thing the Christian faith really is. By 'mystery' the Apostle means something which is concealed from the natural understanding of man but which God in His infinite grace has been pleased to reveal. Now this is a most important matter. In the New Testament, a 'mystery' is something which man's understanding cannot reach, even at the best, but which God has been pleased to make known, clearly and evidently.

Now in the mystery religions, you see, everything depended upon one's understanding and intellectual acumen. One progressed through rites and stages and one could proceed beyond others. Let me put it again in terms of that great statement in the eleventh chapter of Matthew's Gospel where Jesus says, 'I thank thee, O Father, Lord of heaven and earth, that thou hast hid these things from the wise and prudent' – these people who always pride themselves on their wisdom and understanding, and they arrive at knowledge. Not here! 'Thou hast hid these things from the wise and prudent, and hast revealed them unto babes. Even so, Father, for so it hath seemed good in thy sight'.

Now let me give you some other examples from the New Testament of the use of this very term. You find it in the last chapter of this very Epistle. In verses 25 and 26, the Apostle says, 'Now to him that is of power to stablish you according to my gospel, and the preaching of Jesus Christ, according to the revelation of the mystery, which was kept secret since the world began, But now is made manifest, and by the Scriptures of the prophets, according to the commandment of the everlasting God, made known to all nations for the obedience of faith'. There is a perfect illustration of this very thing. We have it in 1 Corinthians 2:6–8 and Ephesians 1:9,10 and 3:4–6. There the gospel of salvation and the inclusion of the Gentiles in its benefits together with the consummation of all things are referred to as something which is beyond man's ability to know, had not God revealed it. The same applies to the resurrection of the body in 1 Corinthians 15:51. A fine example from the Epistle to the Romans is in verses 25 and 26 of the last chapter.

You see, my friends, this is the glory of the Christian position, that this grand mystery of God and His eternal purpose and will is revealed to us. This is Christianity and we have got to exercise ourselves with respect to these things. There are prophecies in the Old Testament about the Gentiles, that the gospel is to be preached to them. Yes, but it is merely hinted at in the Old Testament, now it has been fully revealed. So you must not say that any one of these mysteries is something that was totally unknown before; but what it does mean is, that it was only hinted at, now there is to be a plain and a full and a clear revelation of it. You see, I say that for this reason – that the moment the Apostle reveals this mystery he goes on to say 'as it is written'. It had been prophesied but not very clearly. You could read your Old Testament and not see it, not get it; the Jews had entirely missed it. It is there. It is there in embryo but it is not there in its fullness. But now he says I am going to show it you, I am going to put it before you so that you cannot be ignorant and you will no longer be wise in your own conceits.

What a wonderful difference there is between Christianity and all the mystery religions – past and present for there are still some 'mystery religions' that appeal to people. You know, they have got some great secret, it is not told to everybody, only to those who are initiated. That is the characteristic of false religions always. It is kept to themselves, and there they are, a group on their own. They have got a wonderful secret and they are some special people. They help one another but they do not help other people – all for themselves, the initiated.

Now that is the absolute opposite of Christianity which noises abroad, makes known, reveals, proclaims. What a contrast between Christianity and all these false religions! Indeed we can sum them up like this. The difference between Christianity and every false religion is the difference between mystery 'revealed' and mystery 'concealed'. We should always mistrust any religion that claims to be true or spiritual if it conceals and only gives this information to certain initiated people. Christianity is mystery 'revealed'. It is something which can be shown, says the Apostle. What a contrast there is between concealing and revealing! And this is something, I say, which is of value to us at the present time even as it was in the times of the great Apostle. Let us ever remember this therefore when people tell us that they have got something that is superior to the teaching of the church, something that does more good. The reply to make to such people is this: If it is so wonderful, why do you make a secret of it? Christianity wants everybody to know the truth. It is a gospel which proclaims from the house-tops, it is open, it is free, it is not something to be done behind closed doors and in great secrecy.

What then does this statement tell us about the Apostle Paul? He says, 'For I would not, brethren, that ye should be ignorant of this mystery, lest ye should be wise in your own conceits; that blindness in part is happened to Israel, until the fulness of the Gentiles be come in. And so all Israel shall be saved'. This tells us a great deal about the man who wrote this Epistle to the Romans, and what it tells us about him, of course, is that he is an apostle; and that means that a revelation of the truth had been made to him in order that he could go out and teach others. In other words, the Apostle is not giving a forecast here, he is not sitting down and trying to work out what is going to happen and saying, It is my opinion that this or that is going to take place. No, no, this is a dogmatic pronouncement, it is the utterance of a prophecy. He did not arrive at this either intuitively or even as the result of studying the Old Testament. It was 'revealed' to him.

Now that is one of the things that made a man an apostle. He is called and a revelation is given to him in order that he may teach others. Revelations like that are not given to everybody. 'The church is built', says Paul in Ephesians 2:20, 'upon the foundation of the apostles and prophets.' That means that the revelation of truth was made to them. And it has been made only to them. So there is no fresh revelation to expect. That is one of our reasons for rejecting the church of Rome. She claims that revelation has continued through her. That is why, you see, the Pope is said to be the successor of Peter and so on. They talk about 'a succession of the apostolate' and high church Anglicans do the same. But it is this kind of claim which ultimately carries with it the notion that these men are the successors of the apostles. The answer is, you cannot have successors to the apostles. They were once and for all. The revelation was made to them in order that they might pass it on and send it forward. 'This dispensation of the gospel has been given to me', says Paul, 'in order that I may make known among the Gentiles the unsearchable riches of Christ'. And here the Apostle is, in other words, just telling these Romans that he is an apostle.

So we accept this prophecy of the Apostle Paul in exactly the same way as we accept the prophecy of Isaiah, of Jeremiah, or Ezekiel, or of Daniel or any one of the Minor Prophets. Indeed Peter exhorts his readers to regard the Apostle Paul in this very way when he places the writings of Paul on the same plane as the Old Testament Scriptures, having said that they came 'not by the will of man: but holy men of God spake as they were moved, carried along, by the Holy Spirit'. So the Apostle here is telling these Romans that he is going to make an utterance that is exactly the same as the utterances of the prophets under the Old Testament dispensation. The Christians at Rome are to remember that. They are to believe this as the revealed truth of God. And you and I in our day and generation are to do the same thing. This is not the opinion of Paul, the man; this is the prophetic utterance of Paul the called Apostle of Jesus Christ, unto whom the revelation has been given.

# *Twenty-one*

*

*For I would not, brethren, that ye should be ignorant of this mystery, lest ye should be wise in your own conceits; that blindness in part is happened to Israel, until the fulness of the Gentiles be come in. And so all Israel shall be saved: as it is written, There shall come out of Sion the Deliverer, and shall turn away ungodliness from Jacob: For this is my covenant unto them, when I shall take away their sins.* Romans 11:25–27

We are looking at this great statement which the Apostle declares to be a prophecy and which I have already described to you as his way of expressing his absolute certainty about the restoration of the Jews to the kingdom of God and to the Christian church. In many ways it has occasioned difficulty and there has not only been disagreement about it but even controversy.

The Apostle states his prophecy in the last part of verse 25 and the first part of verse 26. It is then supported in the second half of verse 26 and in verse 27 by quotations from the Old Testament – his usual method. Here, then, is the prophecy – 'that blindness in part is happened to Israel, until the fulness of the Gentiles be come in. And so all Israel shall be saved' and we need to remember that it is a prophecy. It is the revelation of a mystery, something which man can neither foresee nor foretell, but something that has been revealed by God to Paul in order that he might make it known to others.

There are two main ways in which a statement like this can be approached. The first is to give its meaning in general terms and then to support that by means of a detailed examination. That is the method that is adopted by Charles Hodge, for instance, and others. But there is a second method and to me it seems to be the preferable one. It is that we take the statement as it is, break it up into its component parts, try to discover the meaning of the words and of the phrases, and then having obtained an exact meaning, to state and substantiate the doctrine, considering and evaluating rival points of view. It seems to me that that is the better procedure because we cannot present the general meaning of a verse without having determined what that is.

So we start with the word 'blindness'. This is the mystery that he is revealing to them, 'that blindness in part is happened to Israel'. Now 'blindness' is the word in the Authorized Version, and in a sense it is quite an accurate and a good translation; but the word that was used by the Apostle does not mean blindness in and of itself; it means 'hardness', 'obtuseness', 'insensibility' – that is the root meaning. And of course ultimately, therefore, it does come to mean blindness. If you are insensitive to truth you cannot see it. So they were quite justified in using the word 'blindness'. But as they have used 'hardness' in other places it would have been better if they had used 'hardness' here.

Now there is nothing new about this because the idea has already been stated in verses 8–10 of this very chapter. There we read: '(According as it is written, God hath given them the spirit of slumber, eyes that they should not see, and ears that they should not hear;) until this day. And David saith, Let their table be made a snare, and a trap, and a stumblingblock, and a recompence unto them: Let their eyes be darkened that they may not see, and bow down their back alway'. This same idea is expressed except that he puts it more like this, that 'blindness in part is happened to Israel'. The same essential idea appears in chapter 9:18 in the word 'hardeneth'.

Now this is an idea that recurs in the Scriptures, that the trouble with the children of Israel was a 'hardness' that led to blindness, and this, according to statements in the Scripture, is the ultimate cause of unbelief. It is found a number of times in Hebrews 3:8–11 which refers to Israel's disobedience in the wilderness.

Now that is the idea that is conveyed by this word 'blindness'. The reason why the Jews as a nation rejected their own Messiah and His teaching and rejected the teaching of the apostles and dealt with them in the cruel fashion they did was that they had become 'hardened', they had become insensitive to truth and it could make no impression upon them. The same condition is described as a 'veil on the heart' in 2 Corinthians 3. It is a terrible thing this, and it is the ultimate explanation, as I say, of all unbelief.

But there is a qualifying statement. He says 'that blindness in part is happened to Israel'. What does he mean by 'in part'? Once more, there is obviously room for several different interpretations. Some people say that it means a 'partial blindness', that is, the Jews were not totally blind but only partially. They still saw aspects of the truth but they could not see it all.

This view has to be rejected completely because the trouble with Israel was that she was totally blind. To reject the Messiah means 'a total blindness', and that was the charge that our Lord so constantly brought against the Pharisees. They claimed that they had light, were teachers of the people and experts in the Law, but the trouble was they were absolutely ignorant. This is proved by the case of this Apostle Paul himself. You remember how in writing to Timothy he refers to the days when he was 'a persecutor and a blasphemer, and injurious', but you remember what he says. He says, 'I did it ignorantly' – ignorantly! – 'in unbelief'. It was nothing but ignorance and it was a total ignorance. He says the same thing in Philippians 3.

Then others would say that what it means is, 'that blindness is happened to a part of Israel', that is only some, or not all of them, are blind. Well, of course, that was so. We have already seen in this chapter that the Apostle makes that same point himself. He not only says 'I am a believer', but also that 'there is a remnant according to the election of grace'. Some of the Jews had believed. So it is true to infer that it was only 'some' of the nation of Israel who were unable to see the truth of the gospel.

And yet I reject that explanation of the meaning of this term also, for this reason: that the Apostle here is dealing not with individuals but with the nation as a whole. Now I have had to keep on saying that, but in this chapter he is really dealing with the nation as a whole. The fact was that the nation as a whole was outside the church and had rejected the Messiah and the gospel, and he is here dealing with the nation as a whole. So I reject both those suggested explanations as to what he means by saying 'that blindness in part is happened to Israel'.

Well then, what is he saying? It should be read like this: 'That blindness is happened in part to Israel': not 'partial blindness is happened to Israel', or 'blindness is happened to a part of Israel'. What does this mean? Well, it means that he is referring to length of time: not to the intensity of the blindness but to its duration. A better way, therefore, of translating this would be – 'That blindness has happened temporarily to Israel'. That is what he means. What confirms this rendering is, of course, the use of the word 'until'.

'Blindness in part is happened until . . .' The blindness is not permanent, it is not everlasting; it is a temporary blindness.

Now you see that when we come to gather up all these points it will make the exposition, I think, quite inevitable and my method of approach will be justified.

But now we come to the next phrase, which is 'is happened'. You see every single term here is of great importance. 'Blindness in part is happened' to Israel – which means, of course, that something has happened to Israel, rather than something being true of it. He is referring to what was discussed in chapter 9 which we have called a judicial blindness. In other words, it is not something that they have produced themselves, it is something which has been inflicted on them. What we are told in Romans 9:17 and following of God's dealings with Pharaoh is an exact case in point. We read, 'Therefore hath he mercy on whom he will have mercy and whom he will he hardeneth'.

So the blindness which 'is happened' to Israel is something that has been put on them by God. This does not mean that He is the author of unbelief but that He hardens the Jews who did not believe the gospel, just as He did with Pharaoh.

This is something which people do not like. But it is not a question of liking. It is what Scripture says. Nor is it a question of understanding. We dare not reply against God. He has 'power over the clay, of the same lump to make one vessel unto honour, and another unto dishonour.' How foolish it is for people to put their little understanding against profound truth like this!

Now let me show you how our blessed Lord Himself taught exactly the same thing. You remember what He says in the Gospel according to St Matthew in chapter 13 as to why He spoke in parables. We read in verse 10: 'And the disciples came, and said unto Him, Why speakest thou unto them in parables?' How often this has been misunderstood. I have heard evangelists sometimes using this passage to justify their own use of stories. They say, 'But our Lord told stories; didn't He tell the parables? The message has to be made simple'. They think that that is why our Lord spoke in parables. But listen to what He says Himself. They ask Him, 'Why speakest thou unto them in parables? He answered and said unto them, Because it is given unto you to know the mysteries of the kingdom of God, but to them it is not given. For whosoever hath, to him shall be given, and he shall have more abundance: but whosoever hath not, from him shall be taken away even that he hath. Therefore speak I unto them in parables: because they seeing see not; and hearing they hear not, neither do they understand. And in them is fulfilled the prophecy of Esaias, which saith, By hearing ye shall hear, and shall not understand; and seeing ye shall see, and shall not perceive: For this people's heart is waxed gross' – same idea; that is still 'hardening' – 'and their ears are dull of hearing, and their eyes have they closed; lest at any time they should see with their eyes, and hear with their ears, and should understand with their heart, and should be converted, and I should heal them'. It is exactly the same thing as He says at the end of Matthew 11, 'I thank thee, O Father, Lord of heaven and earth, that thou hast hid' – hid! – 'these things from the wise and prudent, and hast revealed them unto babes. Even so, Father: for so it seemed good in thy sight'. This is the deliberate action of God. He blinds, He hardens in a judicial manner the nation of the Jews in order that He may not only punish them but that He may bring His great purposes to pass of sending the gospel to the Gentile, and even ultimately through that to bring back the Jews as a whole. But this, I say, is an example therefore of judicial hardening, or judicial blindness. Our Lord spoke in parables in order that they might not understand. And they didn't. They misunderstood completely, and that was because their hearts were hardened.

So, then, the Apostle's teaching is this: As it is God Who inflicts this judicial blindness upon the Jews, it is God also Who sometime in the future is going to open their eyes and restore them and graft them in again. It is always God's action, both the hardening and the restoring. You notice the phrase in verse 26 of Romans 11: 'As it is written, There shall come out of Sion the Deliverer' – and remember it is the Deliverer Who shall 'turn away ungodliness from Jacob'. It is not that Jacob at some future time is going to decide to believe. No, no; the God Who blinds is the God Who heals. The God Who breaks away the natural branches is the same God Who is able to graft them in again. It is God's action in both respects. It is the Redeemer, the Deliverer, alone Who has the ability to 'turn away ungodliness'. We must not think of it as some voluntary action in the future on the part of the Jews. No, no! They would continue for ever as they are now were it not God's purpose to enlighten them, to drive away their ungodliness and to bring them back into the olive tree to which they originally belonged. 'Christ is set for the fall and the rising again of many in Israel'. It is a mystery, is it not? The next phrase, of course, is 'to Israel', which means to Israel as a whole and not to individuals.

The next word is the word 'until' which links up with the temporary nature of the hardening. But 'until' when? Well, 'until the fulness of the Gentiles be come in'. Now here again is a most important statement. There have been many different explanations of this. Some say that it just means that as long as Gentiles keep coming in to the Christian church, so some of the Jews will also be converted. They say, God has finished with the nation of Israel as such altogether, but still individual conversions will continue among the Jews as long as the gospel is still preached to the Gentiles. That is one explanation that is put forward.

Another explanation which is put forward is this: that 'the fulness of the Gentiles' means that the Gentiles will make up the fulness that has been partially depleted by the defection of the Jews. Here, you see, is the olive tree consisting originally of Jews, and Jews only. But the Jews reject their Messiah and are removed. There is a gap left, the olive tree is no longer full, as it were. And they say that what this fulness of the Gentiles means is that the Gentiles are being brought in to make up that fulness.

But there is an obvious answer to this. Already, centuries ago, far more Gentiles had been converted to Christianity and had entered the Christian church than the total number of the Jews alive at the time of our Lord. Yet the gospel is still being preached to them. Obviously, this explanation is not accurate.

Well then what does it mean? I suggest it means what we interpreted the word 'fulness' to mean back in verse 12. It means the great majority of the Gentiles and of the Gentile nations. It does not mean that every single Gentile who has ever lived is going to be saved nor that all the Gentiles who will be alive at a given point in the future are going to be saved. This word 'fulness' means the Gentiles regarded as a whole. As the fulness of the Jews means the Jews as a nation, as a whole, so the fulness of the Gentiles means exactly the same thing, the Gentiles in general. The Gentile 'world', as it were, will have come in, and it is when that has happened that the same is going to happen to the Jews.

We must now take note of the phrase, 'be come in'. It is a very definite term, almost a technical term. It does not mean merely that a given number of Gentiles will have decided throughout the centuries to come in or that the great bulk of them will decide at some future date. No, the term carries with it the whole notion of being introduced into the kingdom; being introduced or engrafted into the divine life, beginning to partake of the divine glory. It almost carries with it this idea of being 'gathered in'. In other words, the very term that the Apostle used carries this very definite idea, that God has His great eternal plan, He knows the number of the redeemed, there is a complement to come in from the Gentiles, and the Apostle is saying they will be brought in. And when that complement has been brought in, God will then do this other thing with regard to the Jews.

Having looked at these words used in the second half of verse 25, we turn to the beginning of verse 26. 'And so', says the Apostle, 'all Israel shall be saved'. Now what does he mean by 'And so'? I suggest that he means after the 'until' is ended. This blindness has happened temporarily to Israel 'until' the fulness of the Gentiles has been brought in. But when that has happened then 'all Israel shall be saved'.

Now there are those who say that we have no right to translate it like that – that the Apostle says 'And so', not 'And then'. They say he is not so much referring to time as to God's method. I do not deny that, but would argue that the method and the time are both worked together. What the Apostle ultimately is saying is that when this fulness of the Gentiles has come in, the Jews will be aroused to jealousy, and in that way they will be brought in. 'And so' therefore means the time and the method and that is made quite plain in verses 30 and 31: 'As ye in times past have not believed God, yet have now obtained mercy through their unbelief: Even so have these also now not believed, that through your mercy they also may obtain mercy'.

But this brings us to the meaning of the crucial expression 'all Israel'. Here is the thing above all others about which there has been argumentation, and there are three main views with regard to it. The first is that 'all Israel' means the total number of the elect, both Jews and Gentiles. This was the view taught by St Augustine, John Calvin and Martin Luther, and yet I make bold to reject it.

Why do I do so? Let me give you my reasons. First, that interpretation means that the word 'Israel' is given a different meaning here in verse 26 from what it obviously had in verse 25 where it refers to the nation of the Jews. Why change the meaning of a simple word in such a short compass? There is no indication that it is necessary to do that and that fact alone, it seems to me, is enough to set aside such a view. Why did the great Reformers teach that? Undoubtedly it was because they were reacting violently against the very wild teaching about the Millennium that became current in their day and generation. It is always dangerous when correcting an excess, to go to an opposite excess oneself. I believe the great Reformers were guilty of that very thing.

But not only does this interpretation make 'Israel' have a different meaning in verse 26 from verse 25, it makes the statement run counter to the whole argument of the entire chapter. What Paul is dealing with in this chapter, as I have had to go on repeating and still must repeat, is the case of the bulk of the nation of the Jews. That is what he is dealing with here, and he is still dealing with it: Verse 28 really proves this to the very hilt. He says, 'As concerning the gospel, they are enemies'. Who are they? Well, it is the Israel about which he is speaking, and that is the nation of Israel as a whole. 'As concerning the gospel, they are enemies for your sakes: but as touching the election, they are beloved for the fathers' sakes'. This does not include the Gentiles; it is the Jews only. It cannot therefore be the total of the elect, which includes Gentiles as well as Jews. I think those three reasons are more than sufficient to exclude that interpretation altogether.

Let us look at the second interpretation, which is that 'all Israel' means the total number of elect Jews. The argument runs like this. The Apostle has already told us that he was a saved Jew and that there was 'a remnant according to the election of grace'. This has continued ever since. A number of Jews have been saved from decade to decade and century to century, and this will go on right until the end of time, so that when you come to the end you will have a total number of saved Jews. 'All Israel' is the sum total, the aggregate of all the individual Jews who have been saved throughout the running centuries.

Who has advocated this? The great interpreter Bengel took this view, and also the great Dutch theologian Herman Bavinck, contemporary of Abraham Kuyper, and R. C. H. Lenski too.

I am going to reject this interpretation too. Why? Because if this is all that is meant, there is no mystery. But the Apostle says he is telling us a mystery: 'I would not, brethren, that ye should be ignorant of this mystery . . .' This prophetic utterance is a great mystery. It is something that has been revealed to him. Well, if it is just a question of a number of Jews now and again being converted and added to the church and that eventually there will be a sum total of them – well, there is no mystery about that. It is something which is generally known. We can deduce it for ourselves. So the whole element of mystery has completely gone. And that is enough in and of itself to exclude that interpretation.

But there are further reasons for excluding it. That interpretation does not allow for the difference between the 'now' and the 'then' that the Apostle has been putting before us all the way through. Look at it in verse 12: 'Now if the fall of them be the riches of the world, and the diminishing of them the riches of the Gentiles; how much more their fulness?' If it is like this now, what will it be like then? Similarly in verse 15 – 'if the casting away of them be the reconciling of the world, what shall the receiving of them be, but life from the dead?' 'Now' and 'then'. You have the same thing in verses 23 and 24. He says, 'They also, if they abide not still in unbelief, shall be grafted in'. He is talking about something that is going to happen – not something that is happening the whole time. He is contrasting the present with something in the future. It is possible, he says in verse 23; in verse 24 it is probable because God has got the power – '. . . how much more shall these, which be the natural branches, be grafted in?' It is not something continuous, it is a distinct event which contrasts with what is happening now.

But there is an argument which simply demolishes this interpretation completely, and it has got to be driven right out of court. What is it? It is that this verse fails completely to account for the argument of verses 12 and 15, and especially that great statement at the end of verse 15. 'If the fall of them be the riches of the world, and the diminishing of them the riches of the Gentiles; how much more their fulness?' 'If the casting away of them be the reconciling of the world, what shall the receiving of them be, but life from the dead?' You remember we interpreted this great hyperbole as an event which is going to be so phenomenal, so amazing, it will literally be like life from the dead, the most astounding thing that has ever happened. An odd Jew converted today, another one tomorrow, and by the end of time there will be a certain sum total. Now this interpretation does not allow for that at all. Where is the phenomenon, where is the life from the dead in that? You see, it does not account for it at all. We must have an interpretation which does justice to this amazing, this staggering phenomenon which is going to be comparable to 'life from the dead'.

So I reject both those interpretations and suggest to you that the only valid and consistent interpretation is the one I have been suggesting all along, which is this – that he is referring here to something that is going to happen to the bulk of the nation of the Jews. This means that the 'Israel' of verse 26 is the same Israel as in verse 29. It means the bulk of the Jews, the Jews as a whole. It does not mean every single Jew at any given point, or every pure-blooded Jew. But it does mean that those who have Jewish ancestors and those who cling persistently to the Jews' religion will, as a whole, have their eyes opened. The hardness will be removed and they will believe and enter the Christian church. 'All Israel', as we saw in verse 12, where it is put as 'their fulness', means the bulk of the Jewish people. It means that the Jews who still separate themselves and worship after the tradition of the fathers and reject the gospel will, as a whole, become believers and will come in; and its effect upon the whole church will be comparable to 'life from the dead'!

# *Twenty-two*

*

*For I would not, brethren, that ye should be ignorant of this mystery, lest ye should be wise in your own conceits; that blindness in part is happened to Israel, until the fulness of the Gentiles be come in. And so all Israel shall be saved: as it is written, There shall come out of Sion the Deliverer, and shall turn away ungodliness from Jacob: For this is my covenant unto them, when I shall take away their sins. As concerning the gospel, they are enemies for your sakes: but as touching the election, they are beloved for the fathers' sakes. For the gifts and calling of God are without repentance. For as ye in times past have not believed God, yet have now obtained mercy through their unbelief: Even so have these also now not believed, that through your mercy they also may obtain mercy. For God hath concluded them all in unbelief, that he might have mercy upon all.* Romans 11:25–32

---

The only phrase we have not fully considered in verses 25 and 26 is: 'So all Israel shall be saved'. We have given an explanation of what is meant by 'all Israel' but what is meant by 'being saved'? This is most important. What Paul is concerned about is the *salvation* of 'all Israel'. He does not say anything here about the future of the Jewish nation from any kind of governmental point of view, nor even in terms of the land of Palestine. That is not what he is talking about. He is talking about its salvation and Jews are going to be saved in exactly the same way as anybody else.

Now you know that there is a teaching which says that there is a special salvation for the Jews. There are even those who say that, in the future, Jews are going to be saved by keeping the Law, which is to me the most monstrous thing that anybody can ever say. There is only one way of salvation in the whole Bible; it is always by faith and faith in Jesus Christ and Him crucified. There is not, there never has been, there never will be, there cannot ever be any other kind or type of salvation. The salvation that the Jews are going to experience is precisely the same as that which was being experienced then by the Gentiles – and by believing Jews and Gentiles today.

There is no difference. We really must get quite clearly in our minds from the prophecy that at some future time when the fulness of the Gentiles shall come in, then this great movement as it were will take place amongst the Jews and the fulness of the Jews will come in, as he has told us in verse 12. And they will come into the church in exactly the same way as every one of us has come in – namely by repentance toward God and faith in the Lord Jesus Christ. That is the prophecy. That is this mystery that has been revealed to him.

Now the Apostle goes on and does something which is characteristic of him. He wants now to confirm this prophetic utterance of his by means of quotations from the Old Testament. But what is happening here is not simply that the Apostle is interpreting Old Testament prophecy. He is giving a new prophecy; he is uttering something that has been revealed to him in exactly the same way as the truth was revealed to the prophets under the old dispensation. It is a new prophecy but he says that the same thing was taught in the Old Testament.

The very form in which he handles these quotations that we are going to look at proves this point, because we shall see that this is not an exact quotation from the Old Testament. What the Apostle Paul gives us here is the general sense of a number of Old Testament statements. This is important.

We have come across this point before, and you will remember how we saw that it highlighted, rather than detracted from, the doctrine of the inspiration of Scripture. You will often find that the Apostle's quotations from the Old Testament are not exact. Why is that? Is he casting any doubt upon the verbal inspiration of the Old Testament? Well, the answer is of course that he is not. What is happening is this. Here is an Apostle himself under the same inspiration of the Holy Spirit as were the Old Testament prophets. It is not that the Apostle was slack or negligent and trusted to his memory instead of turning up the Scriptures in order to get his exact quotation; that is impossible because he had been trained as a Pharisee and the Pharisees were so meticulous in this respect. It is not that. What is happening is that the same Spirit Who gave the message to the Old Testament prophets is now giving this message to this New Testament Apostle, who is also a prophet. And so the Spirit Who gave the original words sometimes varies the exact expression. Why? Well, in order to show the particular application of the message at this point.

Now this is a most important principle with regard to the whole of prophecy. You remember that in the Old Testament prophecies there are generally two meanings. There was an immediate application to the situation of Israel at that time, but then so often there is this further remote application pointing forward to this very time with which we are dealing here after the advent of our Lord. So it comes to pass that when the Apostle is showing that the fulfilment of a particular prophecy has taken place the words will be varied just a little to show the present, immediate application. In other words, far from casting any doubt at all upon the divine inspiration of the Scriptures and the inerrancy of the Scriptures, he does the exact opposite. No man would ever dare to vary words and expressions like this as the Apostle does, least of all the great Apostle, an ex-Pharisee. No, he is just showing here that he is under the immediate, direct inspiration of the Holy Spirit. And that is why, of course, the Apostle Peter, recognizing that, in his Second Epistle and in the third chapter, refers to the writings of this Apostle as the Scripture, and compares it to 'the other Scriptures'. And this is a very wonderful thing; it helps us to see the uniqueness of the calling of an apostle, how he does correspond in this way with the prophets of the Old Testament. The Apostles were men to whom the Lord revealed the truth in exactly the same way as He did to the Old Testament prophets. So here is the great Apostle writing under divine inspiration and giving this wonderful truth to us.

We come now to the actual quotation. He says, 'So all Israel shall be saved: as it is written, There shall come out of Sion the Deliverer and shall turn away ungodliness from Jacob: For this is my covenant unto them, when I shall take away their sins'. That is the end of the quotation. Now you cannot go to the Old Testament and find just that. What the Apostle has done is to take phrases out of a number of Old Testament statements, namely Isaiah 59:20, 21; Isaiah 27:9; Jeremiah 31:31–34 and Psalm 14:7, and to give their general sense.

Let me show you what I mean. In the Old Testament Isaiah 59:20 reads as follows: 'The Redeemer shall come to Zion, and unto them that turn from transgression in Jacob'. You will notice at once that what the Apostle says here is, 'There shall come out of Sion the Deliverer, and shall turn away ungodliness from Jacob'.

How can that difference be explained? There is no question at all that the Apostle here, as is generally his custom, was using that translation of the Hebrew Scriptures into the Greek which is known as the Septuagint. But why does the Apostle say therefore 'out of Zion'? Now here it seems, and the authorities are agreed about this point, the Apostle had in his mind the seventh verse of the fourteenth Psalm. There, you remember, it is put in this form: 'Oh that the salvation of Israel were come out of Zion! when the Lord bringeth back the captivity of his people, Jacob shall rejoice, and Israel shall be glad'. The great Apostle's mind was filled with these Old Testament Scriptures and what he is concerned about is this general idea.

There is also a variation at the end of the verse we are considering which reads – 'and shall turn away ungodliness from Jacob'. In the Hebrew original, and as the English translators have rendered it, it is 'to such as turn from transgression in Jacob'. But, you see, Paul seems to say the exact opposite. He does not say that in Jacob they are going to turn from transgression; he says that 'the Deliverer shall turn them away from transgression, or ungodliness'. How does he come to do this? Well, here again he follows this Septuagint translation which is: 'and shall turn iniquity, or transgression, from Jacob'. This corresponds to Isaiah 27:9 which is: 'The iniquity of Jacob shall be turned', or 'the iniquity of Jacob shall be taken away', or 'He shall take away his sin'.

Notice this is purely a technical question, but it has got tremendous importance, because it is under this Divine inspiration that the Apostle makes these changes. Let us follow him. 'The Deliverer' – that is clear, that is the Messiah, the one who is going to do this for them. But he is going to come 'out of Zion' rather than 'to' or 'for' Zion. Why does the Apostle do that? What is this coming of the Redeemer 'out of Zion'? Well, there are those who say that this is a reference to the first advent of our Lord; that those prophecies in the Old Testament are a reference to His first coming; that the Saviour came out from among the Jews, and that, indeed, the whole passage that we are dealing with is simply an account of the consequences of the first advent and that the Apostle is just here dealing with the conversions that take place in Jews and Gentiles as the result of the coming of our Lord.

But I must reject this interpretation for two main reasons. First, He is never described as coming out of Zion; out of Galilee, yes, out of Bethlehem, even out of Egypt, but never out of Zion. That is really sufficient in and of itself. But then in addition to that the first advent of our Lord did not do this thing about which the Apostle is speaking.

He says, that when the Deliverer comes out of Zion He shall turn away ungodliness from Jacob. Well if there was one thing that our Lord's coming into this world did not do it was just that. Far from turning away ungodliness from Jacob it emphasized and exaggerated the ungodliness of Jacob. They refused Him, they rejected Him. He did not turn away their ungodliness, He brought it to a head, as you find, for instance, at the end of the twenty-third chapter of the Gospel according to St Matthew where He says, 'That upon this generation shall come all that has been piling up from the day when Zacharias was murdered between the temple and the altar', you remember. That is the teaching of the New Testament. Our Lord's first Advent did in no sense turn ungodliness from Jacob. The whole point, indeed, of this chapter that we are dealing with is to show that the effect of our Lord's coming into this world was, in a sense, to aggravate the unbelief and the unrighteousness of Jacob, leading to its being cast away, torn out of the olive tree temporarily if you like. That is the whole statement not only of this chapter but of the whole of the New Testament. So this cannot possibly be a reference to the first coming of our Lord. And that is why I entirely disagree with those who find a parallel in this statement to the statement made by James in the council of Jerusalem as recorded in the fifteenth chapter of the Book of the Acts of the Apostles. That does not refer to this at all; that is an explanation of why the Gentiles were coming in to the Christian church.

But there are those who say that this is a reference to the Second Advent of our Lord – 'The Redeemer shall come out of Zion'. Well again I must reject this for this reason, that all the references to the Second Coming in the New Testament put it in terms of His coming out of heaven, not out of Zion; not out of the literal Zion, the earthly Jerusalem. And in any case the teaching of the New Testament is, that when He does come again He will come for judgment; not to turn iniquity from Jacob, He will come for final judgment. We are therefore driven to conclude that in saying 'the Redeemer shall come out of Zion' the Apostle is speaking in a spiritual sense. Zion is the house, the dwelling-place of the Lord, where He is amongst His people. This suits the context admirably and it is something which the Apostle does elsewhere.

In Galatians 4 he says, 'This Agar is mount Sinai in Arabia, and answereth to Jerusalem which now is, and is in bondage with her children. But Jerusalem which is above is free, which is the mother of us all'. He says there are two Jerusalems, and of course, Zion and Jerusalem are interchangeable terms. So as the Apostle in Galatians 4 speaks about an earthly Zion or Jerusalem, and a heavenly Jerusalem and Zion, or a Zion or Jerusalem which is above, he shows that he sometimes speaks of Zion in a spiritual sense. And I would not therefore hesitate to say that here in Romans 11 what he is saying is, that the Redeemer will come from that Jerusalem, that Zion which is above – this is the church, the headquarters of the church if you like; it is there. 'Our citizenship is in heaven'. As the author of the Epistle to the Hebrews puts it, 'We come to the heavenly Jerusalem'. When we gather together we come to the heavenly Jerusalem. This idea is characteristic of the New Testament outlook you see. Or, again, in the Book of Revelation that Jerusalem that is going to 'descend' from heaven to earth. In other words, that is where Zion is now. Zion is in heaven, it is the one that is above, and Paul says, You Galatians are thinking of the material, earthly Zion far too much, the heavenly Zion is now there.

You have this same thing here, and so there is no forcing of exposition, it is just following what is done elsewhere in the New Testament. The Zion out of which He will come is indeed heaven itself; His influence will come from there. I am not saying that this is the Second Coming, I am simply saying that the Apostle is saying here that in this spiritual manner the Redeemer will exert this tremendous influence upon the nation of the Jews and will turn iniquity from them and will bring them to faith and salvation and bring them into membership of the Christian church.

Now then, there, it seems to me, is the explanation of this statement, and of course you can see now why the Apostle changed 'to Zion' into 'out of Zion'. He is anxious to show what he now goes on to put plainly in this expression, 'shall turn away ungodliness from'. You remember how I pointed out to you that if he had taken the exact quotation he would have said that He would come 'for those who have turned from ungodliness'. But he is not saying that because he knows that that is not what is going to happen. What is going to happen is, that the Lord will 'turn' Jacob from his transgression.

Now here again we see a principle that we have already met in this exposition. It is His power that is going to do this. It is not going to be the case that the Jews at a given point are going to decide to believe the gospel. They cannot do that. Nobody can ever do that. This is always the action of the Lord. You remember that in interpreting 'blindness in part is happened to Israel' I emphasized the fact that it is God Who does that to them. It is the God Who hardened the heart of these unbelieving Jews. It is a judicial hardening, a judicial blindness. It is God's action. And what the Apostle is saying here is this, that the same God Who is hardening them now is going to soften them. It is He Who is going to 'turn them from iniquity', 'turn away ungodliness from Jacob'.

He is putting in other language what he has already said in verse 23: 'And they also, if they abide not still in unbelief, shall be grafted in' – and he continues – 'for God is able to graft them in again'. And here is how He will graft them in again. He will turn ungodliness away from them, and then they will come in by faith. This is the tremendous action that the Apostle has kept on speaking about; this is going to be the greatest phenomenon of all the centuries of the Christian church; this is the thing that will produce an effect which can only be compared, as he says in verse 15, to 'life from the dead'. That this nation which throughout the centuries has rejected the Messiah and has been still waiting for the coming of the Messiah, these people who have been so bitter in their persecution of Christians throughout all these long centuries, will be brought back, this will be the great phenomenon. We shall find them repenting, turning back to Him Whom they smote and rejected and crucified, and coming like little children to believe in Him. God will have turned away their iniquity and unrighteousness, He will open their eyes, they will see it, they will believe it, as He has done to individual Jews throughout the centuries, as He has done to masses of Gentiles, He is going to do for them as a flock, as a body, and this will be so astounding that it will be comparable to nothing less than life from the dead, and the whole church will be amazed at it and will be filled with a spirit of rejoicing and praise. Now that is what these quotations as handled by the Apostle are saying!

We come now to this further statement in verse 27, which is again difficult. 'For this is my covenant unto them, when I shall take away their sins'. Where do you find that in the Old Testament? And the answer is, you cannot. But what you do find is this: you will find the first part of it in Isaiah 59:21. In other words, he had already been thinking of Isaiah 59:20; he now thinks of the next verse. But he just takes a phrase out of it, the first part, and that is the first part we have got here; but you do not find the second part of his statement in Isaiah 59:21, but in Isaiah 27:9. You find it in both the original Hebrew and in the Septuagint translation. So again, you see, he has taken two bits from different parts of Isaiah, he has put them together, and he has framed this one statement. Again he is doing two things; he is giving the general sense and meaning of the Old Testament on this great question, and stating this prophecy which has been given to him by the direct inspiration of the Spirit.

Now then, how do we understand this? What he is really saying is: 'This is my covenant, that I will take away their sins'. Or here is a literal translation of the Greek: 'This is the covenant from me with them, when I take away the sins of them'. What does it mean? Let me give you the paraphrase of Sanday and Headlam which perfectly conveys the meaning. They translate it like this: 'And whensoever I forgive their sins, then shall my side of the covenant I have made with them be fulfilled'. He is saying this: 'I have a covenant with these people, and when I do turn away iniquity from them and forgive their sins, my covenant with them will be fulfilled.' That is what it really means. 'This is my covenant unto them, when I shall take away their sins'. In other words, when I take away their sins from them what I will be doing will be to fulfil my covenant with them.

So what he is saying, you see, is this – and this is where we see the correspondence between the Old Testament and the New. In the Old Testament we find God casting away His people as it were. Was it not God Who raised up the Chaldeans against the Jews? Was it not God Who brought them to attack the city of Jerusalem and destroy it and rase it to the ground and cause His people to be carried away to captivity in Babylon? God was there, as it were, 'casting away His people', and many of the nations jumped to the conclusion that they were finished as a people. Their land was desolate, there they were in captivity, they had no army, they had nothing at all; but you see God had not finished with them, they were still His people. So God in His own miraculous manner brought them back to Palestine and to the very city of Jerusalem which was rebuilt. God did that in the Old Testament.

Now then what the Apostle is saying is, As God did that with His covenant people in the Old Testament, He is going to do that again. He has for the time being again sent them off to a kind of captivity, He has broken them out of the olive tree, He has cast them aside. But it is not permanent; do not come to that conclusion. He is going to do again in this matter of salvation and the church exactly what He did with them under the Old Testament dispensation. His covenant with them still remains, it is still in force, and it will be fulfilled when He does this great thing to them, when He turns away their iniquity, when He gives them the spirit of grace and of repentance, when He forgives their sins, when He gives them the gift of faith and so brings them to salvation and entry into the Christian church; or if you like when He grafts them back again into their own olive tree. Now that is what the Apostle is saying. That is the prophecy and here he is showing how in this general way the Old Testament prophecies have anticipated this. But the thing that he is anxious to impress upon them is that this is the glorious outcome for this people to whom God has pledged Himself in His covenant.

There are statements similar to this in the Old Testament. You have it for instance in Zechariah 12:10: 'And I will pour upon the house of David, and upon the inhabitants of Jerusalem, the spirit of grace and of supplications: and they shall look upon me whom they have pierced, and they shall mourn for him, as one mourneth for his only son, and shall be in bitterness for him, as one that is in bitterness for his firstborn'.

The Apostle then is saying that the future restoration of Israel as a nation is certain. He puts it in the form of a prophetic announcement of a great mystery in the ultimate plan and purpose of God, something entirely outside the realm of human understanding, something no one would ever have thought of. Now there is no difficulty about seeing how individual Jews can be converted because we see that they are; they were at the beginning as he has told us and this has continued. But this other thing, who would ever have thought of this? Nobody has; indeed it has got to be revealed to us, and it has been revealed to us in this way through this prophetic utterance of the great Apostle. And then he has, as is his custom, confirmed it by saying that it has actually been taught in the Old Testament. This is the same thing as we find in Ephesians 3. There were hints in the Old Testament about the coming in of the Gentiles, but it was specially clearly revealed to the Apostles and Prophets as it had not been so clearly revealed before: it is exactly the same with this. So the Apostle, you see, brings these bits of quotations together. He says in effect: 'This is what the Old Testament says about this. It is an absolute confirmation of what I have uttered to you as the prophecy given to me of the Lord'.

# *Twenty-three*

*

*For I would not, brethren, that ye should be ignorant of this mystery, lest ye should be wise in your own conceits; that blindness in part is happened to Israel, until the fulness of the Gentiles be come in. And so all Israel shall be saved: as it is written, There shall come out of Sion the Deliverer, and shall turn away ungodliness from Jacob: For this is my covenant unto them, when I shall take away their sins. As concerning the gospel, they are enemies for your sakes: but as touching the election, they are beloved for the fathers' sakes. For the gifts and calling of God are without repentance. For as ye in times past have not believed God, yet have now obtained mercy through their unbelief: Even so have these also now not believed, that through your mercy they also may obtain mercy. For God hath concluded them all in unbelief, that he might have mercy upon all.* Romans 11:25–32

We come now to the second section of the tremendous statement found in these verses. It runs from the beginning of verse 28 to the end of verse 32. This can be subdivided as follows: in verses 28 and 29 the Apostle is laying down the principle on which all that he has been saying is going to operate and why it is going to come to pass; in verses 30 and 31 he explains it in practical terms, and in verse 32 he sums it all up in a great overriding principle which governs the whole of God's dealings with the human race.

This is a very important section because it not only gives us an explanation of what the Apostle has just been saying, but it sums up the argument of the entire chapter. In these verses he refers again to things which he has said earlier.

In verse 28 he says: 'As concerning the gospel, they are enemies for your sakes: but as touching the election, they are beloved for the fathers' sakes'. Now you notice the translators of the Authorized Version start off by saying, 'As concerning'; then later they say 'as touching'. Actually it is the same word which the Apostle used in both instances. They may be justified in varying the expression but really there is no difference at all; both of them mean 'As regards' or if you like 'According to'.

Now notice that there is a contrast here. Paul is looking at a body of people, and he says, 'As regards the gospel one thing is true of them; but as regards the election something else is true of them'. Let me give you a literal translation of this verse so that we may see exactly what he is saying. 'On the one hand, according to the gospel, enemies because of you; on the other, according to the election, beloved because of the fathers'.

Now this expression 'enemies' is obviously very important here and we should be clear as to what he is saying. He does not say that they *are* enemies; what he says is that they are *regarded* as enemies. It is not that they are acting as enemies; actually they are, but that is not what he is saying, he is saying that they are being regarded or being treated as enemies. We must say that because the parallelism of the verse demands it; he says about the same people that they are 'beloved'. He does not mean that they are loving but that they are regarded as beloved 'for the fathers' sakes'. The verb is passive in both instances. This is a vital point because, as we shall see, it is an essential link in this great doctrine that the Apostle is laying down in verse 32.

Now the question of the identity of the people to whom he is referring is an important one and must be answered. But let us see what he says about them first, that will help us to see who they are. What he says about them is this, that two things are true of these people *at one and the same time*. He says, that according to the gospel order – what I mean by that is Christ the Risen Lord sending out these chosen representatives, to preach the gospel and found the church – they are treated and regarded as enemies. Why? Well, he says, they are being treated and regarded as enemies 'for your sakes', or as the literal translation puts it, 'because of you'. That is the first part of this statement. In this gospel dispensation they are being regarded as enemies, and that is so for your sakes, for your benefit, because of you and what is going to accrue to you. And when he says 'you' this is undoubtedly a reference to the Gentiles.

But that does not exhaust the meaning. This is true of them because they have rejected our Lord Himself and they have rejected His message and the preaching of the Apostles. Their whole attitude towards the Lord Himself and His followers and the message has been one of opposition, and because of that God regards them as enemies.

This is something which the Apostle has already said. In verse 11 he says: 'Have they stumbled that they should fall? God forbid: but rather through their fall salvation is come unto the Gentiles'. That is the statement that is being repeated here and that is why I say that this is a reference to the Jews. They are regarded as enemies for the benefit of the Gentiles and that is stated in verse 12, 'if the fall of them' – that is to say, the Jews as a nation – 'if the fall of them be the riches of the world, and the diminishing of them the riches of the Gentiles.'

Paul is therefore summing up in order to throw light on what he has been saying in his great prophecy in verses 25 and the first part of verse 26. Verses 28–32 are an exposition of the prophecy that he has just given. He says, If you want to understand this present state of affairs in which you find the bulk of the Jewish nation outside the church and only a very little remnant according to the election of grace inside but the church consisting mainly of Gentiles, this is the explanation of it. God is now regarding the Jews as enemies and He has used that to bring salvation to Gentiles.

There is the first part of this tremendous statement. As regards the gospel economy, they are being regarded as enemies in order that you Gentiles might come in. They have been cast off so that you may be reconciled. But there is another point, and it is that, looked at from the standpoint of election, these same people who are now regarded as enemies are also at the same time 'beloved for the fathers' sakes'.

With the words 'according to the election' he is letting us into the mystery. What does he mean here by 'election'? Well, if you have just used a concordance in a mechanical way, you will rush straight to the fifth verse for the answer. There Paul writes, using the same word for election, 'Even so then at this present time also there is a remnant according to the election of grace'. But it is not the same thing at all, and it cannot be for this reason, that 'the remnant according to the election of grace' have never been regarded as enemies, but the people Paul is talking about are being so regarded. These who are 'beloved for the fathers' sakes' are at the same time now being regarded as enemies, and that, patently, is not true of 'the remnant according to the election of grace' because they, like the Apostle Paul, are in the Christian church and they are receiving all the great and rich blessings. Now what 'election' stands for here is 'the principle of election'. You see there is a parallel here: 'election' is over and against 'gospel'. Looked at in terms of the preaching of the gospel at the present time they are regarded as enemies. Ah yes, but there is another way of looking at these people. Looked at in terms of God's eternal election the people about whom he is speaking are 'beloved for the fathers' sakes'.

This is a really tremendous statement. There were two ways of looking, then, at the Jews, and this is as true today as it was when the Apostle wrote this more than nineteen hundred years ago. You can say this about the Jewish race and nation tonight exactly as he said it then. Looked at from the standpoint of the Christian church and the preaching of the gospel they are outside, still cast away, still regarded as enemies. But that is not the end of the story. God also looks at them from the standpoint of His own eternal election and says that they are regarded as beloved. Why? Well, not because of themselves but 'for the fathers' sakes'. You see the perfect parallel in the two sides of this statement. Looked at from the standpoint of the preaching of the gospel – 'Enemies'. Why? 'For your sakes'. On the other side, looked at from the standpoint of election – 'Beloved'. Why? 'For the fathers' sakes'.

But what does he mean by 'for the fathers' sakes'? Well again, this is something which he has already said in verse 16. He is gathering up all his arguments. In verse 16 he said: 'For if the firstfruit be holy, the lump is also holy: and if the roots be holy, so are the branches'. We saw that the reference to the 'firstfruit' and to the 'root' is a reference to the fathers – Abraham, Isaac, and Jacob. It is out of these, the patriarchs, the fathers, that the Jewish people came. God chose them so that out of them He might produce His people – 'the people of God'. They are the fathers.

The same things was said definitively in 9:4, 5. He describes the Jews who needed salvation as his people but then says: 'Who are Israelites; to whom pertaineth the adoption, and the glory, and the covenants, and the giving of the law, and the service of God, and the promises; Whose are the fathers, and of whom as concerning the flesh Christ came, who is over all, God blessed for ever'. 'The fathers'! He does not forget this, he cannot forget this, because the fathers were the chosen of God. He is not pandering to Jewish nationalism; that is not his argument at all. He is looking at it in terms of God's revelation, and the fathers were chosen by God, it is

God Who set them there as the root and as the firstfruits, as it were, of this race and nation.

But let us go on because in verse 29 he gives the basic reason why it is true that, although God regards them temporarily as enemies, He still loves them as a people. The explanation is: 'For the gifts and calling of God are without repentance'. You see, the whole character of God is involved in this matter. That is why the Apostle has written these three chapters. This is what I described at the beginning of chapter 9 as being a great theodicy, it is a kind of defence of God and a justification of God's ways to man. The Apostle has to do that because he seems to say at the beginning of chapter 9 that it is no use talking about the certainty of God's promises. Does not the whole case of the Jews prove that this is not true? So now he has got to demonstrate this and here he is at last winding up the great argument. He says, 'The gifts and calling of God are without repentance'. That is an absolute. It must be an absolute because God is God.

Now there is just one point to be made with regard to this expression 'without repentance' because, although in one sense it conveys its meaning, in another sense it does not. It would be better to translate it as follows: 'The gifts and calling of God are without regret'. I say that simply because the Apostle actually uses a different word here from the word that is normally used for repentance. It means 'without being sorry afterwards'. Of course in the end that comes to repentance. If you are sorry for something you have said or done, well, you will do your best to undo it.

But let me show you the difference in the shade of meaning which is conveyed here. In 2 Corinthians chapter 7 and verse 10 the Apostle is dealing with the whole question of repentance and says that 'Godly sorrow worketh repentance to salvation not to be repented of'. Now that expression 'not to be repented of' is a translation of exactly the same words as is used here in Romans 11:29. We could therefore say 'the gifts and calling of God are not to be repented of', 'not to be regretted'. This means that God will never feel sorry with respect to them.

But what does he mean by 'The gifts and calling of God'? Well, there is no difficulty about the gifts. They are fully recorded in Romans 9:4, 5. You get them all, of course, described in detail in the Old Testament. Romans 9:4, 5 is one of the most perfect summaries of all that God gave to the children of Israel right through that old dispensation, and that is what he is referring to here.

What is the 'calling'? Well, the calling really explains itself; it means 'calling to be His people'. This term is used constantly in the Old Testament: 'From Egypt have I called my son', and the children of Israel, God's people, are referred to as the people whom He has 'chosen', 'called'. This great word Paul uses so often in this mighty Epistle, for example in 1:6, 7. We are Christians because we have been 'called' and 'the people of God' are the people of God because God has 'called' them. This is the efficacious call; it is the irresistible call; it is because of this call that anybody is a Christian. God 'calls' His people out of darkness into His most marvellous light.

Now the gifts and call of God are without any regrets, and this is because God is God. God's purpose is an eternal purpose. It is never a temporary one. There are temporary aspects to it but concerning the great purpose itself he says, 'The gifts and calling of God' are never regretted. God never changes His mind about this; He never regrets what He has done. What God has decided, He has decided, and He will certainly carry through. There can be no change here. That is the explanation, says the Apostle, of this whole problem of the Jew in the matter of salvation, and if you do not understand this he says, well, you will remain of necessity in the darkness. You have got to look at these things in two ways, the temporary and the ultimate. Temporarily they are regarded as enemies. But in the matter of God's purpose, they are beloved. God's purpose was always this and it cannot change. He has no regrets about it. This is what He decided with the fathers and He made those lavish promises to them and this must be fulfilled. That is what he is saying. He is not only expounding and opening out, as it were, what he has given in his prophecy, but he is giving us the great reason why this of necessity must be the case. The gifts and calling of God are always without any regret whatsoever because God is God.

We are therefore in a position once more to ask the question, To whom does all this refer? Who is he talking about? The Authorized Version translators have supplied the words 'they are'. 'As concerning the gospel, they are enemies: but as touching the election, they are beloved'. Who are they? Who is he speaking about? Well, the answer to that question, I think should now be quite clear to us in view of the statements that he has been making both in the prophecy itself and in these explanations that he has been giving of it and why God works in this way. Surely we must agree that he is referring to the 'Israel' that he has mentioned in verses 25 and 26. 'I would not, brethren, that ye should be ignorant of this mystery, lest ye should be wise in your own conceits; that blindness in part is happened to Israel, until the fulness of the Gentiles be come in. And so all Israel shall be saved'. It is this 'Israel' that is now suffering from this temporary hardness and blindness, which is going to be saved. I think nobody can dispute this; these verses are referring to those same people, the 'Israel' referred to in verses 25 and 26.

Is it not now quite clear that this cannot possibly be a reference to the total number of the elect among the Jews and the Gentiles? It cannot be the 'elect' among the Jews and the Gentiles because they are not regarded as enemies in the gospel order of things. They are in the church, they are the saved. But the Apostle is dealing here with those who for the time being are regarded as enemies. That cannot be said about the elect and about the saved. Not at all. These who are regarded as enemies are being contrasted with those who are saved, the Gentiles and 'the remnant according to the election of grace' that is already in the church. So that it cannot possibly be said that the Israel in verses 25 and 26 is simply the aggregate of the 'elect' amongst both Jews and Gentiles, as is taught by Calvin and others.

But in the same way this cannot be a reference either to the total number of the saved Jews only throughout the centuries, again for this same reason, that the Jews who had been saved up until this point were certainly not regarded as enemies, the Apostle is one of them, they are in the church, and all the others were in the same position. There is no contrast there. But the people he is talking about are those who are now regarded as enemies but who nevertheless are still beloved for the fathers' sakes. But those Jews who have already believed are not regarded as enemies at all because they are already in the church and are coming into the church.

So then, we are left with the same conclusion that we came to before, that this can only be a reference to Israel regarded as a whole, as a nation. This has been the theme of the whole chapter. What the Apostle has told us about them time and time again is this – that they have not fallen away finally, but they have only stumbled temporarily. Now the whole argument is about the bulk of the nation of the Jews as over against the Gentiles with reference to the church. For the time being, he says, the Jews have stumbled, they have been cut out of their own olive tree to which they belonged by nature, and here he says that they are actually being regarded as enemies. Surely this is obvious. Well then, let me anticipate. In verse 30 and 31 he makes this again much more certain. Listen: 'For as ye' – referring to the Gentiles – 'in time past have not believed God, but now have obtained mercy through their unbelief' – that is to say, the unbelief of the Jews who rejected their own Messiah and crucified Him and reviled and persecuted His apostles and would have nothing to do with the gospel; the same contrast is carried on – 'Even so have these also now not believed, in order that through your mercy' – the mercy shown to you – 'they also may obtain mercy'. However, we shall come to that again in greater detail.

But, you see, this is what he is saying: The Jews regarded as a whole, as a nation of people, are still from the standpoint of the gospel, looked at from the standpoint of the church and the preaching of the gospel, regarded as enemies; they are in this condition of blindness or of hardness of heart still; but they are still beloved because of the fathers. God's promises to Abraham, to Isaac and to Jacob still hold and will ultimately be shown to hold. And if they are not shown to hold, well then the Apostle's argument collapses. Look at these great and rich promises to these people in the Old Testament; can you say that they have been fulfilled hitherto in the Christian church? You cannot. The bulk of this people is outside the church. The Apostle says God is going to make it manifest and known to the whole world that they are beloved for the fathers' sakes. They are still His people, they are the natural branches of the olive tree and they will be brought back again. He has already told us that God is able to do so in verse 23 and in other statements.

Here then is the great argument of the whole chapter, that these promises of God remain and are sure. The blindness is only 'in part'. You see he started off the chapter by saying this: 'I say then' – is putting his question – 'Hath God cast away His people? God forbid. For I also am an Israelite, of the seed of Abraham, of the tribe of Benjamin. God hath not cast away (in that final sense) His people whom He foreknew'. That is the thing he is setting out to prove. He starts with it, here he is ending with it, proving that this is still going to be the case. And as he has demonstrated to us in his scriptural quotations, and particularly in the second half of verse 26 and verse 27, what God did with them so many times in the Old Testament He is still doing.

Now that has been God's way of dealing with these people. You would think sometimes as you read your Old Testament that He had finally finished with them. Never! And the Apostle is saying that the same is still true. It is the same argument, 'blindness in part' – temporary blindness for the time being, looked at from the standpoint of how, in the gospel economy, they are being regarded and treated as enemies. And they have been of course. Their city was sacked and destroyed in A.D. 70; they were scattered abroad among the nations. And God did that. That is what we find our Lord saying in Matthew 23, how God said that 'upon you may come all the righteous blood shed upon the earth, from the blood of righteous Abel unto the blood of Zacharias son of Barachias, whom ye slew between the temple and the altar. Verily I say unto you, All these things shall come upon this generation. O Jerusalem, Jerusalem, thou that killest the prophets, and stonest them which are sent unto thee, how often would I have gathered thy children together, even as a hen gathereth her chickens under her wings, and ye would not! Behold, your house is left unto you desolate'. That is the final casting out of them; they are being regarded as enemies. And they were. But it is not the end of the story. Judged from the standpoint of God's eternal principle of election, starting with the fathers and all the gifts, this is not the end of the story – for this reason: because the gifts and calling of God are without any regrets afterwards. What God has promised to the fathers is going to be fulfilled, is going to be carried out. 'All Israel' shall be saved. And this will be such a tremendous thing that when it happens this is all we can say about it, 'what shall the receiving of them be, but life from the dead?'.

# *Twenty-four*

*

*As concerning the gospel, they are enemies for your sakes: but as touching the election, they are beloved for the fathers' sakes. For the gifts and calling of God are without repentance. For as ye in times past have not believed God, yet have now obtained mercy through their unbelief: even so have these also now not believed, that through your mercy they also may obtain mercy. For God hath concluded them all in unbelief, that he might have mercy upon all.* Romans 11:28–32

In these verses the Apostle is expounding the prophecy which he has offered in the latter portion of verse 25 and the first part of verse 26. It is this – 'that blindness in part is happened to Israel, until the fulness of the Gentiles be come in. And so all Israel shall be saved'. He declares that God has two ways of looking upon His people, the Jews. When He looks at them in terms of the gospel dispensation he regards them as 'enemies'; but when He looks at them in terms of His purpose of election which He had revealed especially through the fathers, He regards them as 'beloved'. This is a great biblical principle. You remember those well-known lines in the hymn of William Cowper –

*Judge not the Lord by feeble sense,*
*But trust Him for His grace.*

Why? Well, the answer is –

*Behind a frowning providence*
*He hides a smiling face.*

Cowper is here using the principle in relation to the individual believer. Sometimes, he says, you look up into the face of God and you see nothing but a 'frown'. But do not be misled by that, he says; that does not mean that God has finished with you because 'Behind a frowning providence, He hides a smiling face'. And this, of course, is something which we can well understand in human terms. It is the typical action of any parent, worthy of the name, with a child. If the child is misbehaving, the parent does not smile upon the child, but shows displeasure, 'frowns' upon the child. And the child, of course, jumps to the conclusion that the parent is hard-hearted and has finished with him because of what he has done, and he may break his heart or he may rebel. This is because he does not realize that the 'frown' is temporary and that even while the parent is expressing displeasure there is still in that parent's heart great love for that child. Now that is exactly what the Apostle is saying – that God, as it were, is looking at the same child, or the same children, in two different ways at one and the same time. 'As concerning (as regards) the gospel, they are enemies; but as regards the election and God's ultimate purpose, they are beloved for the fathers' sakes'.

Underlying that is the fact that 'the gifts and calling of God are without any regrets', that God never regrets what He does. So that all His gifts and all His promises to the fathers and the great purpose of election is something that cannot be changed.

We move on now to verses 30, 31 and 32. In verses 30 and 31 he makes this theme even more explicit. Verse 32 is a great general theological doctrinal principle which explains not only this immediate matter but the whole of God's handling of mankind in this whole matter of redemption and of salvation.

Verses 30 and 31 must be taken together. They form one connected statement which is made up of two counter-balancing parts. Those addressed as 'you' are Gentiles; 'they' are the Jews. We will consider each part in turn.

He says, 'As in times past', referring to the time when the Gentiles did not 'believe God'. The word which he uses for 'believe' and its opposite would have been better translated by some form of the word 'obey' giving us the following rendering of these verses. 'For as ye in times past have not obeyed God, yet have now obtained mercy through their disobedience: even so have these also now not obeyed, that through your mercy they also may obtain mercy.' The Apostle has already used this word as a description of what is involved in believing in 1:5 and 10:16. This word reminds us that faith is not merely intellectual, it involves action. The will is involved as well as the mind. If a man really and truly believes in God he submits to God. So 'obeyed' is a better word and actually it carries this meaning. He says, 'As ye in times past did not allow yourselves to be persuaded by the truth of God'. That is what it means. There is an element of resistance implied in the word. 'Ye did not allow yourselves to be persuaded'. That, of course, in turn leads to unbelief and that leads in turn to disobedience.

Now what the Apostle is telling these Gentiles is this: there was once a time when they were disobedient to God. When was that? Romans 1:18 and following describe it. That is the whole meaning of that terrifying passage. He is addressing the Gentiles and showing them how they lived a life which was quite godless in every way. Until the advent of our Lord Jesus Christ the Gentiles were outside the kingdom of God. This is something that is stated everywhere, of course, in the whole Bible. Paul puts it particularly clearly in writing to the Ephesians in chapter 2. Until the coming of our Lord into this world the Gentile races and nations were godless, they were 'aliens from the commonwealth of Israel, and strangers from the covenants of promise,' they were 'without God' and 'without hope', they were 'in the world'. There was an occasional convert to Judaism, an occasional proselyte, but speaking of the Gentiles in general they were in blind unbelief and ignorance and disobedience towards God.

Now he is reminding them of that. But, he says, 'you have now obtained mercy'. What does that mean? A Christian is a man who has 'obtained mercy'. As Paul will go on using this term, we look at it now in particular. What is mercy? It is the pity of God. Were it not for the mercy of God nobody would ever be saved, salvation is always the result of God's mercy, it is never due to anything in man at all. God has looked down from heaven in pity. If He did not do that nobody would ever be saved. So he says, 'You were utterly disobedient, but you have obtained mercy' and that has led to forgiveness, to your being grafted in – new life, and all the other things about which he has been speaking. But it all comes out of the fount of mercy, God is the Father of mercies.

But he also reminds these Gentiles as to how this has happened to them and he says, 'You have obtained mercy *through their disobedience*'. Verses 11 and 12, as we have seen, make this point. Paul is summing up his teaching in these verses. What he is telling these Gentiles is that they were outside the kingdom of God, but now are inside because of God's mercy operating by means of the unbelief of the Jews. This is recounted in Acts 13:45–48 and 18:6.

Now he says 'Even so', 'these also', these Jews, 'through whom the Gentiles had come in'. He says that at the moment their position is that they 'have not believed'. But what is in view in the rest of the statement? He says they are in that position now 'in order that through your mercy they also may obtain mercy'. You have obtained it, they are going to obtain it, and they are going to obtain it through what has happened to you.

We go on, now, to verse 31 which completes the parallel introduced in verse 30. He says 'Even so' meaning 'in the same way' and 'these also' meaning the Jews, that is the bulk of the nation. The parallel is complete. Gentiles were disobedient, but became obedient through the condition of the Jews. But, in turn, the Jews will become obedient by means of the mercy shown to the Gentiles.

In saying 'through your mercy' Paul is not teaching that it is the mercy of the Gentiles that is going to bring the Jews back, for the Gentiles do not possess mercy, and if they had they would not have any power to save anybody else. It is God alone Who has mercy. He is not saying that the Gentiles are going to save the Jews. When he says 'your mercy' he means the mercy shown to you, the mercy which you have had, the mercy which has become yours as the result of the grace of God in the way that He has shown. This is something he has already said in verses 11 and 14.

I want to sum up the position which we have arrived at because people have often been mistaken on this matter. Until the first coming of the Son of God into this world the Gentiles were unbelievers, they were godless, they were outside the covenants of promise, outside the kingdom of God. As I say, an occasional Gentile might become a proselyte but the bulk of them were 'without hope', and were 'without God in the world'. The Jews were God's people, they had the 'oracles of God' as the Apostle has reminded us in the third and ninth chapters of this Epistle. That was the position. But with the coming of the Son of God into this world the position has been entirely reversed. The four Gospels are so important. In the Gospels you see this tragedy taking place. The Old Testament ends with the Jewish nation looking forward to the coming of the Messiah, and they were the only people who were looking for His coming. But in the Gospels you see them rejecting their own Messiah, proving to be utterly disobedient to the gospel. So that when you come to the rest of the New Testament and look at the Christian church this is what you find – that the bulk of the Jewish nation is outside and rejected, branches, as it were, torn out of their own olive tree. They are bitter in their rejection of the Lord and of His truth and of His gospel and they are outside; and inside you have got the gospel appealing to the Gentiles and the Gentiles, as it were, crowding into the kingdom of God. So that as you look at the New Testament church it is mainly a Gentile church, and the Apostle here in writing to this church at Rome is obviously conscious that he is writing in the main to Gentile believers. There were some Jews but in the main it was Gentile. You see the position. Before, Jews with occasional Gentiles; now, Gentiles with occasional Jews; Paul himself and 'the remnant according to the election of grace'. But – and this is the thing that has been revealed to him, this is the mystery which had been hidden and which nothing but the revelation of God would ever have made clear even to the Apostle Paul himself – that is not the end of the story. It is still the truth to say that the Christian church is mainly Gentile, and the bulk of the Jewish nation is rejecting, it is disobedient, it is outside. But that is not the end of the story. As God of old used the disobedience of the Jews to bring in the Gentiles, so He is going to use the belief of the Gentiles to bring in the Jews, He is going to 'provoke them to jealousy'. He is going to use what He has done and is doing to the Gentiles to open the eyes of the Jews and to bring them to a position of obedience and surrender and rejoicing in the gospel. When this tremendous thing takes place it will have this effect upon the whole church, it will indeed be like 'life from the dead', so marvellous that nothing short of such an expression is adequate to describe it.

So there is only one exposition of this passage which is in any sense of the word adequate. This is to understand it as referring to Israel as a whole and not merely to the total number of elect Jews and Gentiles.

But now in verse 32 the Apostle gives us the ultimate explanation of all this and it is one of the most remarkable things in the whole of Scripture, the very centre of God's great and eternal purpose. Take a broad view of history, cannot you see it? All those centuries, the Jews, the Jews, the Jews – and the Gentiles nowhere. Then suddenly this tremendous reversal, and now the Gentiles, the Gentiles, the Gentiles – and the Jews outside. This is a great fact of history, and this is the only explanation of it, and here it is: 'For' – he is going on, you see, he is explaining – 'For God hath concluded them all in unbelief, in order that he might have mercy upon all'.

Now then let us look at this statement. Take this word 'concluded'. It is an archaism. When the Authorized Version was translated it had a meaning which it no longer has. It is a word derived from two Latin words – 'con' which means 'together', 'claudere' which means to 'shut up'. So 'concluded' means 'shut up together'. That is the meaning of the Greek word in the text. It is used in Galatians 3:22, which reads, 'But the Scripture hath concluded all under sin, that the promise by faith of Jesus Christ might be given to them that believe'. The word means 'shut up together', even to inspection. 'For God hath shut them all up completely'. That is what it means.

Well then, to whom does this word 'all' refer? 'God hath shut them all in completely' – all of them – 'in unbelief, in order that he might have mercy upon all'. To whom does this 'all' in both parts of the statement refer? It must have the same meaning. There is an 'all' who are imprisoned in unbelief who are then shown mercy. Well, it cannot, of course, mean everybody who has ever lived or ever shall live; it does not mean all in a universalistic sense. Why? Because then the teaching of this verse would mean that everybody eventually is going to be saved. There are people who believe that, of course; they are called Universalists. But anybody who believes the Bible cannot believe that. Why? Well, because the Bible divides up people into the saved and the lost. That is the great distinction – and the last book of the Bible shows us that some will go to everlasting perdition. This is in the Bible everywhere. Our Lord Himself says it: 'Enter ye in at the strait gate: for wide is the gate, and broad is the way, that leadeth to destruction, and many there be which go in thereat: Because strait is the gate, and narrow is the way, which leadeth unto life, and few there be that find it' [*Matt.* 7:13, 14]. Therefore the 'all' cannot mean everybody; it is impossible. Otherwise the only conclusion you can come to is Universalism, and that simply works havoc everywhere with the plain teaching of the Bible.

What then does the 'all' mean? The Apostle has been talking for some time about Jews and Gentiles. That was the way in which the whole world was comprehended. By 'all' Paul is therefore referring to these groups, to all sorts and types of Jew and Gentile. The Apostle says that God has concluded Jews and Gentiles in unbelief. What then does the 'all' mean? It means 'every type and kind'. The Apostle has been talking about Jew and Gentile – the two great groups in the human race. In saying 'all' he is referring to people of all sorts – who are shut up in unbelief prior to their being shown mercy and saved. Not every individual in the group, obviously, otherwise all would be saved. No, no, he means 'every type and kind'.

Now this is something that we have already had the Apostle saying in chapter 10. Listen to him in verses 12 and 13 – or take, indeed, verse 11: 'For the Scripture saith, Whosoever believeth on him shall not be ashamed. For there is no difference between the Jew and the Greek: for the same Lord over all is rich unto all that call upon him'. Not to everybody in the universe, but 'all who call upon him'. 'For whosoever shall call upon the name of the Lord shall be saved'. That is exactly the same thing and you have another example of it in 1 Timothy 2:4–6.

So what he is saying is this: not that God has shut up the Jews and the Gentiles together, but that rather He has shut up in unbelief all types and kinds of mankind that are to be saved, whether Jews or Gentiles. He is saying, God has shut up the Gentiles in unbelief, God has shut up the Jews in unbelief. That is what he means. God has 'concluded', 'shut up that they cannot escape', Jews and Gentiles in this unbelief and disobedience. Why? Well, 'in order that he might have mercy upon all', the two groups, in exactly the same way.

In other words, he is simply putting in this great statement what he has just been saying. There at one time were the Gentiles shut up in unbelief, but God showed mercy to them. Here now are the Jews shut up in unbelief in exactly the same way, in order that God may show His mercy to them. Notice, the emphasis is always upon what God has done and not upon man. '*God* hath concluded them, shut them up, in unbelief'. It is God Who does it. Why does He do this? His object in both cases is to show 'mercy' and to make it clear that salvation is always only the result of the mercy of God.

Why does he put this in the summing up? I will tell you why. He has been showing us in the body of the chapter how both the Jews and the Gentiles have failed to see this. The Jews tended to say, We are all right, we are God's people; because we trace descent from Abraham as lineal descendants we are all right. The answer is, No, you are not! Then the Gentiles have been brought in and they say, 'Ah, we have been brought in because we are such wonderful people, we are better people than those Jews'. No, you are not, says the Apostle. There is nothing to recommend anybody in the sight of God. Both the Gentiles and the Jews are exactly the same, and they are both equally ridiculous in their boasting. They have nothing to boast of, neither the Jews nor the Gentiles.

Now God, says the Apostle, has shown this perfectly clearly in the very realm and field of history. History demonstrates this. Jews and Gentiles are shown to be absolutely hopeless, and the only conclusion you can come to then is that salvation is solely and entirely the result of God's mercy. The Gentiles were once hopeless, but God showed mercy to them. The Jews are now hopeless, but God will show mercy to them also, in the way that he has been explaining. In other words the Apostle's statement in this thirty-second verse is this: that God has deliberately emphasized the hopelessness and the helplessness of both Jews and Gentiles in order to glorify His own great and eternal name, and show that everything is the result of His grace and mercy and compassion. God has shut them up in this. Look at those Gentiles before Christ came into the world; you cannot imagine anything more hopeless. How did they ever come into the church? They had no background, they had nothing. How did they ever come in? There is only one answer – the mercy of God. Could anything appear more hopeless today than the position of the Jews as a race and as a nation with respect to the gospel? It seems unthinkable that they will ever come in. But they are going to come in! And as there was only one thing that could bring in the Gentiles there is still only one thing that can ever bring in the Jews, it is the mercy of God. That is the statement. 'God hath concluded' – He has put them there into complete helplessness, shut them in so that there is no way out at all. That is how God saves.

In other words the Apostle is saying here precisely the same thing as our blessed Lord is recorded as having said in the Gospel according to St Matthew in chapter 11 verses 25 to 27: 'I thank thee, O Father, Lord of heaven and earth, because thou hast hid these things' – hid these things – 'from the wise and prudent, and hast revealed them unto babes. Even so, Father: for so it seemed good in thy sight. All things are delivered unto me of my Father: and no man knoweth the Son, but the Father; neither knoweth any man the Father, save the Son, and he to whomsoever the Son willeth to reveal him'. It is impossible. No man can ever save himself. That is what the Bible teaches. 1 Corinthians 1:18–30 makes it so clear. Man's strength and wisdom are shown to be weakness and folly by the way in which God sets about saving sinners and by those whom He saves. This is so that 'no flesh should glory in his presence' – neither Jew nor Gentile. We are all born 'dead in trespasses and sins', lifeless, unable to do anything. 'The natural man receiveth not the things of the Spirit of God:

for they are foolishness unto him'. Well, how can he believe then? He cannot believe. He is shut up in unbelief. God has shut up Jews and Gentiles in unbelief in order to show that nothing matters but His mercy. And His mercy can save Jews, His mercy can save Gentiles. It has saved Gentiles, it is going to save Jews, speaking in bulk, of the whole.

# *Twenty-five*

*

*For I would not, brethren, that ye should be ignorant of this mystery, lest ye should be wise in your own conceits; that blindness in part is happened to Israel, until the fulness of the Gentiles be come in. And so all Israel shall be saved: as it is written, There shall come out of Sion the Deliverer, and shall turn away ungodliness from Jacob: For this is my covenant unto them, when I shall take away their sins. As concerning the gospel, they are enemies for your sakes: but as touching the election, they are beloved for the fathers' sakes. For the gifts and calling of God are without repentance. For as ye in times past have not believed God, yet have now obtained mercy through their unbelief: Even so have these also now not believed, that through your mercy they also may obtain mercy. For God hath concluded them all in unbelief, that he might have mercy upon all.* Romans 11:25–32

---

What makes the 32nd verse of this chapter so important is that it gives us an explanation of God's great way of salvation. It not only sums up the argument of this chapter but it lays down a fundamental proposition which enables one to understand the message of the entire Bible. It is that He 'shuts up' in unbelief, or in disobedience, all kinds and classes of people. We interpreted this statement as saying, that the 'all' refers to Jews and Gentiles. That is what the Apostle has been dealing with, Jews and Gentiles – and he says that these two great groups which between them include, of course, the whole world, have been shut up in unbelief, confined in a condition from which they cannot escape. God has done this with the deliberate intention that He might show His mercy to both. And the Apostle explains that there was a time when the Gentiles were shut up in that way but God showed mercy toward them, brought them out, and He is going, he says, to do exactly the same thing with respect to the Jews. But the thing we must lay hold of is this, that what is emphasized in this procedure is the mercy of God. God has chosen this method in order to make plain and clear that great principle of the mercy of God being open to all. In other words there is in this whole section what can well be described as the Apostle's great philosophy of history. Here is a summing up of God's method in His dealings with the whole of the human race. We must therefore pause with this verse and not pass over it because its main point has already been expressed in chapter 3 and in earlier verses of this eleventh chapter. This is a definitive summary and great and high doctrine is involved in it.

We understood verse 25 to be referring, like verses 8 to 10, to a judicial blindness. Verse 32 is dealing with the same thing and we must consider this because many stumble over this point and are tempted to say, as the disciples said to our Lord when He was preaching to them on one occasion, 'This is an hard saying; who can take it' (or, 'who can hear it') and many 'went back and walked no more with Him'.

Now we are still in the flesh and we are much too like some of those people. When we come across something we do not understand we say that too much is being asked of us. Many people have stumbled at this kind of statement and have turned their backs upon the truth and that is a very serious and a very terrible thing to do. So let us look at this for a moment in a spirit of reverence and a spirit of godly fear.

What does this mean? Does it mean that God is the author of sin, or is the author of unbelief and disobedience? Is that what the Apostle is saying? That is what so many people take it to mean and they stumble at it, they say, 'This is impossible', and they either dismiss it on the grounds that the Apostle Paul was just writing his own thoughts here, a typical Pharisee, legalist and so on, or attributing things to God which may have been true of himself. That, of course, is to us unthinkable, being a complete denial of the whole doctrine of inspiration and of the fact that the man who is writing even goes out of his way to remind us that this is a revelation that was made to him as an Apostle and not his own thoughts at all. But people do not hesitate to say this sort of thing because the Apostle is contradicting what they believe about the love of God.

But what exactly is the Apostle teaching? Now he is not saying here that God permits sin in general for the sake of or with a view to redemption. Some people have taken it to mean that. The problem of sin and of evil is a very great problem. Let us admit that quite frankly. God is all-wise, God is holy, God is light, God is all-powerful – well then, the question that people ask is, if that is so why is man as he is, where has sin come from? Now the temptation in the light of a verse like this is to say that what the Apostle is teaching is that God has created sin in order that He might show forth His own grace and mercy and power to save. But that is a thought that we of necessity must reject immediately. God is not the Author of evil. God is the eternal antithesis to evil. I say it with reverence, God cannot create evil, God could not have created sin for any purpose. Sin, I say, is always rebellion against God, disobedience to God, the eternal antithesis to God. So the Apostle is not teaching that God has brought in sin in order that He might show forth the riches of His grace and His amazing mercy. What he is saying is that though God is not the Author of sin, nevertheless it is true to say that sin is not outside His control. He is even going further and saying that God can and has used even sin to serve and to suit His own purpose and to help to bring it to pass.

Now you notice the distinction. He does not say God created sin, but he does say that, sin having come into the world, God has used it for His own great and glorious purpose and to display the riches of His grace and of His mercy. Now that is what the Apostle is actually saying; that sin and unbelief, not created by God, have entered the world and that it is entirely man's responsibility for having listened to the devil. But here it is, here is the fact: God in order to bring His great purpose to pass has made use of this, even at times aggravating it, in order to bring out still more clearly His mercy and the riches of His grace.

There are many statements to this effect in various parts of the Scriptures. Many of them are in the book of the prophet Isaiah, for example chapter 45 which contains the phrase 'I create evil', which alarms so many people. What this means is, that God creates evil consequences. He does not create the evil itself but He is involved in the consequences of man's sin and evil, He is in control of it all: even the devil is under the control of God.

But, of course, the case of Pharaoh is the classical example and illustration of this. In chapter 9, verse 17 we read: 'For the Scripture saith unto Pharaoh, Even for this same purpose have I raised thee up, that I might shew my power in thee, and that my name might be declared throughout all the earth. Therefore hath he mercy on whom he will have mercy, and whom he will he hardeneth'. That is it. He hardened the heart of Pharaoh. He did not make Pharaoh an unbeliever and a sinner, but, Pharaoh already being that, God hardened him, aggravated it. Why? Well, in order that He might show this great contrast between sin and grace. In that same context the Apostle puts up the case of the objector. 'Thou wilt say then unto me, Why doth he yet find fault? For who hath resisted his will?' and he answers those of us who tend to be philosophers and who want to understand fully the mind of God and comprehend all truth, 'Nay but, O man, who art thou that repliest against God? Shall the thing formed say to him that formed it, Why hast thou made me thus?' Let us beware, if we think we can fully understand the mind of God.

This great mystery of God and His ways with respect to man is staggering doctrine. We should never be upset by this but rather be amazed that God gives us the privilege of being allowed to enter at all into these things. He need not have done so; He need not have told us. But He does, He wants us to understand what He has been doing in history, and this is one of the most wonderful aspects of it all.

Now in order to make this matter clearer I want to quote to you some words which were written by Professor James Denney which I think put this matter very well. He says: 'Divine necessity pervades and controls all the freedom of men. It is a Divine purpose mastering all the random activity of human will'. Now what he means by that is this – that God allows a measure of freedom to us, and there is no question about that. Man is responsible and as we have had to emphasize throughout our discussion of these three great chapters 9, 10 and 11, man is responsible always for his damnation; he is not responsible ever for his salvation but he is always responsible for his own damnation.

But while God allows this measure of liberty to man He is over it all. He allows liberty to the devil but it is liberty within limits. You see that in the case of Job, do you not? As you read the first chapter of the book of Job, even the devil is only allowed to do things, but God is over all. In other words this 'Divine necessity' is found to be 'pervading and controlling' all the freedom of men. There is a Divine purpose which masters 'all the random activity of human will'. But Denney has then one very good statement which is: 'God subordinates sin to His purpose, but it is not a subordinate element in His purpose.'

This distinction is crucial because if sin were a subordinate element in God's purpose, it would mean that God is the Author and the Creator of sin. You must not say that sin is a subordinate element in God's purpose, but you must say – and we are told it here by the

Apostle – that God can and does subordinate even sin to His own purpose and for the sake of His own great and eternal purpose.

What the Apostle is teaching us is that God presses man's unbelief and disobedience to the very point at which it becomes quite clear that nothing but God's own mercy can ever give us salvation. He makes that point in many other familiar portions of Scripture, for example Ephesians 2:1–10.

In other words the purpose of this activity of God is to show that we are entirely what we are because of the mercy of God alone. He has shut us up in unbelief and disobedience and we cannot get out of it. 'The natural man receiveth not the things of the Spirit of God: for they are foolishness unto him'. If you say that you are a Christian because you are such a wonderful man with such an understanding and so on you are denying the Scriptures. Salvation is solely due to the mercy of God, and God has made that clear by shutting up the Gentiles in unbelief, shutting up the Jews in unbelief also.

Having dealt in that way with the actual statements in this great portion of Scripture we now try to establish the exposition that has been given. Our contention all along has been that what the Apostle is saying is that a day is coming when the bulk of the nation of Israel is going to believe the gospel. But there are people who do not accept that, but hold other views. There are those, Martin Luther and John Calvin included, who say that 'all Israel' means the total number of the elect, both Jews and Gentiles, while others say that 'all Israel' means the total number of the elect Jews only.

Which view should be adopted? This is a very important matter because the view that we hold will affect our understanding of the Apostle's great doxology that starts in verse 33. That is a good test of our exposition with regard to 'all Israel' – it has to lead you on to this tremendous doxology. So let us look at these two views in the light of our detailed exposition.

First: Why do I say that 'all Israel' is not a reference to the total number of the elect both Jews and Gentiles? Well, let me give you the reasons. To say that 'all Israel' of verse 26 is a reference to the total number of the elect of all nations including the Jews, means that the word 'Israel' is being understood in a different sense in verse 26 from that which it has in verse 25 where it clearly means the nation of Israel. I am arguing that the Apostle does not suddenly change the meaning of a word like that without indicating that he is doing so. 'But', says somebody, 'what about verse 6 of chapter 9 where Paul says, "Not as though the word of God hath taken none effect. For they are not all Israel, which are of Israel"? Is he not using the same word there in two different senses?' My answer to that is that he is not. He is not changing the meaning entirely. All he is showing there is that there is an Israel within the Israel. There are no Gentiles involved there at all. But the other argument which I am rejecting involves including Gentiles in 'Israel' while still calling them Israel. The Apostle does not do that sort of thing.

Again, someone may say, 'What about Galatians 6:16 where the Apostle talks about "the Israel of God"?' There is no difficulty because of the addition of the words 'of God'. When he is talking about the nation he says 'Israel', but when he says 'the Israel of God' he is indicating that he is not talking about the nation but the people of God. In Galatians 6 he has not been discussing the nation at all and so there are different contexts between Galatians 6 and Romans 11.

But then my second reason for rejecting this exposition is that if 'all Israel' in verse 26 means the total number of the elect, the statement becomes bathetic; that is, instead of leading up to a climax it becomes something quite ordinary and the argument is not completed. He says, you see, in verse 25, 'I would not, brethren, that ye should be ignorant of this mystery' – 'this mystery'! – 'lest ye should be wise in your own conceits; that blindness in part is happened to Israel, until the fulness of the Gentiles be come in. And so all Israel shall be saved' – and on he goes, leading to the doxology. But if he is merely saying that a number of Jews and Gentiles are going to be saved, well, that is no climax, it is bathos. Why does he say, I am going to tell you a mystery which, had it not been revealed to me, I would never have thought of, nor would anyone else and then say something so ordinary? It empties the term 'mystery' of its meaning and in no way accounts for the statement of verse 15. 'If the casting away of them be the reconciling of the world, what shall the receiving of them be, but life from the dead?' There is no room for that, it is not there, it has disappeared altogether. And yet that is the greatest thing of all that the Apostle is concerned to say.

So, finally, my third reason for rejecting that exposition is, that it does violence to the argument of the entire chapter. The problem at issue not only in this chapter but in chapters 9 and 10 is the Jews as a nation. 'Hath God cast away his people?' The nation! That is what he is talking about, that is what he is interested in. And so if it is just to end by saying that a given number of Jews and Gentiles are going to be saved, well, the Apostle has not answered the question, it is not really an answer at all. So we reject that exposition for that reason.

We come now to the second alternative exposition, the one which says that 'all Israel' means the total number of the elect Jews. This view has the advantage of not suddenly changing the meaning of 'Israel' in mid-stream without given any reason for doing so at all. It does recognize that he is talking about the Jews and therefore has that great advantage over the other. But I still reject it.

I have come to the conclusion that the most convenient way for me to respond to this view is to quote a statement of it from William Hendriksen, the excellent New Testament commentator. He presents this view in a book of his entitled *The Bible on the Life Hereafter*, but first responds to what he calls a 'wrong view'. That is the view which I have been presenting to you and Hendriksen uses five arguments against it.

First, he says that 'It is contrary to the context of Romans 11'. Here we have a flat contradiction. I say that the context of Romans 11 makes me say what I have been saying; he says, 'it is contrary to the context of Romans 11' and goes on, 'The context nowhere speaks about national salvation or even about mass salvation. On the contrary, it speaks about mass-hardening and remnant-salvation'.

Now this really does astound me, for this good reason: he says this chapter speaks about 'mass-hardening' and 'remnant-salvation' (quite the reverse of this mass redemption) but the Apostle goes out of his way to tell us that the 'mass-hardening' is only temporary, is only 'in part', it is only 'for a while', and he keeps on contrasting what is happening for the time being, which is the 'mass-hardening' and the 'remnant-salvation', with what is going to happen. Hendriksen says this chapter is not concerned about 'national salvation' or 'mass salvation' but, on the contrary, with 'mass-hardening' and 'remnant-salvation'. But what the Apostle says is that at the present time a mass-hardening has happened to Israel and there is only a remnant-salvation, but there is something going to happen. There is my first answer.

Secondly, Hendriksen says: 'Our Lord nowhere predicted a national conversion of the Jews. Jesus loved the Jews. He Himself was a son of Abraham, Isaac, Jacob, and Judah. If the Jews are going to be converted in large masses as a sign of the end, one would expect Jesus to have said so, especially when the disciples asked him to tell them about the sign of his coming and of the end of the world. But he said the very opposite. He indicated everywhere that the privileges which once belonged to the ancient covenant people would be transferred to a new nation (namely, the church), gathered out of Jews and Gentiles (Luke 19:43, 44; Matt. 8:11, 12; 21:32).'

Well, what about this? Well, here it seems to me there are two answers. He is quite right in saying that our Lord in His teaching as we have it in the Gospels did not deal with this question. But why not? We have a specific statement from our Lord to this effect, that there were many other things that He had to teach to His disciples – which at that time they were not able to understand [*John* 16:12]. There were things that He could not teach them before His crucifixion and before the resurrection. They were not clear about His Person, they therefore could not possibly be clear about the Jews' rejection of Him in the way it was going to happen. So He did not pretend to teach them everything. He says specifically there were certain things that He could not teach them then, but that, giving the Holy Spirit, 'He would lead them into all truth' and would reveal unto them 'things to come'. And I am suggesting that in Romans 11 we have a perfect illustration of that very thing. He says, I am going to send the Spirit, He will lead you into all truth, He shall tell you things to come. So this very prophecy of something that was going to come was revealed to the Apostle.

There is a most interesting statement in Acts 1 from the very lips of our Lord Himself which seems to me again to be relevant. Acts 1:6, 7: 'When they therefore were come together, they asked of him, saying, Lord, wilt thou at this time restore again the kingdom to Israel? And he said unto them, It is not for you to know the times or the seasons, which the Father hath put in his own power'. You notice that He does not say that Israel has no more concern with the kingdom. All He says is, you must not be concerned about times and seasons.

Now if Hendriksen were right there was a wonderful opportunity for our Lord to say, Look here, do not ask about the restoration in any sense of Israel in terms of the kingdom, for Israel is finished as regards the kingdom. He does not say that. So I am suggesting that that is a complete answer to the second objection.

Thirdly, he says: 'According to the uniform teaching of Paul, special promises or privileges for this or for that national or racial group – say, the Jews, or the Dutch, or the Americans – do not exist in this new dispensation (Romans 10:12, 13; Galatians 3:38; Ephesians

2:14).' These are the statements about there being 'neither Jew nor Gentile, Barbarian, Scythian, bond nor free, male nor female' in Christ, and of God having broken down the 'middle wall of partition' and statements to that effect, including the one we have already looked at in Romans 10:12.

But there is a very complete answer to this. None of the statements quoted has anything whatsoever to do with the matter that is being dealt with in Romans 11. All the Apostle is teaching in those other statements is that everybody is going to be saved in the same way. The Jews think that they alone are to be saved because they are Jews. That is wrong. From the standpoint of salvation all have got to come through faith in Christ, Jew and Gentile, Barbarian, Scythian, bond or free, it does not matter. There is only one way. Salvation is only in Christ and by faith. There is no other. That is what all those statements are saying. That is not what we are concerned with here. The Apostle in this eleventh chapter of Romans is saying that very plainly and clearly. It is all by the mercy of God, and nobody can claim merit or any goodness in and of himself. But when Hendriksen goes beyond that to say that God is no longer interested in particular in 'this or that national or racial group' he is then simply contradicting what the Apostle says. Where? Well, in this chapter, first in verse 16: 'If the firstfruit be holy, the lump is also holy: if the root be holy, so are the branches'. That is all, you remember, about the nation of the Jews. Then, of course, in verse 25: 'I would not, brethren, that ye should be ignorant of this mystery, lest ye should be wise in your own conceits; that blindness in part is happened to Israel'. Why does he bother to treat Israel separately if there is no purpose in doing so? If all this has ended, why does he have this great argument about the place of Israel if the statement is true that God no longer looks upon any people in a different way from others? There would be no purpose in making such a statement. And then of course, the statement in verse 25, that 'All Israel should be saved'. But still more important, verse 28, 'As concerning the gospel, they (the Jews) are enemies for your sakes: but as touching the election, they are beloved for the fathers' sakes. For the gifts and calling of God are without repentance'. God still loves these people though at the moment they are enemies from the standpoint of the gospel. Why? Well, because of the fathers! God does take still this special interest in the Jews in the way that we have been indicating, namely, that they are going to be brought back as a people into the church through belief and faith in Christ. They will not come in in a special way, they will not even have a special position in the church. But they are going to come back because God still loves them for the sake of the fathers.

His fourth objection is: 'God does not reward disobedience!' to which I have added a little sentence of my own – 'Nor obedience either!' What is the whole point of verses 30 to 32? 'Ye in times past have not believed God, yet have now obtained mercy through their unbelief: Even so have these also now not believed, that through your mercy they also may obtain mercy. For God hath concluded them all in disobedience'. God is not 'rewarding' disobedience, he has 'concluded them all in disobedience in order that He might have mercy upon all'. Mercy is not a reward. Mercy is entirely free, mercy is entirely undeserved. God does not reward anything, either disobedience or obedience. It is all of mercy. There must be no talk about rewarding when God's way of salvation is being dealt with. It does not come in and should not be mentioned.

His last argument is that 'The text – Romans 11:26a – does not say, "And then all Israel shall be saved", as if the Lord will first deal with the Gentiles and, when he is through with them, will start thinking about the Jews once more. It says, "And so all Israel shall be saved". The meaning of the word "so" must be derived from the context'. I agree and that is exactly what I say, claiming that it must be derived from the context and not from some preconceived notion and idea. And the context, as I say, demands that the element of time be included. So Hendriksen's reasons are not valid.

Now what is his positive view? It is this: that throughout this Christian era as Gentiles believe there will always be just a few Jews who will believe in every generation, and that will go on. While the gospel is still being preached to the Gentiles there will always be just a few – he emphasizes this – 'just a few' Jews who will believe. So that when the time comes that the gospel era is finished and the fulness of the Gentiles will have been gathered in, you will be able to add up the total number of just this odd little number of Jews who have believed from age to age and generation to generation, and that constitutes 'All Israel'.

Now that is his explanation of this 'great mystery', but there is no mystery about that. Everybody knew at this time that a number of Jews had believed. The Apostle tells us that at the beginning of the chapter. 'I myself also am an Israelite'. That was known. He also says in verse 5, 'Even so then at this present time also there is a remnant according to the election of grace'. They knew that; there was no mystery about this. And yet Paul says he has a mystery to show them. We have known that throughout the centuries an occasional Jew has believed the gospel, perhaps two or three in places, and that that is still going on. But we do not need to have a revelation to tell us that, we know that, and we could therefore say ourselves, Well, this no doubt will go on until the end of this age and while large numbers of Gentiles will believe there will always be a number of Jews who will believe. You see the explanation completely fails to account for what Paul calls this 'mystery'. And again I must remind you, it completely fails to deal with what we are told in verses 12 and 15: 'Now if the fall of them be the riches of the world' – if their present fall has led to the riches of the world – 'and the diminishing of them the riches of the Gentiles; how much more their fulness?' If we are getting this benefit now, oh, how much more when their fulness comes in! And then verse 15: 'If the casting away of them be the reconciling of the world, what shall the receiving of them be, but' – and then the hyperbole – 'life from the dead?' This will be the most amazing thing that will ever have happened in the long history of the Christian church.

This explanation misses what is to me the main emphasis of the whole chapter. What is that? It is this: The Apostle is all along contrasting Now and Then. This is how it is now – then that is going to happen. There is no such structure in Hendriksen's exposition. All he presents is a continuation of what had already happened.

In other words, he misses entirely the whole object of chapters 9–11, which is the problem of the nation of the Jews rejecting the Messiah and remaining outside the church, and the Gentiles, of all people, coming in. How can that be reconciled with the promises of God made to the fathers? All this explanation tells us is that there will be a kind of 'all Israel' which will just be the sum total of these few that have believed from age to age and generation to generation. Surely that cannot lead up to the tremendous doxology with which Paul concludes his discussion: 'O the depth of the riches both of the wisdom and knowledge of God! How unsearchable are his judgments, and his ways past finding out! Who hath known the mind of the Lord? or who hath been his counsellor? Or who hath first given to him, and it shall be recompensed unto him again? For of him, and through him, and to him, are all things: to whom be glory for ever. Amen'?

# *Twenty-six*

*

*As concerning the gospel, they are enemies for your sakes: but as touching the election, they are beloved for the fathers' sakes. For the gifts and calling of God are without repentance. For as ye in times past have not believed God, yet have now obtained mercy through their unbelief: Even so have these also now not believed, that through your mercy they also may obtain mercy. For God hath concluded them all in unbelief, that he might have mercy upon all.* Romans 11:28–32

Our great contention in expounding these verses has been that the Apostle here, as indeed in the whole chapter, is dealing with the case of the Jews as a whole and as a nation. We have seen reason to reject both the view that 'all Israel' (verse 26) means all the elect, or saved Jews and Gentiles, and the view that it means all the elect Jews, the aggregate of the Jews who had become Christians throughout the entire period of the preaching of the gospel. We have therefore said that the prophecy is to the effect that at some time in the future God is going to do a marvellous thing, He is going to restore as a whole, the Jews whom He has temporarily cast aside. 'Blindness in part is happened to Israel, until the fulness of the Gentiles be come in'.

But there is one further objection which has to be considered. It has been suggested that to understand this prophetic declaration as we have seems to be in conflict with what the Apostle has been teaching, particularly at the beginning of chapter 9. We now take this up.

All are agreed that chapters 9–11 constitute a whole and a part of this great Epistle. In the early part of chapter 9 the Apostle's case has rested upon what he says in verse 6: 'They are not all Israel, which are of Israel'. He proved that by referring to the cases of Isaac and Ishmael, Jacob and Esau and so on. That is the key verse and we emphasised it.

Now this is how the contrary argument runs. They say, Surely this is the Apostle's fundamental answer to this whole problem – that we must not think of Israel as a whole, that the real Israel, the true Israel consists only of the elect Israel and that when you come therefore to say (as we have been saying here in chapter 11) that a day is coming when Israel as a whole, as a bulk, is going to be brought in, we are running contrary to this great basic argument of the Apostle especially as it is expounded at the beginning of chapter 9.

Now then what is the answer to that? Well it does not seem to me to provide any real difficulty whatsoever. I answer it in this way. The Apostle in these three chapters is dealing with this whole question of the Jewish nation. That is obviously the question. He starts off by saying, 'I say the truth in Christ, I lie not, my conscience also bearing me witness in the Holy Ghost, that I have great heaviness and continual sorrow in my heart. For I could wish that myself were accursed from Christ for my brethren, my kinsmen according to the flesh, who are Israelites'. Now there is the introduction. You remember how he repeats that at the beginning of chapter 10: 'Brethren, my heart's desire and prayer to God for Israel is, that they might be saved'. He is considering Israel as a nation.

In other words the big problem is this, that at that time the bulk of the people of Israel rejected the gospel and so were outside the Christian church. Now that was the tremendous problem and while we can well understand it, there is a sense in which it is difficult to do so because we are so accustomed to thinking of the church in terms of Gentiles with the Jews outside. But at the beginning it was the exact opposite. There was this great tradition coming down the centuries in this nation. The Lord Himself was a Jew. These first preachers were all Jews, and yet here is the bulk of the nation outside and it is only a remnant that is to be found inside the church.

Now that was the staggering problem with which the Apostle has to deal. There are different views as to why he dealt with it. There are those who say that he just felt after coming to the end of chapter 8 – 'Well now, I cannot stop without dealing with this whole question of the nation of the Jews.' That is a possible explanation and I am prepared to accept it but I do not think it is the real explanation. My contention is that the Apostle raises this whole matter because he has been dealing with the glorious doctrine of assurance at the end of chapter 8. He has been glorying in the certainty and triumph of the purposes of God. But, with regard to the nation of Israel they seem to be contradicted and to have gone entirely astray if the gospel is true and if the church is the people of God.

That was the problem which was inescapably raised, and the Apostle deals with it in a most thorough and systematic manner in chapters 9–11. At the beginning of chapter 9 he starts dealing with the problem and therefore what he says there is not the whole story. It is only a part of it and it is only the beginning. We must therefore realise that in verse 6 of this chapter Paul is only introducing the matter and that there is a very definite progress in his argument. What he does is to start with the immediate situation. Somebody may come along and say, 'You claim that Israel is the people of God and that the purposes of God are always sure, that they cannot fail. You cannot have it both ways. If you say Israel is the people of God and the purposes of God are sure, well then, why is the bulk of Israel not in the church? You must be wrong somewhere.'

And the first part of the Apostle's reply is that there is another Israel, a 'spiritual Israel', within the natural Israel. God is interested in both, but his argument there is this, that even though the number of the spiritual Israel may be very small indeed it is still the true Israel. God has never promised that He would save every single Israelite who has ever lived. So he demonstrates in the whole of that argument in chapter 9 until he comes to the very end, that the fact that there has always been this 'remnant according to the election of grace' is a proof that God's purposes have stood. That answers the objection raised as well as satisfying the original challenge. He says, 'You know, what is happening now is not happening for the first time; there have been other times in the history of this people when the true Israel was indeed nothing but a very small remnant. And that is sufficient. God's promises to Israel are still being fulfilled even though it be in a remnant.

But you see that is not the whole story. To get the big argument you go straight from chapter 9 to chapter 11 where he says, 'Even so then at this present time also there is a remnant according to the election of grace' (verse 5). You see, that is a summing up of the whole argument of chapter 9, this 'remnant' that God has kept going. He says it is like that at present. But – and here is the startling thing – it is not always going to be that, it is not always going to be a remnant. So he introduces this great idea in verse 11 where he talks about 'provoking them to jealousy'. 'They have not stumbled that they should fall'. They are not finished with. And then, you see, in verse 12: 'if the fall of them be the riches of the world, and the diminishing of them the riches of the Gentiles; how much more their fulness?' And he repeats that, you remember, in verse 15: And then, that there should be no doubt at all about it, in verse 25 he says, 'I am going to let you into the secret. I have received a revelation. I am speaking as an Apostle, I am speaking as a prophet. I am not arguing any longer'. He had been arguing in terms of the Old Testament. He says this is no longer argument, I give you a revelation. The mystery which he is revealing is, as we have seen, that Israel as a whole is going to be brought in.

Now, my contention therefore is that there is no contradiction at all between what he says at the beginning of chapter 9 and what he says here in chapter 11 and especially towards the end. It is not a contradiction, it is an addition, and an addition is not a contradiction. Paul is not saying that it is always going to be a remnant, and only a remnant of Jews that believe. 'At the present time it is', he says, but this other event is going to take place. He says, What is happening now has proved to be a great benefit to the Gentiles but it is nothing in comparison with what will take place when that happens. So you see it is a question of the progression of the argument: reason capped by revelation; the great manifestation of something that was secret and that was hidden and which is revealed to the prophet by the Holy Spirit.

There is no reason whatsoever for saying that the true Israel must always be a remnant. All Paul is saying is this, that that has often been the case. It was the case when he was writing, it would continue to be the case until the fulness of the Gentiles had come in. Then it would not merely be a remnant of Israel that would believe, it would be the whole of Israel. 'All Israel shall be saved'.

Now having dealt with that, there seem to me to be a number of general lessons taught here, and especially with regard to this whole question of prophecy and its interpretation, to which we must pay attention. You are all familiar with the way in which prophecy has not only often confused people but has, unfortunately, often divided people. So it is important that we should know something concerning the way in which we should approach the whole matter of prophecy and its interpretation, for that is what we are dealing with here.

Now what is the way to interpret prophecy in general? Here I can do nothing better than to quote to you Charles Hodge who seems to me to have put this very perfectly indeed. Listen to Hodge: 'Prophecy', he says, 'is not proleptic history'. Now that is a most important statement and he explains what he means by saying, 'It is not designed to give us the knowledge of the future which history gives us of the past'. Now that is what he means by 'proleptic history'. 'History is concerned to give us knowledge of the past'. That at any rate is the real business of history. Modern historians are turning it into all sorts of other things. They are turning it into philosophy, as they are turning science into philosophy. But the business of history primarily is to give us a knowledge of the past. You may, if you like, afterwards try to draw deductions and lessons, and we should do so. But of course the trouble today is that the historians, instead of really dealing with the past as it is and giving us knowledge of the past, start with their theories and they twist and mould and manipulate the facts of the past to fit their theory. Now that is bad history, and when they do the same thing with science it is bad science. According to Hodge the business of history is to give us 'knowledge of that which has happened in the past'. 'Now', he says, 'prophecy must not be thought of as doing that with respect to the future in terms of details'.

Listen to him as he goes on: 'Great events are foretold but the mode of their occurrence, their details and their consequences can only be learned by the event'. Now history, you see, tells you not only about the great events it gives you the details. It tells you the order in which the events happened and how they happened, and it gives you the details and the consequences of what happened. With history, you look back and you see it all. Now he says prophecy is not like that. Prophecy tells us about the great events that are going to happen, 'but the mode of their occurrence, their details, and their consequences can only be learned by the event' – by when it happens. 'It is in the retrospect that the foreshadowing of history is seen to be miraculous and divine'.

What he means is this: it is only when prophecy has been fulfilled and you look back across it that you see how wonderful it is. Let me take the obvious illustration. Take the prophecies in the Old Testament about the coming of our Lord and so on. Now the people who read those prophecies or to whom they were read or expounded did not see the great significance of what was happening. All they knew was that there was a promise concerning a Messiah. But you and I with the Gospels in our hands and the knowledge of the story, look back and read the Old Testament prophecies and see the amazing character of it all, the detailed information that was given: hidden of course at that time, but to us perfectly clear because we are looking at it in retrospect. That is what Charles Hodge is saying. He says you must not go to prophecy and expect it to be a sort of detailed account of what is going to happen and all the consequences of what will happen in the same way as you have in the history of the past. The principle, he says, of the interpretation of prophecy therefore is this, that it is concerned with the big things not with the details.

I hope that is understood and appreciated because there are so many people today who regard prophecy as something detailed. Once I was travelling to the West Country to preach. We arrived in the train at Reading and a young man came into my compartment holding in his right hand a Bible and a copy of *The Times* and I knew immediately what he was going to do that day. He was going to give an address on prophecy and I turned out to be right. There was nothing clever about my deduction. It was the fact that the man had a Bible and *The Times* together and I happened to know the mentality which did that! The detailed news and information in *The Times* all foretold in the Bible, in the prophecy of the Bible. And so people expect to find these details and so on, and thus they have identified Napoleon with the man of sin, and then Hitler and perhaps Stalin after that. It is a wrong approach to prophecy altogether because prophecy does not give us those details. The Scriptures themselves say so. We are not to be concerned about the times and the seasons. There is the general principle which we must bear in mind as we are dealing with this particular passage. It is a major statement but we have got to be very careful when we come to details.

Let me put that in the form, then, of a second principle. Our greatest danger in the interpretation of prophecy always is to 'read in' to the text things that are not there. Why do we do that? Well, we do that, of course, because we have got a scheme in our mind and we then tend to look for this and to find it everywhere, and if it is not there, in a very subtle way we can put it in; and it is astounding to notice the way in which this is done. I am going to give you an illustration or two in a moment.

Now let me again remind you that this tendency is not peculiar to students of the Bible. Some time ago I read a review by Mr A. J. P. Taylor of a monumental ten-volume study of history by Arnold Toynbee, and the point made by Taylor was this. He said, 'Of course if a man dealing with history starts off with the theory in his mind he can make the facts of history prove his theory'. And he said that the trouble with Toynbee was, 'that he started out with the preconceived notion, idea and prejudice, and in this great review of the history of the world he has just manipulated and twisted the facts to fit into his theory'. To which the answer of course is that Taylor does exactly the same thing himself, and both are wrong. The historian must not do that. But they do it, and they say that about one another, and to that extent it is bad history.

You notice what his charge was? He said that he was 'manipulating the facts to fit into his theory'. Of course it can be done very cleverly; you slide over this and you put unusual emphasis there. You are still in a sense dealing with the facts but – oh, an underlining here, inverted commas there, you can make the whole thing look so different. This is what is being done, incidentally, with the theory of evolution which so many scientists are teaching as facts today. They start rightly by saying it is a theory, a few pages further on you will find them referring to it as a fact. Now that is the thing that people tend to do with prophecy. It is the danger of 'reading in' something that is not there in order to support our own particular theory. Now my contention is that here the Apostle is dealing with one big thing only and nothing else.

So my third principle is this, it is important to notice what a prophecy does not say, and not to go beyond that. Let me show you what the Apostle does not say here. The first thing he does not deal with at all here is the Millennium and the Second Advent. He does not deal with them here at all. But here is the comment of the late Dr Kenneth Wuest of America, who was a most distinguished Greek scholar, on this passage we have been dealing with. 'Israel as a nation will in the sovereign grace of God be regenerated and filled with the Spirit to become again the channel through which God will operate for a thousand years to bring salvation to a Christ rejecting world'. Again he regards 'All Israel' to mean that all, every single individual Jew alive at that time will be converted. I took some time in showing that it does not mean that and cannot, but he takes it that it does. Then he goes on: 'This individual cleansing from sin will be followed by a national restoration to the Messianic Kingdom with the Messiah reigning on the throne of David in Jerusalem as King of kings, and Lord of lords, for one thousand years'. You see what I mean by 'reading in'. Where is there any mention of a thousand years here? It is just not here at all. Where is there any mention here of our Lord's Second Advent? It is not here. Indeed it seems to me that the twenty-fifth verse is enough in and of itself to exclude this interpretation. You see the interpretation is that God is going to use this converted nation of Israel for a thousand years to bring salvation to a 'Christ rejecting world'. Whereas Paul says that 'blindness in part is happened to Israel until the fulness of the Gentiles be come in'. The 'Christ rejecting world' will have received and believed before this happens to Israel. But according to this other interpretation it is the other way round.

Now why does a man do a thing like that? Well he does it because he starts off with his particular theory about the Millennium, and once you have got that you find it everywhere. Any vague reference which seems in any way to point in that direction is taken hold of. Here it is, the nation of Israel is going to be saved. That is a perfectly correct statement. But then you see he adds to that what is not mentioned in the text. He reads it in as a part of his interpretation. He puts it in. This is the kind of thing I say we must not do.

Or take a second point. Where do you find any reference whatsoever to the land of Palestine or of Israel in this section? Where is there any mention of the restoration of the Jews to the land? Where is any mention of Jerusalem as such and the reigning there of the Lord for a thousand years? And yet, you see, those of you who read the notes in the Scofield Bible will find that Scofield says in connection with verse 26, 'According to the prophets, Israel regathered from all nations, restored to her own land and converted, is yet to have her greatest earthly exaltation and glory'. Where do you find that in the text? It is not there, not there at all. We are not told that 'all Israel' is to be saved in this way, 'after they have all been gathered back into the land of Israel'. We are not told that. They will be saved wherever they are – scattered throughout the whole world as far as this passage is concerned. And yet you see it is dragged in. And this will be used then as an argument for saying that people will be taken back to the land and then they will be converted, and then they will do this wonderful thing and they will know their greatest earthly exaltation and glory. There is not a word about this in the whole section. It is entirely read in. Now this is the kind of thing which is happening and which is always liable to happen and against which I am trying to warn you.

Take that last point, which is my third point – this idea that we are told here that the Jews, the nation of Israel, is going to have a unique and separate position of exaltation. Again I suggest there is not a single word about that here at all. What the Apostle actually says is this – that the Jews are going to be converted in exactly the same way as the Gentiles have been converted, with no difference at all. There is only one way of salvation, and Jew and Gentile enter into it in exactly the same way. And there is only one position for Christians, whether Jews or Gentiles, and that is 'members of the Body of Christ'.

So you see there is nothing here to teach us that the Jews are going to be in some special position in the kingdom of God. We are told the exact opposite. All we are told about the Jews is this, that 'for the fathers' sakes they are beloved' and God is going to bring them in. He is going to convert them, He is going to add them to the church, and that that in turn will be a wonderful means of blessing to the whole of the Christian church. That is what the Apostle is saying, and he says no more than that. These other items are not mentioned at all. But men, in the interests of a theory, read them in.

The lesson I trust that we are all learning from this is: Listen to the Scriptures and do not go beyond them. Do not detract, do not add. Both are equally wrong. The Scripture must be allowed to speak for itself.

Let me deal with one other question which is this: When is all this going to happen? That is a question that naturally suggests itself to our minds. If this is going to happen to Israel as a whole, as a nation, when is it going to happen? And the only real answer we can give is this, that we are not told. All we are told is, that it is 'after' the fulness of the Gentiles has come in. That is plainly stated in verse 25: '. . . blindness in part is happened to Israel, until the fulness of the Gentiles be come in'. We are told that they will be brought in by a kind of jealousy. He has been saying that several times over.

Nevertheless, though we are not told anything about it, there are those who would say that we are entitled to deduce from what we are told here that this will happen at the time of the Second Coming of our Lord. They tend to quote what we are told in the second part of verse 26: 'There shall come out of Sion the Deliverer, and shall turn away ungodliness from Jacob'. But we have already dealt with that when we were doing the detailed exposition so I need not go over it again.

Let me therefore bring some other arguments to bear upon this matter. I would say in the first place that if the Apostle here is really dealing with the Second Coming of our Lord he would say so. The Apostle deals with the doctrine of the Second Coming of Christ in many places, and he does so quite plainly and quite clearly. When he is dealing with that he says so. He does not hint at it or deal with it indirectly, he makes plain statements. And that is why there is no difficulty about believing in the literal physical coming again of the Lord Jesus Christ. This Apostle of all apostles has dealt with that. So I am arguing that if that is what he had in mind here, if he is saying that when the Lord does appear again Israel seeing Him will then believe, he would have said that. He does not do so; and that to me is really enough, in and of itself.

But in addition, secondly, the teaching about the coming of our Lord in the New Testament is always to the effect that He will come 'as a thief in the night' – suddenly, unexpected; when men shall say 'Peace and safety' – then. Or 'as the lightning flashes from one end of the heaven to the other'. That is the way in which this doctrine is always presented. There is nothing like that here at all: nothing whatsoever. You rather are given the impression that the preaching of the gospel goes on and the fulness of the Gentiles comes in, then in some way that is not explained to us the Jews as a whole are going to be converted. But there is nothing here to suggest some sudden event, some sudden appearance. That I feel is an argument that militates against it also.

But, thirdly, I have a strong feeling that verses 12 and 15 definitely exclude this supposition altogether, the verses I have quoted so often to you. 'If the fall of them be the riches of the world, and the diminishing of them the riches of the Gentiles; how much more their fulness?' 'If the casting away of them be the reconciling of the world, what shall the receiving of them be, but life from the dead?' Now the emphasis there is, of course, upon the conversion of the Jews and this astonishing phenomenon that is going to have such an invigorating effect upon the life of the church. But, you see, when the Lord Jesus Christ Himself will come again, when He makes His appearance, it is perfectly clear from the whole teaching of Scripture that when that happens the centre of interest will not be the Jews but the Lord. Nobody will be looking at the Jews whatever happens to them. Everybody will be looking at Him. This will be the phenomenon, He shall have appeared. But you see according to this teaching when this happens to the Jews they will be the phenomenon and everybody will be looking at them, and will be amazed at them; and the thing that happens to them will be the cause of the blessing. 'If the casting away of them be the reconciling of the world, what shall the receiving of them be, but life from the dead?' But believe me my friends, however wonderful that will be, and it will be wonderful, it will pale into insignificance by contrast and comparison with what will happen when He Himself will appear. This will be the Phenomenon of phenomena, and every eye shall see Him and look upon Him and we shall forget everybody and everything else. Now the Apostle here is not talking about our Lord's Second Coming, he is talking about this thing which is going to happen to the Jews as a whole and as a nation, and it seems to me that his whole emphasis and description precludes the possibility even of its being associated with the Second Coming.

And then I have another argument which to me carries very great weight. In Luke 18, after the Parable of the Importunate Widow who kept on worrying the judge, we read, 'The Lord said, Hear what the unjust judge saith. And shall not God avenge his own elect, which cry day and night unto him, though he bear long with them? I tell you that he will avenge them speedily. Nevertheless when the Son of man cometh shall he find faith on the earth?' [verses 6–8]. Now that is a tremendous and a staggering statement. It is to the effect that when the Son of man does come, when He makes His second appearing, there will not be much evidence of the faith upon the earth. Whereas what the Apostle is telling us here in Romans 11 is this: That the fulness of the Gentiles will have come in, and all Israel will have come in. It will be a tremendous period of belief and of rejoicing in the faith. That seems to me to be enough to exclude the possibility that the Apostle has in his mind here the Second Coming of our blessed Lord and Saviour. The teaching about the Second Coming is this, that it will not only be unexpected and sudden, it will be in a time of great declension of the faith. Not only is that taught in the Gospels, you have the same thing in the Book of Revelation. You get this terrible warfare and the people of God seem to be on the point of extinction, when suddenly He will come and He will destroy all His enemies.

So that I am arguing that I cannot see any possibility that what we are told about here in this prophecy in Romans 11 is a reference to something that is going to happen when our Lord's Second Coming takes place. I confess freely I cannot go any further. All I am prepared to say is this: it seems to me that what we are told here in the prophecy of Romans 11 is something that must take place before – well before – our Lord's Second Coming. For it appears that after this glorious period there will be a period of declension and He will come at that time and period of declension. But what we are told about here is that the revivifying effect upon the church of the conversion of the bulk of the nation of the Jews is going to be one of the most astonishing phenomena in the whole long history of the Christian church. That is all we are told, and anything beyond that is either reading into the text what is not there, or else it is mere speculation.

# *Twenty-seven*

*

*As concerning the gospel, they are enemies for your sakes: but as touching the election, they are beloved for the fathers' sakes. For the gifts and calling of God are without repentance. For as ye in times past have not believed God, yet have now obtained mercy through their unbelief: Even so have these also now not believed, that through your mercy they also may obtain mercy. For God hath concluded them all in unbelief, that he might have mercy upon all.* Romans 11:28–32

We have drawn some general lessons from the Apostle's great prophecy about the ingathering of Israel into the church and have emphasized that he does not tell us when this is going to happen. It is also true that he does not tell us *how* – and we turn to consider that. We know that now for a number of years there have been various Missions to the Jews which are doing excellent work – may God continue to bless them. It may be through such activities that this great event is going to take place in connection with the nation, or the bulk of the nation, of the children of Israel. We do not know. We are simply not told. All the Apostle is concerned to say here is that it is going to happen. When and how, whether it will be sudden or whether it will be gradual we just do not know; and therefore any ideas that we may put forward with regard to that are nothing but sheer speculation. It is tempting to speculate but we must resist the temptation. We do not know. All we know is this – that when it does happen it will be solely the result of God's great mercy. Nothing else will account for it because, as he tells us in the thirty-second verse, 'God has concluded them all in unbelief that (in order that) he might have mercy upon all'. So however it happens, whenever it happens, it will be entirely the result of God's mercy.

The thing therefore that we have got to hold on to is this – that this is going to happen and it is going to be an amazing thing; so amazing that no terms are adequate to describe it save the terms that he used in the fifteenth verse; it will indeed be 'life from the dead'. It will be a most revivifying event in the life and history of the church. It will be such a phenomenon that it will fill God's people not only with astonishment and amazement but also with wonder, love and praise.

Now then there are certain general lessons which we learn from this all-important passage, but I want to go still further. I think that at this point now it behoves us to make a kind of general review of the teaching in particular of this chapter but in a sense also of chapters 9 and 10 as well, because this is indeed a most important statement. You can describe it if you like as the Apostle Paul's 'Philosophy of History'.

There is a great deal of interest at the present time in the philosophy of history. Books are constantly being published dealing with this very subject and it is not surprising because you and I are living in a century when there is no problem that is more acute for any thinking person than this whole problem of history. I mean by that – Is there any explanation of history? Is there any way of understanding what is happening? Why are these things happening – world wars, crises, tension and so on and so forth? Now all this has caused people to examine this whole problem of history and it is obviously a vital and urgent matter for people to be considering in a century such as this present one.

Our position as Christians, then, is this, that there is only one real philosophy of history, and it is the one that is found in the Bible. All the others break down. It would be very simple indeed to show that. Indeed there is a tendency on the part of most great historians at the present time to say that they can find no meaning in history at all, no purpose. Some have put forward their theories, for example Oswald Spengler, who prophesied a sort of doom and the end of Western civilization; and then you have had a great man like Professor Arnold Toynbee in his monumental *Study of History*.

Now these are just attempts to explain what is happening. They are not adequate even as that, and they disagree amongst themselves. The prevailing tendency seems to be to say that there is no meaning at all, it is all accident, there is no great purpose. If you have ever read the *History of Europe* by the late H. A. L. Fisher of Oxford, once a Cabinet member during the First World War, you will remember that he says in his Introduction that having spent his life-time in studying history, he had come to the conclusion that there is no purpose that he could discern at all in it, things just happen, but there is no plan and there is no direction. That, then, is the kind of prevailing philosophy of history, and you see it is finally hopeless and does not give us any help whatsoever.

On the other hand the Bible deals with this in a very specific manner and one of the most notable passages in the whole of the Bible in which a philosophy of history, or if you like an outline of history, is provided is the one under examination.

What does the Apostle teach on this subject? Well here, it seems to me, are the principles which he presents, and I know of nothing that is more comforting and consoling at the present time than this teaching. The first great or overarching principle is that everything is under the hand of God.

As we have been working at the details of this passage you must have been impressed by this fact. Indeed, it is the characteristic of all the great reviews of history in the Bible. In the book of Psalms when the Psalmist is dealing with a very depressed state and condition in the life of the children of Israel what he so often does is to review the whole of their history. There are many synopses of the history of the children of Israel scattered about the Psalms, and when you come to the New Testament you find the same thing. In chapter 7 of the Book of the Acts of the Apostles you find Stephen reviewing the whole story and in chapter 13 the Apostle Paul did exactly the same thing in Antioch of Pisidia. In other words their point is that there is a scheme discernible and it is all under God. God is over all and everything is under His almighty hand. That is the thing that they keep on saying. Of course, this is the great message of the Bible and that is why it starts as it does with the words 'In the beginning God . . .' It starts with God and it ends with God. All is under the hand of God. That is its unique message. He reigns and He rules over all.

Now you cannot read the passage that we have been dealing with without seeing that. The prophecy implies that immediately. Nothing seems so impossible or so unlikely to happen when the Apostle was writing as that the Jews as a nation should ever believe the gospel and become members of the Christian church, but Paul said it was going to happen. And why was it going to happen? The answer is, 'God is able to graft them in again'.

Here, then, is the great first principle. But immediately you have to say more about this because if you just leave it at that people will be in difficulties. They will say, If that is so, well then, why does this happen, or why did that happen? The answer is this. God, while being over all, permits many things to happen which seem to be the exact opposite of His own purpose. We have seen instances of that. The fact that the children of Israel reject the gospel has been permitted by God, otherwise it would not have happened. But though God permits many things to happen, that does not mean that they are out of control. The great principle always is that even these things are still under the governance of God.

Now in many ways the classic statement of this is the book of Job, where it is made quite plain in the first chapter that the devil is under the rule of God. The devil has great power but he is not a free agent. The devil could not deal with Job without getting permission to do so from God. God has permitted evil. Now this is a great mystery and nobody can explain it. We are too small to understand. All we know is that God in His infinite wisdom has permitted evil and sin. We may speculate as to why He did so; we may argue that because He created man perfect He had to create him free, and that freedom includes the possibility of saying No as well as Yes. All right! That is philosophic speculation. It may be right, it may not be right. All we know is that God has permitted evil. But – and here is the essence of the biblical message – though He has permitted evil, and though evil is very powerful and works much havoc, it is still under the almighty hand of God.

However, this is not to say that God created evil. God permits it and then overrules it; He can take it and bend it to His own will and use it for His own great and wonderful purposes. Now that is what is to be seen in this chapter. Paul, you remember, says it quite plainly and clearly in the eleventh verse: 'I say then, Have they stumbled that they should fall? God forbid: but rather through their fall salvation is come unto the Gentiles'. There is our first principle then, and it stands out in this chapter as it does in this section, as it does in the essential biblical message. Everything is under the hand of God. He lives. He reigns. He is over all. 'The Lord reigneth; let the people tremble'. There is the first great principle.

Then, secondly, and this, of course, in a sense comes out of the first – God has a great plan and purpose which will certainly be carried out. This is the great comfort. You cannot read this chapter without seeing that at a glance. But look at things as they are and you say, What is happening? You may look back in history and you say I still do not understand it, I do not see any purpose. But as I have quoted to you, that is what the secular historians have to say. If you know your Bible and understand this central biblical message you say, Oh yes, God has got a plan, He has got a purpose, and its execution is absolutely certain. That is what the Apostle has been trying to argue. He says: 'Look here, you are only looking at things as they are – listen to me'. And then he brings in his great prophecy – This is what is going to happen in spite of all that is true now. Why is it going to happen? Well, because it is God's plan. He says, you remember, 'As concerning the gospel, they are enemies for your sakes: but as touching the election, they are beloved for the fathers' sakes'. That is it. What is this 'election'? Well, that is God's plan and purpose. That is what God determined way back in eternity, began to put into practice in Abraham and Isaac and Jacob. They are 'the fathers' the Apostle is referring to.

Now if you have not got hold of this you have missed the central biblical message. The danger is that as we read our Bible we miss the wood because of the trees; we become immersed in problems and in details here and there. My method is, as you know, to go into great detail in all these matters but having done that, it is our business to do what we are doing now. We stand back and see the whole again, and that lets you see with increasing wonder and amazement how every single detail is a part of a great whole and it is only as the parts are seen in the light of the whole that they are properly understood. We therefore emphasize this great plan and purpose of God which He had in His mind before the very foundation of the world and which He will certainly, by His almighty power, carry out in every single detail.

But while we can be absolutely certain about the great fact of the plan of God we are left in considerable ignorance as to the time when He does various things, and this is where we become bothered and unhappy because things do not happen according to our little timetables. The history of biblical exposition and God's people is strewn with those who have been fixing times and seasons and who have always been wrong; and they always will be. We are not meant to know these things – we are told that. What we are told is times and seasons belong to God and that everything happens according to His perfect time-table.

I could illustrate this to you at great length but I must not do so. You find it in many places in the Old Testament. For example the Psalmist could not understand it so he cries out, 'How long, O Lord?' He says, 'Why are you like a stranger? Are you asleep', as it were, 'what is the matter?' Well, that is because of his impatience, but God always has His time, and He suddenly acts when nobody expects it. He sometimes allows a situation to become the very worst conceivable, and then He acts, but He had known it all along. He sees the end from the beginning and when the saints are in the right spiritual condition they not only recognize that, they celebrate it and they thank God for it.

So all we are left with is great phrases like this: 'When the fulness of the time was come, God sent forth his Son, made of a woman, made under the law, to redeem them that were under the law . . .' What is this 'fulness of time'? Well it really means 'God's hour', 'God's appointed time', the time that was originally in the mind of God. He gives indications of it in prophecy but never too clearly. Take the prophecy of Daniel for instance where figures and days are mentioned. Now there is a sense in which they are detailed, but they are never so specific that men can tell exactly when things are going to happen. Looking back they can but never otherwise. What makes prophecy possible is that God has a perfect plan and He knows the exact time of everything. But it is God alone Who knows the time.

The crucial verse about all this is a statement of our Lord Himself as recorded in the Gospel according to St Mark chapter 12 and verse 32. He says: 'Heaven and earth shall pass away: but my words shall not pass away. But of that day and that hour knoweth no man, no, not the angels which are in heaven, neither the Son, but the Father'. This time, this day, and this hour are not only not known to man, not known to angels, they are not even known to the Son. These are a day and a time known to the Father alone.

We therefore hold on to the main thing, which is that God has this plan and He knows the end from the beginning, the time, the date, everything is known to Him. It is not to be known by us. As our Lord goes on to say, we should be in this position, 'Take ye heed, watch and pray: for ye know not when the time is'. But though we do not know the time, look at the consolation and the comfort of remembering that God knows! And because He is God and because He is over all, nothing can ever upset His purpose.

My third deduction under this particular heading follows from this and it is that salvation is altogether and entirely of God. Here is biblical history, here is Paul's philosophy of history: with man fallen in sin, God has a plan of redemption, He is forming a new humanity. God is saving people out of this present evil world for that world to come. That is the plan in its essence. God is not giving in to the devil; the devil is not to be allowed to be the final conqueror. Of course not. God is going to have a restored, renewed heaven and earth, and a new humanity that is perfect, the Head of the new humanity being Christ. All else shall be destroyed, eternally destroyed.

So the great matter of interest to us is this salvation. Who are these people who are going to belong to this new humanity and who will dwell in this renewed and restored universe? Well there is only one answer here and the Apostle has kept on saying it in this chapter and in these three chapters, and what he has always emphasized is that their salvation is altogether and entirely of God. That is what makes it certain, that is what guarantees it. If it were dependent upon man in any sense it would fail for certain because although we are born again we still sin and so we would forfeit salvation. It is because it is of God that it is sure and it is solely the result of God's mercy. 'God hath concluded them all in unbelief, that he might have mercy upon all'. This is the word he keeps on repeating. 'For as ye in times past have not believed God, yet have now obtained mercy through their unbelief: Even so have these also now not believed, that through your mercy they also may obtain mercy'. It is all due to the mercy of God. And were it not for the mercy of God not a single soul would ever have been saved, not one. We are all lost, we are all born in sin, we are all the children of Adam and we have all died in Adam, and it is the mercy of God alone that makes salvation possible to anybody.

But salvation is not only due to His mercy but to His 'election'. 'Jacob have I loved, Esau have I hated.' Before Jacob and Esau were born, while they were still in their mother's womb together, God said, 'Jacob have I loved, Esau have I hated'. It was not as the result of their actions that God said that. He said it before they were born and before they could act. The great election of God is a great mystery that foolish people try to understand. We are not to understand it, we are to recognize it, we are to look at ourselves and say, Why am I a Christian? Is it because there is some innate goodness in me? Is it because I am better than the other people who are not Christians? Is it because I am a better fellow? What utter rubbish that is and we know it is. 'I am what I am by the grace of God', and if you are not amazed at yourself, I would say that you had better examine the foundations again. It is all of the mercy of God and it is all the result of His election and it is all brought about by His almighty power. That is what he has been proving in this chapter. 'Look', he says, 'at you Gentiles; you in times past did not believe God', and the whole of the Old Testament period the Gentiles rejected the teaching concerning God, which was possessed only by the Jews. There they were, entirely hopeless, how did they even come into the church? There is only one answer. It was the mercy of God, it was the election of God, above all it was the power of God. God took them, the unnatural branches, and He grafted them in to this olive tree. This explains why Gentiles become Christians.

But in exactly the same way it explains why any Jew ever becomes a Christian and why the nation as a whole will become Christian at some future time. What is happening in other words is that God is calling out a people for Himself, out of the Jews, out of the Gentiles, and eventually this great influx – the fulness of the Gentiles, the fulness of the Jews, and there you will have this completed people of God. And this is the thing that he keeps on emphasizing – it is all entirely of God and not at all of man. He proves that. 'Look at you Gentiles', he says, 'you rejected it all, you were in unbelief; so do the Jews now. So that the fact that you ever become Christians is entirely and solely the result of God's grace and mercy and power'.

There is our general philosophy of history. Man made perfect, he sins, the world becomes chaotic. Civilizations try to put things right – it is no good, they are only going round in circles, or think that there is no purpose at all. But then you come to the Bible and you see this great purpose going right through, ending in the vision of the Book of Revelation; the final deliverance, the return of Christ, the conquest and destruction of evil and the setting up of this glorious kingdom which is eternal. That is the biblical view or philosophy of history.

But now I want to be a little more practical, I want to be more of a pastor. I want to draw certain inferences or deductions from this wonderful teaching, and oh, how consoling and wonderful it is. I am sorry for people who do not understand the Bible. I really find it increasingly difficult to know how they have managed to live at all, in days and times like this particularly. But once you get hold of this great teaching, that it is all under God and that His purposes are sure you are able to draw deductions like this.

Things are not always what they appear to be on the surface. I have felt that tremendously during the weeks that we have been working through this eleventh chapter of the Epistle to the Romans. This is the great teaching that comes out in the Bible so constantly. So many times it looked as if God had failed completely. His people are defeated, they are spat upon, they are despised and derided, and the enemy is loud and proud and arrogant, and the whole world says, 'God, if there is a God, is defeated'. The children of Israel felt that He had been defeated. That is what appearances seemed to say and it seemed an unanswerable argument. But you cannot read a chapter like this and understand it or know your Bible without seeing what utter folly that is. Once you get this other viewpoint, things are not what they appear to be. It looks today as if the Jews as a nation will never become Christians, does it not? But they are going to be. It looked absolutely hopeless at the time of the Apostle Paul. They had crucified their own Messiah, they were vilifying the Christians and persecuting them – the thing seemed impossible. Things are not as they appear to be. That is the whole statement here, once you see it from God's side. And you can put that if you like in a still more personal and individual way. Take that hymn of William Cowper, *God moves in a mysterious way*. There is the line 'Behind a frowning Providence . . .' and I would like the next line to be – 'He hides a Father's face', not a smiling face but a Father's face! You think at times that God is against you because circumstances seem to be indicating that. Do not jump to conclusions. Once you get this message you will never feel that again. You will say, That is how things seem to be; it does not guarantee that they are. Behind a frowning Providence He hides a Father's face.

But I will put it like this in the second place. What appears to be thoroughly bad may, in a sense, be produced by God for the furtherance of His own purposes. Now this is the great point which we have seen emerging so many times in this eleventh chapter, where he says quite specifically in verse 11 that 'rather through their fall salvation is come unto the Gentiles'. He repeats that in verse 12: 'Now if the fall of them be the riches of the world, and the diminishing of them the riches of the Gentiles; how much more their fulness?' Verse 15: 'If the casting away of them be the reconciling of the world'. That is how it turned out to be and this is a tremendous thing; this is where we with our small minds so constantly tend to go astray. This principle of God even works like this – that things that seem to be the most antagonistic to God's purpose are actually serving His purpose. Now the Apostle has already told us that in chapter 8 verse 28: 'All things work together for good to them that love God'. That is another way of putting it. Everything!

In history this can be seen very plainly. The Roman Empire

persecuted the Christians in a very grievous manner; it did its utmost to exterminate Christianity. And yet, it is equally true to say this, that the Roman Empire provided the most perfect machinery for the evangelization of the then known world that one can possibly imagine. I mean they were such wonderful road builders. They had conquered most of the world, and they had built their roads. They seem to have provided the very machinery that was necessary for the spread of the gospel. It is an astounding thing. That is not an accident, my friends. God allowed this tremendous empire that did its best to exterminate Christianity to rise. Why? Well, He knew He was going to use it. And you might very well say the same thing about the Greek language. He had allowed that great flowering period of Greek culture to take place in order that when His Son came, and the gospel, the language and the roads were ready, out it went. What appeared to be against the interests of the church when seen from this angle are in the very best interests of the church. That is the philosophy.

But here is another point. You remember the destruction of the City of Jerusalem in A.D. 70 – the greatest calamity that ever happened to the Jews; something that it is very difficult to understand when you regard the Jews as they are as God's people. And yet it was the destruction of Jerusalem and the scattering of the Jews that turned out to be the best thing possible for the spreading of the gospel amongst the Gentiles. There were all sorts of difficulties as we have seen, which continued and persisted while the church was mainly Jewish. The Jewish prejudices were doing great harm. Once you get the destruction of Jerusalem the whole position changes. It was one of the best things that ever happened from the standpoint of the evangelization of the Gentiles. Historians are agreed, further, that the Arian persecutions had a very direct influence again upon the conversion of the Goths. Now the Arian heresy was a bad thing, but the persecutions connected with it were used by God in the conversion of the Goths.

In the same way we are entitled to say that the declension of the Roman Catholic Church in the Middle Ages and right up to the period of the Reformation led to the Reformation, which turned out to be possibly, next to the Apostolic era itself, the greatest ever period of evangelization, and it has continued almost up until our very day. Now this is just illustrative of the fact that what appears to be utterly inimical to the interests of the gospel turns out to be in the highest and best interests of the gospel. The diminishing of the Jew has meant the salvation of the Gentiles. This is how God works and it is marvellous.

So I come to my third deduction under this heading. I have hesitated a little bit about this but I am sure I am right. Extreme and violent rejection of the gospel may in a sense be a good sign. What do I mean? I mean this. 'God hath concluded them all in unbelief, that he might have mercy upon all'. You remember we interpreted that as meaning that God shuts them up. There are certain instances of persons and of groups of people who have first of all to be shut up in violent unbelief before their conversion takes place. I always feel that the Apostle Paul himself is the most notable instance of this. You read the beginning of the ninth chapter of the Book of the Acts of the Apostles and you see Saul of Tarsus setting out on a journey from Jerusalem to Damascus 'breathing out threatenings and slaughter'. Violent! That was the prelude to what happened a few hours later when he suddenly saw the light from heaven and the fact of Jesus Christ, and was turned into the Apostle Paul. That is God's way of acting.

So I end on this note – the comfort which we must draw from all this personally is that no case is hopeless. Now that is to me the most wonderful thing of all. Here is the argument you see. No case appears to be as hopeless as that of the nation of the Jews. They were looking forward to their Messiah. He came and they were the very people who rejected Him. They hated the gospel, they rejected it, they persecuted His followers. Nothing seemed so hopeless as the case of the Jews, and they have persisted more or less like that. But you see you must not say they are hopeless. Why? Well, 'God is able to graft them in again'. And He is going to do it because 'they are beloved for the fathers' sakes'. No case is hopeless. The fact that a man like Saul of Tarsus was ever converted means that no one is ever hopeless. You may say, 'But look at him; look at the attitude; the thing is impossible. It is impossible', you say, 'that that man can become a Christian'. It is not.

Now of course, if you believe that a man determines himself whether he becomes a Christian and that it is his own great brain and understanding and goodness that makes him a Christian you cannot say this sort of thing. You have then got to say about certain people that they are absolutely hopeless. But if you agree with the Apostle Paul in the statement he made in the sixteenth verse of the first chapter of this great Epistle, 'I am not ashamed of the gospel of Christ: for it is the power of God unto salvation to every one that believeth; to the Jew first, and also to the Greek', having studied this chapter, you must come to the conclusion that no case is hopeless. I am probably speaking now to people who have got some loved one and dear one who is not a Christian and you have been praying for this loved one for many years, but he or she seems to be getting further away from it instead of nearer to it, and the devil is telling you to give up, stop praying, there is no point; he or she is absolutely hopeless. My friend, give the answer of Romans 11. Nothing is impossible with God. 'He is able to graft them in again'. 'He concludes all in unbelief, in order that he might have mercy upon all'. There is no such thing as a hopeless case.

This to me is one of the most thrilling and amazing things about the Christian faith and particularly about the work of a preacher or of a minister. People come and tell me about those they are interested in and how utterly and completely and finally hopeless they seem to be. I always reply – and this is why – There is no such thing as a hopeless case where God is concerned. It takes the power of God to save anybody, and therefore the power of God can save anybody. Thank God there is no such thing as a hopeless case. The power of God is a final answer to all such pessimism and hopelessness.

And this is a comfort not only with respect to individuals but it is equally a comfort with respect to the church as a whole, the church at large. We are living in probably one of the most evil periods in the long history of the Christian church. Look at the world and its attitude to Christianity, look at the power of unbelief, look at the organization behind everything that is opposed to God and His Christ. If you look at the present position merely with the eyes of man and human reason and understanding you would be bound to come to the conclusion that the Christian church is finished. People are always pointing that out to me, and when I have a Sunday holiday, as I had recently, and I go to some simple service in other parts of the country – in the country and the small towns – I can see exactly what they mean. You look at the little congregations and they are all middle-aged or old people, very few young people if any at all; and you say, Well, in another twenty years the whole thing will be finished. And that is how many people reason and argue and they get excited and they propose to do this, that and the other. And they have been doing that for years but they do not make any difference at all, things go on from bad to worse.

My dear friends, there is only one answer to all that and it is this:

that God's purpose is sure and nothing can stop it. But it is, you see, a part of His method to allow things to go to the very limit in favour of the enemy and the adversary. And then when everybody says, 'It's all up, it is finished', God arises and His enemies are scattered, and the church experiences a new period of revival. That is how revivals have always come, and the reason is quite obvious. If they came in any other way, some of us would be claiming that we had produced it, that something we were doing had led to the revival. God always sees to it that nobody can ever claim it. He does it in His own way and He allows things, He shuts us up in unbelief until the whole thing seems hopeless, then suddenly He appears. You remember the notable instance of that in the twelfth chapter of the Book of the Acts of the Apostles. King Herod raised his hand against James the Apostle and put him to death for no reason at all, and then arrested Peter and threw him into prison and appointed four quaternions of soldiers to look after him; and there he was, chained to a soldier on each side and he was to be put to death the next morning. The church had been praying from the moment of his imprisonment but nothing happened. They went on praying, and now it is only a matter of hours before Peter was going to be killed as James was and everybody probably was beginning to feel hopeless. But suddenly a light shone in the prison, an angel appeared and touched Peter on the side, had to wake him up even, and his chains fell off him and the door opened, and the keepers seemed to be asleep, and a mighty gate shutting up the whole prison from the city opened on its own hinges. And Peter could not believe it himself, he thought he was seeing a vision. But he was actually all there and walking on his own feet, and found himself at the house of John Mark, and there that girl Rhoda could not believe it; and when she went in and told the very praying church that Peter was knocking at the gate, they said, 'You are mad'. But it had happened, God had done it. But He had let it continue until the very last moment, as it were. And that chapter ends in a most magnificent manner. This Herod, who thought he was so powerful, when certain people who lived nearby and were dependent on him came to him and did their obeisance, made a great oration to them, and they said, 'This is the voice of a god and not of a man'. Here he is, almost turning himself into god. God allows all this; He allows this man to inflate himself almost to the heavens, but the next thing you read about him is this: 'And immediately the angel of the Lord smote him . . . and he was eaten of worms, and gave up the ghost'. What is the next word? It is this. 'But the word of God grew and multiplied'.

Now these are but illustrations of the philosophy of history outlined in the eleventh chapter of Paul's Epistle to the Romans. There is no such thing as hopelessness. This is how God has always acted. Men have frequently predicted the end of the church and prepared their funeral orations for it. God allows it all, and then when they think they have got everything, God arises. He blows and they vanish, they have gone. And the Christian church goes on to another period of mighty revival, reawakening, evangelism, success and spread. Whatever the appearances today, I say, do not look at them. Look at this great scheme, this plan, this purpose, and realize that God is over all, He can never fail, His purposes are forever sure and will certainly be brought to pass.

Yes, the Jews as a people are going to be brought into the Christian church, and it is such an incredible thing that when it happens, we will all feel that it is exactly like 'life from the dead'. May that day soon dawn.

# *Twenty-eight*

*

*O the depth of the riches both of the wisdom and knowledge of God! how unsearchable are his judgments, and his ways past finding out! For who hath known the mind of the Lord? or who hath been his counsellor? or who hath first given to him, and it shall be recompensed unto him again? For of him, and through him, and to him, are all things: to whom be glory for ever. Amen.*
Romans 11:33–36

We come now to this great doxology at the end of this eleventh chapter of the Epistle to the Romans. It is beyond any question one of the most glorious, wonderful and exalted statements which is to be found anywhere in the Bible and I could give you many illustrations from the writings of learned and saintly men of God to support that view. They have vied with one another in giving expression to their feelings and thoughts as they have studied these verses. Henry Alford, the well-known Anglican commentator of the nineteenth century, seems to me to put it better than anybody else. He refers to this as 'the sublimest apostrophe existing even in the pages of inspiration itself'. I am in entire agreement with that statement.

A number of questions face us at once as we read this great statement. The first one obviously must be this: What led to it? What made the Apostle utter this sublime apostrophe?

There has been a good deal of discussion amongst learned commentators as to one of two answers to this question and I suggest to you that both of them are right, so that we do not have to be pressed to one or the other. The first answer is that it was the immediately preceding context which led to the doxology. Obviously, that is something which is to be taken for granted unless there is some very good reason for not doing so. I have no doubt at all that it was what the Apostle had just said about God's great purpose with regard to the Jews as a nation, about God having concluded Jew and Gentile in unbelief that He might have mercy upon all, that prompted him to express amazement and astonishment. This explanation provides a test of any exposition of the preceding verses because if it does not lead up to the doxology there must be a defect in it.

This then is the first reason for this doxology. But I am also in entire agreement with those who say that what the Apostle is doing here is to give expression to his thoughts and feelings as he contemplates everything that he has been saying in this Epistle. This is certainly the case because in verse 32 he really seems to come back to the point from which he originally set out, and that is the proof that he is winding up his great doctrinal exposition. Where did he set out? Well, he set out in the sixteenth verse of the first chapter. You remember how he puts it. He says, 'I am ready to preach the gospel to you that are at Rome also'. Why? Here is his answer: 'I am not ashamed of the gospel of Christ: for it is the power of God unto salvation to every one that believeth; to the Jew first, and also to the Greek'. He tells us at the outset that he is going to expound this great gospel which is God's way of salvation to every man who believes, whether he is Jew, whether he is Greek. Now that is the theme, and you see in the thirty-second verse he has come back to that, 'For God hath concluded them all in unbelief, that he might have mercy upon all' – Jew and Greek, Jew and Gentile. So that there is no question that he is here bringing to a conclusion and a climax what he originally set out to do.

He has kept reiterating this and it is very important that we should notice it. In the ninth verse of the third chapter he says, 'What then? are we better than they? No, in no wise: for we have before proved both Jews and Gentiles, that they are all under sin'. He says it again in chapter 3 verses 22 and 23. He wants them to know at the beginning that this is his great theme. 'Even the righteousness of God which is by faith of Jesus Christ unto all and upon all them that believe: for there is no difference', that is between Jews and Gentiles, 'For all have sinned, and come short of the glory of God'. It appears again in verses 29 and 30 of the same chapter: 'Is he the God of the Jews only? is he not also of the Gentiles? Yes, of the Gentiles also: seeing it is one God, which shall justify the circumcision by faith, and uncircumcision through faith'.

That has been the teaching he has been setting out to demonstrate. Having done so and reflecting on the great thing which God has done, there is nothing left for him to do but to worship and praise God.

The next thing therefore that concerns us is this: How do we approach this doxology? This is a very important question. I think there are two main dangers at this point. One danger is just to regard it as a piece of magnificent writing, as a masterpiece of eloquence, and to say that it is so wonderful and so amazing that you must not dream of analysing it.

There are people who always take that attitude with regard to any piece of Scripture such as this. They just like reading it or repeating it, but they say you must not try to analyse it. To do so is like trying to dissect a rose, when you have done so you have nothing left. In pulling off the petals you have destroyed the rose.

There are people, then, who approach every great passage of Scripture in that kind of way. They are particularly liable to do this with a book like the Psalms which many use in a purely psychological manner. They say it gives them great comfort just to recite, 'The Lord's my Shepherd, I'll not want'. They are not interested to know what exactly that means but the words come to them as a kind of incantation and it soothes their troubled spirits and it helps them to sleep at night and to take a happier view of life. That is the first danger.

But secondly, there is the danger of doing the very thing against which that first one warns us, and to come to a passage like this with some kind of pedestrian outlook, only being interested in the words and their exact meaning. The result of that is like the dissection of a rose.

But surely we are not driven to a choice between those two approaches. I want to suggest to you that if we listen to the great Apostle we shall do both those things, and that seems to me to be the only right and true thing to do with all such great statements in the whole of the Scripture. We must take the whole, but we must also take the parts, and I would argue that you cannot really appreciate the whole unless you understand the parts. You do not put these things as opposites, you take them together. What the Apostle does himself is to give details in his statement. He does not just stand back and say, 'For of him, and through him, and to him, are all things: to whom be glory for ever'. In addition to that general statement, he goes into details. He speaks of 'The depth of the riches, . . . wisdom, . . . knowledge of God, . . . [his] judgments, . . . and ways'.

Indeed, I am prepared to go as far as saying that none of us will appreciate the glory of this doxology unless we understand these particular statements that the Apostle makes. An example of the wrong approach is found in a popular modern writer, Professor William Barclay of Glasgow. This is how he puts it, and I am suggesting that this just means that he has entirely misunderstood what the Apostle is saying. He says, 'Paul never wrote a more characteristic passage than this; here theology turns to poetry'. (I am going to show you that it does not.) 'Here', he says, 'the seeking of the mind turns to the adoration of the heart'. Now that sounds very wonderful, does it not? But do you see the fallacy? He says that before this Paul has been seeking with his mind but now stops doing that and he just allows his heart to speak. There is a contrast between the heart and the mind. I am going to try to show you that what kindles the Apostle's heart is his mind. It is the understanding that moves his heart. You must not put mind and heart in contrast when you are dealing with Scripture. But let us go on. Barclay says, 'In the end all must pass out in a mystery that man cannot now understand, but it is a mystery at whose heart is love. If a man can say that all things come from God, that all things have their being through God, and that all things end in God, what more is left to say? There is a certain paradox in the human situation. God gave man a mind and it is man's duty to use that mind, to think to the very limits of human thought. But it is also true that there are times when that mind can only go so far, and when that limit is reached all that is left is to accept and adore. How could I praise if such as I might understand?' Now listen: 'Paul has battled with a heart-breaking problem with every resource which his great mind possessed'. You see the picture – that in the previous portions Paul has been battling with a problem with his great mind. 'He does not say that he has solved it, as one might neatly solve a geometrical problem, but he does say that having done his best he is content to leave it to the love and power of God. At many times in life there is nothing left to do but to say, "I have thought and I cannot see the reason and the way. I cannot grasp Thy mind but with my whole heart I trust Thy love. Thy will be done"'.

Now you see the picture, that in the previous section the Apostle has been trying to understand this problem, he has used his great mind to its uttermost limit but he cannot solve it. So he says, 'Very well, I give up; I know that God is love, I leave it in His hands'. In other words, there is a contrast here between what the Apostle has been struggling with and his giving up the struggle and just worshipping God. Like a man who tries to understand the ways of

God in ordinary life and cannot do so, he just submits and says 'Thy will be done'. 'Though I do not understand I know Thy name is love'. In other words there is a break; you stop thinking, you stop understanding, and you allow your heart to speak in the language of devotion.

Now what I am trying to say is that that seems to me to be the exact opposite of what is happening here. I am putting it to you rather that this doxology, this sublime apostrophe, is the direct and the immediate outcome of everything that Paul has been saying. He is not saying, 'Ah well, we have to give up, we cannot go any further. We cannot understand and follow with our mind, but let us worship God'. It is not that. Paul says, 'Let us worship God because of all that we have been saying.'

In other words, the Apostle Paul was not struggling with a problem. This man is the inspired Apostle. You see, these other people do not believe in inspiration; that is their whole trouble. They think of the Apostle Paul as if he were a man like themselves, struggling with problems. He was not. He has told us in verse 25 that he is letting us into the secret of a 'mystery' which has been revealed to him. These are not Paul's thoughts. We are not dealing here with Paul's reasoning and understanding. Paul is writing Scripture – as Peter said of him [*2 Pet.* 3:15, 16]. In Romans 11 Paul records a revelation of God's great plan and purpose of redemption. He has been unfolding it, he has been expounding it, and having done so he is amazed at it himself and he feels there is only one thing to do, and that is to praise God with the whole of his being.

In other words, there is nothing that we must condemn more strongly than to put the heart and the mind against one another. The Apostle is always moved in all his Epistles. Notice this as you read his epistles and also the rest of the New Testament. It is the contemplation of the truth with the mind that always moves the heart. There is none of this dichotomy, there is none of this rejecting of the mind in order to speak the language of the heart. Romans 6:17 shows that it was doctrine which came to the mind and captivated it, moved the heart and changed the will that was responsible for people being saved.

That is the invariable order of the Scripture. Mind, heart, will. And we must always be very careful and very wary of any teaching that by-passes the mind and goes to the will, or puts these things in antithesis, or as if they were different. The glory of the Christian salvation is that it deals with the whole man. The enlightened mind sees the glory of the truth and that moves the heart to worship and praise and adoration. This is what we are dealing with in this great doxology. The great Apostle stands back for a moment and looks at this wealth of revelation that he has been writing or dictating, and seeing it all he himself is once more carried away by its glory and immensity, by its splendour and wonder.

Now all this is of tremendous importance because it shows at once what view we take of the Apostle himself and of the Scripture itself, whether we regard it as divinely inspired or as just the thoughts and meditations of men. These things are important for that reason.

Let me now suggest a division of the contents of this great doxology. The first division is that the Apostle notes and celebrates the depth of God's riches, wisdom and knowledge which have led to this glorious salvation. The second division relates to the incomprehensible character of all of this. Thirdly, it is entirely independent of man. And lastly, it is nothing but a manifestation and an exhibition of the glory of God Who is to be adored because of who and what He is. There I suggest are the natural divisions of this great doxology.

We take up the first of these divisions which arise from the first part of verse 22: 'O the depths of the riches both of the wisdom and knowledge of God!' There is a slight preliminary difficulty over which the commentators are about equally divided. It relates to how the statement should be rendered. The Authorized Version translates it as if it read: 'O the depth of the riches of God's wisdom, and the depth of the riches of God's knowledge!' Another rendering, to which I incline, runs as follows: 'O the depth of the riches and the wisdom and the knowledge of God!' In this 'the depth' includes what he calls 'the riches of God', 'the wisdom of God', and 'the knowledge of God'. It is not 'the depth of the riches', because that is in a sense almost tautology, but it is 'the depth of the riches and the wisdom and the knowledge of God'.

Why do I prefer that? For this reason. This term 'riches' is generally associated with the idea of 'grace' and of 'mercy'. So I am arguing that 'riches' here stands for that and brings out that vital element, so prominent in this Epistle, that vital element which this other view does not bring out quite as clearly. The great word that arrests us at once of course is this word 'depth'. 'O the depth' – the fathomless character! That is what he means. One of these commentators – I think it was Godet the nineteenth-century Swiss commentator –

compares the Apostle here to a man standing on a great mountain-peak in Switzerland and looking down into some great abyss, and then looking to some great old mountain-peak stretching up on the other side. And there it is – from the almost illimitable depth to an illimitable height. Depth! The only way to think of everything that God does.

This is so typical and characteristic of the Apostle's language. He finds that, whenever he stands back and looks at what God has done, language fails him, he is forced to use superlatives, and then he still feels he has not said it. He talks about 'the exceeding riches of God's grace'; he talks about 'the unsearchable riches of Christ'. But then there is his tremendous statement, very similar to the one we are looking at here, in the First Epistle to the Corinthians and in the second chapter. Dealing with the mystery and the marvel of the gospel and contrasting this 'wisdom of God' in salvation with the wisdom of the world, he is led to say: 'But as it is written, Eye hath not seen, nor ear heard, neither have entered into the heart of man, the things which God hath prepared for them that love him'. But God hath revealed them unto us by his Spirit: for the Spirit searcheth all things, yea, the deep things of God' [*1 Cor.* 2:9–10]. That is it! It is the same idea. 'O the depth!' 'The deep things of God!' These 'infinities and immensities', as Thomas Carlyle once called them. That is what we are dealing with, and the Apostle was never tired of using these great expressions. We have it in Ephesians 3:18 where he is praying for those Ephesians 'that they may be able to comprehend with all saints what is the breadth, and length, and depth, and height' of the love of Christ. 'Depth' in Romans 11 includes every dimension – breadth, and length, and depth, and height. It is this vast ocean of the deep things of God.

Looking back across all that he has been saying in this Epistle and in particular the mystery of God's purpose with regard to the nation of Israel, the Apostle says, O! what immensity, what profundity! What a glorious thing this is, this depth of God and all that is true of Him! What a privilege it is to be entering into this uncharted ocean, this never-ebbing sea, this eternity of God! We are having the privilege of entering into these 'deep things of God'. They have been revealed to us and recorded for us – the ultimate mysteries and all the everlasting glories.

What great shame attaches to modern Christians! Any Christian who is ashamed of the fact that he is a Christian is just saying that he does not know anything about this depth. Look at the men of the world even at their best; look at the sophisticated people who talk with disdain about Christianity and are sorry for people who still believe it. What do they really know? What are they dealing with? Think of the people who spend their Sundays reading the learned articles in the supplements to the Sunday papers which they think are very profound. Borrowing books from libraries and so on! What are they reading about ultimately? Christians have these 'deep things of God' here before us in this Epistle. Think of it as a sea, and you go on swimming, and you know you are never going to cross it, but you are 'in the deep', you are in 'the deep things of God'.

What are these depths? They are in God's great purpose of salvation, His way of restoring to sinful man that original righteousness which he has lost as the result of his rebellion and his folly in listening to the devil. What is it? Well, he says at the very beginning, it is 'a righteousness from God'. Now the law talked about righteousness, and a way of righteousness but he says it is not that. It is 'the gospel of Christ'. Why? 'It is the power of God unto salvation to every one that believeth, to the Jew first and also to the Greek. For therein is the righteousness from God revealed from faith to faith: as it is written, The just shall live by faith'. Here is the secret: This is God's way of making men righteous; that is the message.

You can compare this Epistle if you like to a great mountain-range, for example the Alps. All the mountains are elevated and lofty but there are certain peaks that just stand out. I will pick out some. I believe the Apostle was doing so in his mind when he uttered this great apostrophe. There is the key thing – 'a righteousness from God'. Well, how does it come?

That is what he introduces in the third chapter from verse 21 onwards, and it is a most important section. Do not overlook the argument of chapter 1:18 to the end of chapter 3:20. That is so important because it puts the Jews and Gentiles into the right position which is, 'The whole world lieth guilty before God'. But suddenly he turns at the beginning of 21 and says, 'BUT NOW the righteousness of God without (apart from) the law is manifested, being witnessed by the law and the prophets; even the righteousness of God which is by faith in Jesus Christ'. This is God's way of saving and it is the most amazing thing in all history. There is nothing comparable to it. God's way of giving righteousness to man through His own Son, and especially through His death on the cross; his blood shed as a 'propitiation'. That is God's way.

And then of course what follows from that is that a man is justified by faith only. This is the great single theme, in a sense, of this Epistle. It is what produced the Protestant Reformation. It was through studying this Epistle that Luther came across this truth, was led to it by the guidance and illumination of the Spirit – Justification by faith only! This amazing thing, this staggering thing! 'By the law shall no flesh be justified in his sight: for by the law is the knowledge of sin'. 'Being justified freely by his grace'. The great and glorious doctrine of justification by faith only.

But it does not stop at that; having worked out that he comes in chapter 5 to what is, in many ways, the centre of the whole letter – our incorporation in Christ! What a tremendous review of the whole of history. Man created; but Adam, the man, the representative, sinning, bringing death upon himself and upon the whole of his progeny; 'so death came upon all men'. What is the way of deliverance? There is only one – there must be a new Adam, a new man. There is, he is Christ. 'As we were in Adam, even so we are in Christ'. That glorious contrast is worked out there.

And then he goes on to work out how this new people is being prepared for its inheritance in the glory. In other words, sanctification by the Spirit of God. He starts with that in the seventh chapter, particularly in verse 6: 'We are now delivered from the law, that being dead wherein we were held; that we should serve in newness of spirit, and not in the oldness of the letter'. And then the triumphant cry of chapter 8 verse 2: 'For the law of the Spirit of life in Christ Jesus hath made me free from the law of sin and death'. That is how sanctification is possible. That is it; life in the Spirit.

And then comes the tremendous principle of adoption: 'As many as are led (in this way) by the Spirit of God, they are the sons of God'. This leads in turn to this tremendous doctrine of our final glorification which includes even the redemption of our body. Finally the certainty of all this is driven home in a great hymn of praise at the end of chapter 8. 'I am persuaded, that neither death, nor life, nor angels, nor principalities, nor powers, nor things present, nor things to come, nor height, nor depth, nor any other creature shall be able to separate us from the love of God, which is in Christ Jesus our Lord'. The absolute certainty of this to all the elect – 'the fulness of the Gentiles' and 'All Israel' – is argued out in chapters 9–11, and the work will be complete.

I do trust that, by now, we all have very clearly in our minds this principle that runs through the whole Epistle. It is like constructing a great building, or a great symphony. He lets you know what he is going to do, and when he has finally done it he says, 'There it is. This is the thing I said I was going to do, I have done it.' It is God's way of salvation to every one that believeth, to the Jew first, also to the Greek. 'He hath concluded all in unbelief, that he might have mercy upon all'. So there is nothing left but the final doxology.

What has made this immense salvation possible? Paul uses three terms; there are three things which have made all this possible. What are they?

The first is God's riches which I suggested just now stands for God's grace. That is the source of everything. What is grace? It is 'undeserved favour'. Grace means God's kindness to people who deserve nothing but punishment, retribution, and everlasting woe and misery. So what has led to it all is 'the grace of God'. He keeps on saying this and does so supremely in chapter 5 where he says, 'Where sin abounded, grace did much more abound' and in chapter 10 where God is described as 'rich' in mercy to Jew or Gentile who call on Him.

This is one of the Apostle's great themes. He can never really refer to the gospel without mentioning grace. The opening three chapters of his letter to the Ephesians are a case in point. The riches of grace and mercy are described in superlatives. The riches are unsearchable. That is the source of it all. Were it not for that there would be nothing to say; man would just have festered in sin and iniquity and vileness into nothing.

But the second is 'wisdom'. What does wisdom mean? It means the ability to deal with a situation. A man may have great knowledge but if he lacks wisdom his knowledge is going to be no use to him. I remember a man once who did very well in his medical examinations, he used to learn his textbooks by heart, but when you put a patient in front of him he could not do anything, he could not apply his knowledge. In other words, he lacked wisdom.

Now the grace of God and the compassion of God created a desire within Him to do something for sinful man but the question is: How could it be done? The answer is, God's 'depth of wisdom'. It is only the wisdom of God that is adequate to devise a plan and a scheme that can save man and restore him to this righteousness; and not only devise it but carry it out. This is one of the most amazing things of all.

Paul keeps on saying this. 'We preach Christ crucified, unto the Jews a stumblingblock, and unto the Greeks foolishness; but unto them which are called, both Jews and Greeks, Christ the power of God, and the wisdom of God'. This is where you see God's wisdom in devising this plan of salvation. The first man fell. It was no use making another perfect man; he would be no better than the first. The law has been given a trial, it cannot do it; it is 'weak through the flesh'. How can man be saved? God's wisdom sees the way. I will send My Son. He will be born as a man; He will take human nature to Himself. The incarnation! – and all that followed, including the death, burial, resurrection. This is God's wisdom in a mystery.

Now it is not surprising the Apostle celebrates this and glories in it, and worships God on its account. It is 'not the wisdom of this world, nor of the princes of this world, that come to nought'. It is God's wisdom. Hidden wisdom! It is a mystery! And God has so contrived it, that it is sufficient to save us all because it does not depend upon us. It depends upon Christ and His saving work and His power. Therefore there is hope for anybody, for everybody. And the result is, as Paul told those Ephesians in chapter 3 verse 10, 'To the intent that now unto the principalities and powers in the heavenly places might be known by (or through) the church the manifold wisdom of God'. Did you know this: that the good angels, the perfect angels are going to be instructed in the manifold wisdom of God through the church, through what God has done in Christ through people like you and me? They are in His Presence, they have always been there and they are obedient and they worship; but it is as they see what has happened in the church that they begin to understand the wisdom of God, 'the manifold wisdom of God'.

Very well, what has produced this great thing is the desire of God according to the riches of His grace, leading to the wisdom which devises the plan of salvation.

And then the knowledge. 'O the depth of the knowledge of God!' What is this? Well, this is most wonderful. God is omniscient, God knows everything, there is nothing that He does not know. Thank God for this. Why? Well, you see, it means that God has been able to produce a plan of salvation which caters for every eventuality and every possibility. There is nothing that God has not foreseen because there is nothing that is unknown to God. There is a very powerful adversary against God, and against God's people; he is the devil – brilliant, subtle, powerful, knowledgeable; and he is doing everything he can to frustrate God's plan and purpose and to bring it to nothing.

So my security then is this – that God knows everything! 'The depth of God's knowledge!' There is nothing that He does not know. He is omniscient. Everything is before Him always at all times; nothing is outside His knowledge. There is no trick the devil can play but that God already knows all about it. There is nothing that he can conjure up; there is no invention that he can produce. There is nothing that can ever be done by the devil or hell or anything else that can in any way take God by surprise. When God planned He knew it all and He has prepared for it all. And the result is, because of God's perfect knowledge, His plan is complete in every single respect. Nothing can ever go wrong with it, and nothing can ever prevent its perfect execution in every one of us who is 'the called of God'.

It was something like that, I venture in humility to suggest to you, that the Apostle felt as he contemplated this great and glorious plan in general. There is only one thing to say as you look at the range and the peaks – 'O the depth of the riches both of the wisdom and knowledge of God', ever to have produced such a glorious, such a perfect plan!

# *Twenty-nine*

*

*O the depth of the riches both of the wisdom and knowledge of God! how unsearchable are his judgments, and his ways past finding out! For who hath known the mind of the Lord? or who hath been his counsellor? or who hath first given to him, and it shall be recompensed unto him again? For of him, and through him, and to him, are all things: to whom be glory for ever. Amen.*
Romans 11:33–36

I have suggested that you can divide this doxology into four main sections and we have considered the first which emphasizes the depth of it all. The second section, to which we must now address ourselves, is one that follows, of course, of necessity from what we have just been saying. It is the utter incomprehensibility of God's great plan and purpose of salvation. The Apostle puts that in these great words: 'How unsearchable are his judgments, and his ways past finding out'.

Now that is another way of representing this category of depth and of profundity, but he elaborates it by the addition of two words. The first word is the word 'unsearchable', which means 'inscrutable'; all one's investigation and examination will never bring one to a full understanding of it; it is beyond us. Or if you like you can say that it is, in terms of the idea of depth, 'unfathomable'. You can go down as far as your measures will take you but still you have not plumbed the depth. As the same Apostle puts it in writing to the Ephesians in chapter 3, it 'passeth knowledge'. He is very fond of saying that. You remember, 'the peace of God, which passeth all understanding', and the love of God in Christ, again, 'passeth knowledge'. Well, it is the same idea that we have in this word 'unsearchable'.

But there is the other interesting word – 'past finding out'. It seems, according to the authorities, that this is a word which carries the original meaning of 'tracing out' or 'tracking down'. You know how huntsmen in ancient days used to track down an animal. There would be the imprint of the foot of the animal and they would follow that and doing so carefully and perseveringly they would find their prey eventually.

Now that is the word that the Apostle uses, and what he says is that God's ways are untraceable or untrackable. You think you are on the scent and the track and think you have only to keep going and you will arrive at the goal. You never will. You will end your life, says the Apostle, still on the track that goes on into eternity, into infinity.

What I want to put to you now is a most vital statement with regard to the gospel, one that is all-important at the present time. It seems to me to point to what is dividing the Christian church at the present time and which will do so more and more in the future. It is also the dividing line between all who are truly Evangelical and those who are not, and that is the only ultimate division. There are many other divisions but they seem to me to be comparatively unimportant. The Christian church as you know is divided up into many groups and denominations and they differ about various matters of ceremonial and have different points of view about this and that. I am saying that, as I see things at any rate, and as I believe the Bible teaches, as I am going to try to show you, there is only one vital real division; it is between those who hold what I am describing as the Evangelical view of salvation and those who do not; and I think all the other issues can be subsumed under these two main headings.

Now the point I am establishing is that in this particular statement we are given the great divide. Our attitude towards this statement of the great Apostle determines which of the two sides we are on.

Let me illustrate what I mean. There are disagreements amongst people with regard to sacraments. Take baptism for instance. Whom do you baptize? When do you baptize? There are differences with regard to the Lord's Supper and differences on prophetic matters and so on. And not only that; there are certain divisions about particular statements that men have made with regard to many other aspects of the Christian faith. Now what matters above everything else before you come to such details is your total view of the gospel of salvation, and that is the thing which is held before us here because, you see, the Apostle makes this statement. He says not only, 'O the depth of the riches both of the wisdom and knowledge of God', but he goes further, he says, 'how unsearchable are his judgments, and his ways past finding out'.

I want to try to show you that this statement of the Apostle's which is characteristic not only of the New Testament but also of the Old Testament as well, is precisely the statement that is not only being questioned but actually being denied at the present time. To me there is nothing more important than this. What is at issue at the moment is, the whole nature of Christian salvation.

Now let me show you what I mean. Let me quote some words of a religious dignitary from a leading national newspaper. Here are his words:

'The secular world is, for all its estrangement from religion, still God's world. It is for the Christian teacher to be a person of sympathy and sensitivity; not to talk too much, but to listen and learn. The way of approach from the Christian to the secular world is the way not of proclamation but of dialogue.'

Now there is a perfectly clear statement. We agree, of course, entirely with the statement that the teacher should be 'a person of sympathy and sensitivity'. That is quite all right. That carries universal assent. But what about the rejection of proclamation in favour of dialogue? That is the popular attitude at the present time and it has been for some years. It has been given wide publicity. It is the prevailing teaching in the Christian church.

It means that our starting point must always be 'the man of today', and our whole approach must be governed by modern knowledge. What may have been all right in the past, we are told, is no longer acceptable. Because we are in this new, scientific age, there are certain things that are quite impossible for modern man to believe, so he must not be approached along those lines. He does not believe in the miraculous and the supernatural and so on. Very well, it is no use speaking to him in such terms, he will not have it. In other words, you start by saying, What about modern man? What is his position? And the whole of your attitude and approach, your message and method must be governed and controlled by that.

Now this is most serious because it is the exact opposite of what the great Apostle says, which is typical of the whole of the teaching of the Bible. Nothing can be more serious than this. Here is something that is bound to make an absolute division.

Therefore let me put it like this to you. Why do I say that this modern teaching is a denial of the New Testament teaching? Well, I say so for these reasons. It is first of all a flat contradiction of the practice of the apostles which we read of in the Book of the Acts of the Apostles. There you have this great standard and pattern as to how

Christian teachers and preachers must always conduct themselves, and you find it immediately on the day of Pentecost in Jerusalem when Peter gets up with the eleven and lifts up his voice and says, 'Ye men of Judaea, and all that dwell at Jerusalem, be this known unto you, and hearken to my words.' He does not suggest a dialogue, a discussion. He is going to preach, he is going to address them, and he calls upon them to listen to his words.

But there is a still more striking illustration of this in the seventeenth chapter of the Book of the Acts of the Apostles where we find the great Apostle Paul in no less a place than the great and famous city of Athens. Here is the home of the philosophers, the men who spent their time in discussing and in arguing and debating. Dialogue! That has always been the great word of the philosophers. But what did the Apostle do? Well listen: 'Paul stood in the midst of Mars' hill, and said, Ye men of Athens, I perceive that in all things ye are too superstitious. For as I passed by, and beheld your devotions, I found an altar with this inscription, TO THE UNKNOWN GOD'. Then: 'Whom therefore ye ignorantly worship, him declare I' – proclaim I – 'unto you.' Now we are told we must not proclaim. But the Apostle Paul proclaimed, he 'declared'. He said, You are ignorant, you do not know what you are doing. I have come to proclaim to you this God Whom you are fumbling after and Whom you ignorantly worship. Listen, says the great Apostle.

And again to make it abundantly clear that this was his universal practice, as it was of all the other apostles, the Apostle reminds the Corinthians: 'And I, brethren, when I came to you, came not with excellency of speech or of wisdom, declaring unto you the testimony of God' [*1 Cor*. 2:1]. And again in the fifteenth chapter: 'Moreover, brethren, I declare unto you the gospel which I preached unto you, and which ye also received, and wherein ye stand' [*1 Cor.* 15:1].

What you get, in other words, in the whole of the New Testament is that apostolic practice consisted of proclamation. And, of course, that has been precisely the same in the great periods of reformation and revival ever since in the long history of the Christian church.

But secondly, this modern thinking not only contradicts the practice of the apostles, it contradicts their plain, direct teaching concerning this very matter. What did Paul say to the Corinthians about his practice in the opening chapter of his first Epistle? He said that Jews wanted a sign and Gentiles wanted wisdom. That meant they wanted a discussion. Did he comply? No, he said, 'But we preach Christ crucified to the Jews a stumblingblock and to the Greeks, foolishness'. And then he goes on to say, and this is absolutely crucial in this matter – 'Ye see your calling, brethren, how that not many wise men after the flesh, not many mighty, not many noble are called: But God hath chosen the foolish things . . . That no flesh should glory in his presence. But of him are ye in Christ Jesus, who of God is made unto us wisdom, and righteousness, and sanctification, and redemption: That according as it is written, He that glorieth, let him glory in the Lord' [*1 Cor.* 1:22–31].

Now the whole purpose of that statement is to say that man as he is by nature is incapable of understanding God's truth and it therefore has to be declared to him. And then he says exactly the same thing in the second chapter in verse 14: 'The natural man receiveth not the things of the Spirit of God: for they are foolishness unto him: neither can he know them, because they are spiritually discerned'. Now the Apostle wrote this whole section of the First Epistle to the Corinthians to say that you must not bring in this philosophy and dialogue, this listening to the other side. He says the thing is impossible because of the condition of the natural man. There is only one thing to do, and that is to proclaim to him the message that has been delivered unto you.

But not only does that idea contradict the practice and the direct teaching of the Scripture on this point, it also contradicts the indirect teaching of the Scripture too. What do I mean? Well, I mean this: here is typical characteristic New Testament teaching – Matthew 18:3: 'Verily, verily, I say unto you, Except ye be converted and become as little children, ye shall in no wise enter into the kingdom of heaven.' Could anything be plainer? You have got to be converted, says our Lord, you have got to become as little children; it is the only way of entering into this kingdom.

Then this is put yet more plainly in the famous incident of the interview between our blessed Lord and Nicodemus, recorded in the third chapter of John's Gospel. Here is this man going to our Lord by night and praising Him and saying that He is 'a teacher come from God: for no man can do these miracles that thou doest, except God be with him'. Our Lord interrupts him and says: 'Verily, verily, I say unto thee, except a man be born again, he cannot see the kingdom of God'. Can anything be more explicit than that? Here comes this great ruler, you see, and he approaches our Lord more or less as an equal. He praises Him of course because he admits that our Lord has worked miracles that he has not been able to do, and that He is obviously 'a teacher come from God'. But he is somewhat perplexed so he wants to discuss this matter with our Lord. Our Lord rejects a discussion, He will not have it, He will not have a dialogue. He breaks across him and He says, 'Verily, verily, I say unto thee, Except a man be born again, he cannot see the kingdom of God'. Then Nicodemus puts his clever questionings but our Lord keeps on answering, 'Verily, verily I say unto thee, Except a man be born of water and of the Spirit, he cannot enter the kingdom of God. That which is born of the flesh is flesh; and that which is born of the Spirit is spirit. Marvel not that I said unto thee, Ye must be born again. The wind bloweth where it listeth, and thou hearest the sound thereof, but canst not tell whence it cometh, and whither it goeth: so is every one that is born of the Spirit' [*John* 3:5–8]. You see there is no discussion, there is no dialogue. Our Lord is just telling him, He says, As you are you are hopeless, you have got to be born again. And Nicodemus can only ask plaintively, 'How can these things be?' And the answer he receives is, 'Art thou a master of Israel, and knowest not these things? Verily, verily, I say unto thee, We speak that we do know, and testify that we have seen; and ye receive not our witness'.

You see, the thing is perfectly plain and clear. This is the doctrine of the absolute necessity of regeneration. Even a master and a teacher of Israel needs a new beginning, a new life. As he is it is hopeless. Paul puts it in other terms in 1 Corinthians 3 – that if anyone wanted to be wise, 'let him become a fool, that he may be made wise', which means that one has to become a fool to the world's eyes, for Christ's sake, dismissed by the learned and the philosophical, regarded as a fool. But no matter, it is the only way to get this knowledge.

Therefore, to say that when you approach the unbeliever you have a dialogue and a discussion, you listen to him and learn from him even, instead of proclaiming to him, is really a denial of the doctrine of the regeneration which is the plain teaching of the Scripture. The natural man must be 'born again' before he can possibly receive these things. He is that 'natural man who does not and cannot receive these things, because they are spiritually discerned'. Very well.

But furthermore, unregenerate man proves that the biblical teaching is right and that this modern teaching is wrong by his very attitude to the gospel when he hears it. What is that? Well, he does not understand it, he does not know what it is all about. He understands politics, he understands political sermons, he understands morality in a sense so he can understand moral and ethical appeals, and he approves of them and thinks that that is Christianity. But when he hears a doctrine such as is unfolded in the Epistle to the Romans he does not understand it, as Nicodemus did not, and thereby he proves the truth of what the Scripture teaches. The natural man constantly misunderstands God's way of salvation.

Now we have seen that at great length many times over in the Epistle to the Romans. Take the Jews; they completely misunderstood the purpose of the law. Men are still doing the same. They think they can make themselves Christians by keeping a law. That is to misunderstand the whole of God's way and plan of salvation. Man by his misunderstanding constantly reveals that he cannot receive it. And when you come to the other great doctrines that we have been considering together and how men argue against them and say, 'I cannot see this', they are really saying that what the Apostle says is true. 'How unsearchable are his judgments, and his ways past finding out!' The natural unregenerate man himself gives proof of the truth of the statement.

But still further, he does not merely fail to understand it, he goes further, he ridicules it. As the Apostle says there, 'The natural man receiveth not the things of the Spirit of God: for they are foolishness unto him'. And they are still foolishness unto him. The natural man ridicules this gospel. Listen to men and women speaking about 'the blood of Christ', and the sarcasm with which they do so. The way in which they ridicule a gospel that says that it is the death of our Lord upon the cross that in particular saves us and that without that we are lost. They rise up in fury against it. And likewise with the doctrine of regeneration and all these great doctrines that Paul has been unfolding to us in this Epistle to the Romans. So, you see, the natural man by his very objection to the gospel, and especially by his ridicule and contempt, is demonstrating what the Apostle says here, that God's judgments are unsearchable, and his ways past finding out!

But let me come to my fifth point, which is the conclusive argument in this matter it seems to me. It is that what the Apostle says is of necessity true. Why is this of necessity true? Well, for this reason, that these matters which we are considering together are not ultimately a matter of the intellect or of knowledge at all, but are entirely a matter and a question of man's relationship to God. All this modern popular teaching starts on the assumption that it is an intellectual matter; so you find out your modern man, what does he know, where he is, what does he believe, what views does he hold . . . Now then you have got to make contact, you have got to accommodate to that. It is purely a matter of understanding and reasoning it out together. Now the whole of the Bible says it is not that. What is it then? Well, it is a matter of man's relationship to God, not of grasping certain ideas or accepting a point of view or a teaching, but a man's total relationship to God. And the moment you put it like that you see that what Paul says must be right, for this reason. He says, 'How unsearchable are his judgments, and his ways past finding out!' Why must this be true? Well, because God is God, He is infinite and eternal in all His attributes and powers. He is from everlasting to everlasting, He is omniscient, He is omnipotent, He is 'Light, and in Him is no darkness at all'. God is absolute and perfect in every respect, and He is holy, and just, and righteous, and pure.

But man is finite, he is limited. There is a very definite limit to all our knowledge. Even at our best we are small, we are limited, how little we know. And the more that is being discovered, the more it reveals to us our ignorance and how little we really do know. Man is a very finite creature, he is a small creature. But unfortunately that is not the only thing that we have to say about him. He is a sinful creature, he is a perverted creature; he is a creature whose faculties have all been tarnished as a result of the Fall, and none of them is working perfectly. You get that brought out in statements like this: 'The fool hath said in his heart, There is no God'. It is not his mind that makes him say that, it is something deeper; it is the state of his *heart*. The Apostle puts it like this in this Epistle to the Romans in chapter 8 and verse 7; he says, 'The carnal mind is enmity against God: is not subject to the law of God, neither indeed can be' [*Rom.* 8:7]. Now that is the whole trouble. Becoming a Christian is not a question of understanding a certain philosophy but of the whole relationship of one's mind to God, and by nature man is at enmity against God, inveterately opposed to His law.

In addition to all that there is something which is even worse, and that is the power and the activity of the devil. That is what makes this same Apostle say in the Second Epistle to the Corinthians in the fourth chapter verses 3 and 4: 'If our gospel be hid' – and it is hid! The gospel is hid to the natural unregenerate man. The vast majority of the people in this country do not believe the gospel because it is hidden from them. 'If our gospel be hid, it is hid', he says, 'to them that are lost: in whom the god of this world hath blinded the minds of them that believe not, lest the light of the glorious gospel of Christ, who is the image of God, should shine unto them'.

Now that is the trouble with the modern man. It is that man, by nature, is sinful, has got a carnal mind, hates God, and the devil whom he unknowingly serves, has blinded the minds of them that believe not. It does not matter how clever or able he is. The devil has blinded his mind 'lest the light of the glorious gospel of Christ, who is the image of God, should shine unto them'. That, according to the Apostle and according to the whole of the scriptural teaching, is the one and only explanation as to why men and women do not believe. Therefore what have I to learn from such a man? What has a man who is blinded by the devil got to tell me about these matters? Why should I have a dialogue with him? No, no, I am sorry for him. The man is blinded, he is ignorant, he knows nothing. I have the knowledge which alone can help him. It is not mine, it has been given to me, it has been revealed to me, and it is my duty to tell him. I am doing him a disservice by letting him talk. He is not capable of expressing an opinion. He is in the dark, 'dead in trespasses and sins'. That is the whole of the scriptural teaching.

But, the modern teaching denies this utterly and absolutely, and this is the spectacle by which we are confronted, that the modern church is paying compliments to the unregenerate man and says, 'Now we must preach less to you, we have been speaking too much, let us sit down, you talk, I want to listen, I want to learn from you'. I do not hesitate to assert that that is a denial of Christ. Not only do I not learn from the natural unregenerate man, I do not learn from the Hindu or the Muslim, the Confucian or the Buddhist; they have nothing to tell me. The Bible, and the Bible alone, contains the knowledge and it is given by God. And it is our business to call upon the natural unregenerate man to be silent, to listen, to learn. We are to say to him, 'Hearken unto me'. 'Whom ye ignorantly worship, him declare I unto you'. The greatest need in the world tonight is the authoritative proclamation of this one and only gospel.

You see the importance of this statement? 'How unsearchable are his judgments, and his ways past finding out!' We must not be interested in what the unregenerate man has got to say. He knows nothing. Man at his best can never reach it. He cannot possibly understand it. Indeed the Apostle drives this home with great thoroughness in the next two verses. The Apostle says, 'Who hath known the mind of the Lord?' Where is the man who has understood and known the mind of the Lord? 'Or who hath been his counsellor?' Who can add anything to Him? Who can give Him any knowledge or information, can any one of His people? There is no one. And to suggest that the unregenerate man has any contribution to make is, as I am saying, a denial of the very heart and centre and foundation of this gospel of salvation.

But then let us look at what the great Apostle is saying positively. What he asserts, of course, is nothing but simple fact and it is proof positive of what I have been trying to say. Paul says: 'How unsearchable are his judgments!' The natural man cannot understand them. What are they? Well, they are His decisions, His thoughts, His plans. The Psalmist had already said it: 'Thy righteousness is like the great mountains; thy judgments are a great deep' [*Psa.* 36:6]. Even they had seen it, and they were only looking at it and seeing it afar off. Who can search this? It is impertinence, it is ignorance, it is arrogance to suggest that anybody can!

His judgments – what are they? Well, look at what He allows. How can a man understand God? Look at what God allows. He has allowed evil. You and I would never have allowed evil, would we? That is why we argue so much about it: 'Why has God allowed evil?' you ask. 'If God is God, and God is perfect, as you say, well then why did He ever allow evil to come in, why didn't He make this perfect world and leave it at that? Why did He ever allow it?' But He has done it, you see! You cannot understand it, can you? I cannot. And I am not fool enough to try to! I know that His judgments are 'unsearchable'. He decided to allow it. It is a standing mystery and we will only know the answer when we get to the glory.

And look at the devil. How did God ever allow the devil to come into being and to work as he has worked and to do what he did? Why did He ever allow him to go and tempt Adam and Eve? Why didn't He protect them against him? Those are the questions of the natural man. We do not ask them any more, do we? Of course not! We know that this is a great mystery. And look at the way that God has tolerated the manifestation of evil. Look at the world before the Flood and how God allowed it to develop and to fester. Why? I don't know! 'How unsearchable are his judgments!' He decided, it was His judgment. And look what He has tolerated and allowed since.

Oh, His judgments are unsearchable! Look at the whole plan of salvation! Who would ever have thought of it? In Jesus Christ, sending His own Son! By faith alone! You and I would never have planned a salvation like that, would we? We would have planned a salvation of good works, good behaviour, doing good deeds, and thereby putting yourself right with God and making yourself a Christian. God does the exact opposite. 'How unsearchable are his judgments, his decisions!' By faith alone!

Then the mighty doctrine of election. The whole world is not to be saved. There are the elect and the lost. Why? The answer of Paul is, 'How unsearchable are his judgments!' What amazes me is that He ever decided to save anybody; none of us deserve it. We were none of us righteous, 'no, not one', and if you feel like arguing, the Apostle has already answered you in chapter 9: 'Who art thou, O man, that repliest against God?' 'How unsearchable are his judgments!'

But then take another aspect of His judgments, look at the people He does choose! Fancy choosing the Jews! But they were the people He chose; they are His chosen people. 'How unsearchable are his judgments'! Fancy choosing Jacob rather than Esau! There was no comparison between them as nice fellows and decent men. Esau – an open air man, a huntsman, a man enjoying a free life; and the other, a schemer, staying at home, always at his mother's apron-strings. Jacob! Yet he is the one that God has loved and has chosen and not your fine fellow Esau. 'O how unsearchable are his judgments!'

Then you come to the New Testament, and the Apostle puts it all before us. God acts in a way that nobody can understand. 'Ye see your calling, brethren, how that not many wise men after the flesh, not many mighty, not many noble are called'. You would have thought, and I would have thought by nature, that the first people to be saved would be the Greek philosophers and the Roman government authorities. They were not. The people who were saved were the offscourings of society in seaports like Corinth and other places. 'God hath chosen the foolish things of the world to confound the wise; and God hath chosen the weak things of the world to confound the things which are mighty'. Do you understand that sort of thing? Are you mad enough to try to? No, no, there is only one thing to say: 'How unsearchable are his judgments!' And look at a man like Saul of Tarsus. Who would ever have thought that he would have become a Christian, and not only a Christian but an apostle, and the greatest of them! The thing is madness, the thing is impossible. It is the sort of thing God does. That is one of His judgments, His decisions. Oh, how unsearchable they are!

And as regards 'His ways', says the Apostle, 'they are past finding out'. What is the difference between judgments and ways? Well, it is the difference between decisions and methods. 'Ways' means plans, or methods, or dealings, or if you like paths; and what he says about them is that they are untraceable and untrackable. Job has already said it: 'I would seek unto God, and unto God would I commit my cause: Which doeth great things and unsearchable; marvellous things without number' [*Job* 5:8–9].

And Isaiah in his day and generation, looking at the ways of God, says, 'Verily thou art a God that hidest thyself, O God of Israel, the Saviour' [*Isa.* 45:15]. He says, You know I have given up trying to understand You. I thought it was going to be hopeless. You are a God Who makes streams in the deserts, You turn the mountains into plains and you exalt the plains into mountains. 'Thou art a God that hidest Thyself, O God of Israel, the Saviour'. His ways are past finding out.

Have you ever considered the ways of God? He does not always act in a direct manner, does He? He sometimes acts indirectly. He seems to be doing the opposite of what we would expect. 'Whom the Lord loveth he chasteneth.' He seems to deal very hardly with His chosen children and gives a very good time to those who are not. His ways are past finding out. 'Whom the Lord loveth He chasteneth, and scourgeth every son whom He receiveth' [*Heb.* 12:6]. Watch the way in which He allows evil apparently to triumph. Oh how many times has He done this! The Apostle has used the case of Pharaoh in chapter 9; the poor children of Israel, taskmasters, whips, bricks without straw, everything shutting in upon them. And then they seem to have a way of escape and on they go, but suddenly they are in front of the Red Sea. There they are absolutely shut in: they are finished! Not at all. But God allows it to develop until it seems completely hopeless, and then suddenly and unexpectedly He tells Moses to turn to the children of Israel and say, 'Speak unto the children of Israel, that they go forward', and the sea opens. His ways are past finding out.

A man who tries to understand the ways of God is a man who had better discover whether he does really believe in God or not. The very fact that you are trying to shows that there is something radically wrong with you somewhere. You see, you cannot understand Him. God sometimes uses His enemies. It was God Who raised up the Chaldeans to destroy Israel and to take them to the captivity of Babylon. It was God Who did it. He raises a pagan nation to destroy His own people temporarily. He uses a man like Cyrus. He raised him up and called him by name. You cannot understand, the children of Israel could not understand, and because they kept on trying to, they got into trouble. Oh that they had come to see, as Job saw at the end, as this great Apostle sees from the very beginning: 'His ways are past finding out!' And we have already seen in this chapter He uses unbelief. He used the unbelief of the Jews to bring in the Gentiles. He is going to use the Gentiles again to bring in the Jews. The whole chapter has been devoted to this great theme. His ways are, indeed, past finding out. It is not surprising the Apostle says this at this particular point.

And then look at His patience, and what we regard as His delays. The answer is, of course, that 'with God a thousand years are as one day; and one day is as a thousand years'. You cannot understand Him. The whole Bible is a Book of romance and of mystery. Take the case, the whole story, of Gideon. You remember what happened, the Midianites come up and attack and Gideon has an army of thirty-two thousand and you and I would have said, let us get our strategy and our tactics in order. But God does not, He says, Look here, get rid of those men. He reduced thirty-two thousand to three hundred against the hosts of Midian. And how were the three hundred to fight? Well, you remember, it was with a trumpet in one hand and a pitcher with a lantern in the other, and they were to smash the pitcher, show the light and blow the trumpet; and they had done that. He that dwelleth in the heavens shall laugh', says the Psalmist [*Psa.* 2:4]. I believe He does, and especially at our foolish questionings and our attempts to try to understand His ways.

The ways of God are past finding out. You see it supremely, of course, in the case of our Lord. Having planned in His judgment this way of salvation He sends His Son into the world. How would you have sent the Son of God into the world? You would have sent Him to Buckingham Palace, would you not, or some other palace. But He wasn't sent to such a place. He was sent to a stable. You would have sent Him to a place of wealth and of affluence; He was born in abject poverty, in the most lowly manner conceivable. You would have sent Him to study in the greatest schools of rhetoric and of philosophy. He was a carpenter and had no learning. You would have arranged that He should save the world by uttering some great statement, some liberating word. He did not. He saved the world by dying in utter weakness upon a Cross. His ways are past finding out!

And then when the Son of God goes back to heaven and the glory who is going to carry on His cause? Well now, surely at this point you must call in the philosophers and you must call in the best men that Rome can provide. No, no; ignorant and unlettered men, fishermen, the most ordinary men conceivable. And how is this message to be made known? How is this great salvation achieved by the Son of God on Calvary and in the resurrection and ascension – how is this to be made known unto the world? Well now surely at this point you must call in these great philosophers. No, no! Well, it must be a dialogue at any rate, there must be a discussion, give-and-take, listen and learn, share, exchange of views. No, no! The foolishness of preaching! 'When the world by wisdom knew not God, it pleased God by the foolishness of preaching', which means not only the foolishness of the thing preached but even the very method. Preaching! Proclaiming! Declaring! These ignorant and unlettered men. And yet they turned the world upside-down.

You see, the moment you come to look at God's judgments and God's ways you come to this only and inevitable conclusion, that 'His judgments are unsearchable, and his ways past finding out!'

Let me end on this note. Why should we rejoice in this? Why should we reject this modern accommodation of the gospel to the modern man and listen to him and learn from him, instead of proclaiming to him? Why must we reject this? Why ought we to rejoice in the fact that the gospel is as it is and not as we are being told today? Well, here is my answer – because the gospel is God's power unto salvation and not man's. Because it is God's, Whose judgments are unsearchable and Whose ways are past finding out, there is hope for all of us. There would not be hope for many of us, you know, if the philosophers had their way. It would be a salvation for just a handful of philosophers and the vast majority of us would be outside and without any hope. Thank God the gospel is entirely unlike everything that man has ever thought of. It is something that man cannot understand, he cannot receive, he cannot grasp; he cannot trace or track it out, it turns him upside-down, it shocks him, it amazes him. Thank God for it. It is because it is like that, that it holds out a hope for everybody. You can take this gospel to the heart of Africa. You do not ask for a dialogue there, do you? The poor man brought up there is unable to have a dialogue with you. But you know, that poor man is in exactly the same position as your great philosopher in London, or your great scientist wherever he may happen to live – in exactly the same position. God knows this. We do not. Thank God He does know. And what you do to the man in Africa is what you do to your philosophers in Oxford and Cambridge, you address them, you proclaim to them, whether they will hear or whether they will not hear. Here is the only hope for all kinds and conditions of men; here is a hope for all.

Oh, I want to test you, my friend. Now, I do not ask you merely to accept what the Apostle says; I am going to ask you something much deeper. Do you rejoice in what he says? Do you with him burst out into acclamation and praise as you realize that God's ways are past finding out and that His judgments are unsearchable? Are you moved by it? Do you rejoice in it?

*And can it be, that I should gain*
*An interest in the Saviour's blood?*
*Died He for me, who caused His pain:*
*For me, who Him to death pursued?*
*Amazing love! how can it be*
*That Thou, my God, shouldst die for me?*

You see, the Apostle, knowing that the judgments of God are unsearchable, and His ways past finding out, feels that he must speak like that, or in the words of another hymn-writer:

*Jesu, what didst Thou find in me*
*That Thou hast dealt so lovingly?*
*How great the joy that Thou hast brought,*
*So far exceeding hope or thought.*

Samuel Davies brings in his note:

*Great God of wonders, all Thy ways*
*Are godlike, matchless, and divine;*
*But the fair glories of Thy grace*
*More godlike and unrivalled shine.*
*Who is a pardoning God like Thee?*
*Or who has grace so rich and free?*

That is why we should rejoice in it.

And lastly, we should rejoice in it because it is the only thing that guarantees our ultimate glorification in spite of everything that may happen to us; and the world and the flesh and the devil and modern man and science and knowledge, they are all against us and would rob us of the glory that awaits us; but they cannot. Why not? Well, because it is God's way, not ours. We think the end of the church is coming; people say that. I read another article this week which says that the church is obviously finished, there is no point in having the church any longer. People can read now so you do not need a Christian church. All this is said in the name of Christianity, and you see, if it were our way it would have finished, collapsed long ago and none of us would be finally saved. But when I look at it all this is what I say. I am amazed at God's tolerance of it all but I have given up trying to understand:

*God moves in a mysterious way*
*His wonders to perform;*
*He plants His footsteps in the sea,*
*And rides upon the storm.*

Listen to this. Listen to William Cowper stating it:

*Deep in unfathomable mines*
*Of never-failing skill,*
*He treasures up His bright designs,*
*And works His sovereign will*

*Judge not the Lord by feeble sense*
*But trust Him for His grace;*
*Behind a frowning providence*
*He hides a smiling face.*

On he goes:

*His purposes will ripen fast,*
*Unfolding every hour;*
*The bud may have a bitter taste,*
*But sweet will be the flower.*

*Blind unbelief is sure to err,*
*And scan His work in vain;*
*God is His own interpreter,*
*And He will make it plain.*

Man cannot interpret it. 'Who hath known the mind of the Lord? who hath been his counsellor?' What has your unbeliever to say? Why should I listen to him? He cannot understand God's ways. 'God is His own interpreter', and here is the inspired interpretation. 'God is his own interpreter, and he will make it plain'.

'O the depth of the riches both of the wisdom and the knowledge of God! how unsearchable are his judgments, and his ways past finding out!'

# *Thirty*

*

*O the depth of the riches both of the wisdom and knowledge of God! how unsearchable are his judgments, and his ways past finding out! For who hath known the mind of the Lord? or who hath been his counsellor? or who hath first given to him, and it shall be recompensed unto him again? For of him, and through him, and to him, are all things: to whom be glory for ever. Amen.*
Romans 11:33–36

Let me remind you that in this great statement the Apostle is standing back as it were and looking first of all at what he has just been saying about the astonishing and apparently incredible thing that is going to happen to the Jews as a nation. He has been given to see that 'All Israel' in that sense is going to believe the gospel, is going to become a part of the Christian church with the Gentiles, and that is the first thing that makes him burst out like this.

But in addition to that he is also standing back and looking at all that he has put before these Roman Christians of the tremendous plan and purpose of God in redemption in Christ Jesus. As he does so he feels amazed and can only exclaim with a sense of utter astonishment. He speaks of the 'depth' of God's mercy, His wisdom and knowledge, the incomprehensibility of His thoughts and ways. He now moves on to stress that all of this is completely independent of man.

This theme follows on topically from all that has gone before. Because of the depth and the utter incomprehensibility of God's thoughts and ways, it is clearly something that is entirely independent of man. But, as we know, man is very slow to see that, and is still slower to admit it, so the Apostle is anxious that this should be brought home to these people and to all Christian people in all ages and generations. He is particularly concerned to stress this, and this I believe we can say quite rightly has been one of the leading themes of the whole of the Epistle – that salvation is totally independent of man and is altogether and entirely of God.

Now the way the Apostle introduces that to us is put here in verses 34 and 35. 'Who hath known the mind of the Lord? or who hath been his counsellor? Or who hath first given to him, and it shall be recompensed to him again?' These are quotations from the Old Testament. The first comes from the prophecy of Isaiah chapter 40 and verse 13 and the second comes from the book of Job chapter 41 and verse 11.

Before we proceed to examine the doctrine stated here, there is an extremely interesting technical point to note. The authorities point out quite rightly that in quoting from Job 41:11 the Apostle did not quote from the Septuagint translation. He generally does that in his quotations; here he has not done so. Why not? Well, there is no doubt that he knew that it was not a good translation. The Septuagint translation of Job 41:11 is not an accurate rendering. The Apostle, knowing that, took the Hebrew and translated it himself, and the translation that we have here in our English version of what the Apostle wrote is an accurate translation of the original Hebrew. This is an argument for the inspiration of the Scriptures.

Now these two quotations which the Apostle picks out here and uses are, of course, very germane to the point which he is making. He has already spoken of profundity and incomprehensibility and now to press the argument right home he asserts that God's purpose is altogether apart from man.

Now there is no doubt whatsoever but that in these two quotations there is not merely a statement of fact but there is an element of divine irony, divine ridicule. It is important that we should bear that in mind. Man's arrogance needs to be humbled, and here the Scripture does that. 'Who hath known the mind of the Lord?' Who dares make such a suggestion! 'Who has been his counsellor?' 'Who hath first given to him, and it shall be recompensed unto him again?' I believe that that is how we should read this. The same thing is found in 1 Corinthians 1:20 which also quotes from the same source.

Now let us again remind ourselves of why it is the Apostle says this at this point. It follows immediately on verse 32. 'For God hath concluded them all in unbelief, that he might have mercy upon all'. This divine arrangement of showing mercy to Jew and Gentile alike is something which is totally and entirely and completely independent of man.

It is very interesting to notice the way in which these two quotations selected by the great Apostle under divine leading and inspiration deal in a very wonderful way with the three points that he has put before us in verse 33, but he deals with them in the reverse order. What is the order in verse 33? Here it is: 'O the depth!' The depth of what? Well, we saw, the depth of the 'riches', the depth of the 'wisdom', and the depth of the 'knowledge'. But in the quotations they come the other way round. 'Who hath known the mind of the Lord?' That corresponds, you see, to the knowledge in verse 33. He starts with that and works backwards. And this is a most important point; this is what he is driving home with his quotation. He has put it positively in verse 33: that our salvation is the result of this great knowledge of God who knows everything and therefore has catered for every possibility and every eventuality and this is the thing that renders our ultimate salvation and glorification certain.

And, he says, is it not obvious that this puts man right out altogether? What knowledge does man possess that he can give to God? What addition can man make to God in this matter of knowledge? You see he is ridiculing the thing. And the implied answer is, the question implies the answer, that man not only has no knowledge that he can give to God but that his essential trouble is due to his ignorance, and the Apostle has been working this out for us in great detail. Man's troubles ultimately all come out of his ignorance. Man, modern man, twentieth century man, man 'come of age' and all the rest of it – the real trouble with him is his ignorance, his ignorance of God, his ignorance of the being of God. He would not speak about Him as he does were he not so utterly ignorant of Him; he would not express his confident, pompous, blasphemous opinions if he knew anything. The more man says about God the more he displays his utter ignorance. If he knew more about God, like Job of old, he would put his hand upon his mouth, he would become silent before God. But it is his ignorance that makes him speak, and the more he speaks the more he betrays the ignorance. Not only is he ignorant of the being of God, this God of Whom we sing:

*Immortal, invisible, God only wise,*
*In light inaccessible hid from our eyes,*

he is ignorant of himself. He knows nothing about God's purposes, He knows nothing about God's ways. Little man is busy trying to put his universe in order and he cannot do it; he is showing that he cannot do it. And the tragedy is that he does not know that God has a great plan and purpose which is in execution and which is going to be finally completed. Man is ignorant of all that.

And he is ignorant of himself in the same way; he is ignorant of his true nature. He even glories in the theory of evolution which tells him that he is just something that has evolved out of an animal and does not know that he has been created in the image and likeness of God; he is ignorant even of that. He is ignorant of his condition, he is ignorant of his need; never has he been more ignorant of that than today. He thinks he needs knowledge and education; that is not his real need; but he is ignorant of all this. And still more vital in a sense, he is ignorant of the devil, he is ignorant of the forces of evil and of hell and their malign influence in this world, the things that the Apostle speaks of in chapter 6 of Ephesians, that 'We wrestle not against flesh and blood, but against principalities, against powers, against the rulers of the darkness of this world' [*Eph.* 6:12]. Modern man knows nothing about them, hence the condition of his world. He is ignorant of the judgment that awaits him, he is ignorant of the eternity of punishment that awaits all who die in this darkness and ignorance of sin; he is ignorant of all that, and ignorant of what God has planned and purposed with respect to it all. So you see the Apostle ridicules this – 'Who hath known the mind of the Lord?' Where is the man who feels that he can stand up as an equal and say 'I know as God knows'? He does not! The only way man can ever have this knowledge is that it is given to him. The Apostle works that out, as you know, in 1 Corinthians 2 and ends with the statement, 'We' – Christians, the ones who have received the Spirit – 'we have the mind of Christ'. But if a man has not got the mind of Christ he knows nothing: 'He that is spiritual judgeth all things, yet he himself is judged of no man'. 'For who hath known the mind of the Lord, that he may instruct him? But we have the mind of Christ'. He deals, then, with the knowledge.

Then you see he comes to deal with the 'wisdom, and he does that in this question: 'Who hath been his counsellor?' A counsellor is someone from whom you expect wisdom, who is of value to you when you are confronted by a difficult situation and you do not quite know what to do. You need advice or counsel. So the Apostle puts his great ironical question: 'Who claims that he can give any counsel or help or advice to God?' And the answer is again implied in the very question; it is of course that man has got none to give! Because of his ignorance he cannot possibly have any advice to give that is of any value at all. And indeed man unconsciously betrays this very thing. He thinks he knows. He is always ready to give his advice. And modern man in his inflated arrogance is always giving advice even to God as to what He should do. They do not hesitate to do that. They criticize God, they say, 'Why does God allow this?' – these blasphemous questions. It is all based, as I say, upon ignorance and they are ready to give advice and to make their suggestions. But notice how man betrays his folly in all his attempts to give advice or counsel to God. Listen to the modern man in his cleverness giving advice to God as to how a man can be saved. How does a man become a Christian? Well, the modern man thinks he knows and, alas, there are many such in the Christian church. How does a man become a Christian? His answer is, by living a good life, by obeying a moral code, by obeying some kind of law. Is not that the way? Is not that what man thinks? Is not that his instinctive idea as to how a man becomes a Christian? – you make yourself a Christian. Perhaps you are made a Christian by being born in a certain country, to some it is pure nationality. As it was with the Jews of old so it is to many today – Christian countries, non-Christian countries; but especially this, our good works. And so they talk about their rights and their demands, and they believe they can present the account to God. 'This is the life I have lived' – like the Pharisee of old. 'I fast twice in the week, I give a tenth of my goods to the poor . . .' What a good man I am! I am philanthropic, I am always out to help people. And they think that in that way they save themselves and they make themselves Christians and assure themselves of a hope of heaven. To which the simple answer is this, that if God were prepared to accept that suggestion that man makes there would not be a single Christian. Nobody would be saved. We would all go to hell. If God adopted man's advice and suggestion and counsel the whole of mankind would be irretrievably doomed and damned. That is a measure of the folly of man, you see, in putting forward his suggestions.

But he shows this folly equally in this way – that when you do present him with God's way he regards it as unutterable foolishness. 'We preach Christ crucified, unto the Jews a stumblingblock, and unto the Greeks foolishness' and they are still saying the same thing.

This idea that God has sent His Son into the world, the incarnation, the two natures in one Person, God and Man, the sinless life, the substitutionary, atoning death, the resurrection, the ascension, the Holy Spirit, new life, being born again . . . the world ridicules it. And thus it shows, you see, the truth of what the Apostle quotes here, 'Who has been his counsellor?' Every suggestion man makes would but lead to his damnation, and when he is confronted by God's way he dismisses it as folly and still he claims that he is able to tell God what He ought to do. There is only one thing to say to a man like this: 'Who hath known the mind of the Lord? or who hath been his counsellor?' So he deals with the second matter.

And that brings us to the one that is first in verse 33 but which is taken here last. 'Who hath first given to him, and it shall be recompensed unto him again?' And here, you see, this attitude of modern man to this matter of 'riches' is dealt with and finally ridiculed out of court entirely. Man in other words has nothing to give to God at all. Not only has he no knowledge, not only has he no wisdom to give, he has nothing to give at all in any way; he has no righteousness to give, he has nothing!

Now the Apostle has been emphasizing that this is as true of the Jew as it is of the Gentile. 'We have before proved', he says, 'that both Jew and Gentile are in exactly the same case'. You remember he goes on repeating this. It is in chapter 10 in verse 12: 'For there is no difference between the Jew and the Greek: for the same Lord over all is rich unto all that call upon him'. The Apostle has proved in the first three chapters that the Jew is as condemned and as hopeless as the Gentile. No difference! 'All have sinned and come short of the glory of God'. He has concluded them all 'under sin' [*Rom.* 3:23, 9].

But this has to be impressed upon the mind of man because of his foolish pride and arrogance and his misplaced confidence in himself. What has man to give to God? – that is what he is really asking. Who has given first to God and God, as it were, just rewards him because of what he has given? Who has any claim to make upon God? What is it? What is man, what kind of claim can he make upon God? The great answer that runs through the whole Bible is this, that man not only has nothing at all to give but he is a hopeless debtor. He is in a most terrible precarious impecunious position in every conceivable respect. He is a debtor. He is one who has not paid his dues. He was made to live and to pay glory to God, he has not done it. 'All have sinned and come short of the glory of God'. The law makes its demands and man cannot pay them. No man has ever done so. The Apostle has proved that with regard to both Jews and Gentiles once and for ever. But not only is man a debtor, he is a thief, he is a robber. He has taken things that do not belong to him, he has appropriated them to himself. The gifts that God gave him that were intended to be used to the glory of God, man has used for his own glory, and he is a thief, he is a robber; and on top of it all he is ungrateful.

Now this of course is the great theme of the whole of the gospel. Our Lord Himself puts it unforgettably. In Luke chapter 8 we read that a certain Pharisee invited our Lord to go into his house to dine and our Lord accepted. And when the Pharisee saw who had come along and had washed our Lord's feet with her tears and had wiped them with the hair of her head, – 'he spake within himself, saying, This man if he were a prophet would have known what manner of woman this is that toucheth him: for she is a sinner'. And then our Lord you remember spoke a parable: 'There was a certain creditor which had two debtors: the one owed five hundred pence, and the other fifty. And when they had nothing to pay, he frankly forgave them both' [*Luke* 7:39, 41–42]. Now that is the point. Neither had any means to pay the debt. And that is the position of the whole of mankind, as our Lord goes on to prove in that particular case. Mankind is like the Prodigal Son who had lost everything, all his money had been spent, he had got nothing left 'and no man gave unto him'. He is completely destitute. That is mankind in sin.

And yet, you see, men go to God and they claim, they demand, they say, 'Look at the life I have lived, look what I have done, look at my disposition', and they present their bills to God, they say 'This is what I have done for You; now then I expect to go to heaven because of that'. And they claim forgiveness if they should fall into sin in terms of this 'goodness' of theirs and this 'merit' that they have been accumulating.

Now this is the thing that is here being ridiculed again, I say, out of court. 'Who is there', says the Apostle, 'who can present a claim to God or a demand or a bill and say, "I have given; give me back, or give me a reward for what I have done".' And his answer is, you see, that there is none, there is no one. Man is a pauper, a debtor, he is nothing, and having nothing he is still in this awful debt and he has got nothing whatsoever to pay. That is just his way of saying, you see, that salvation is entirely of God, it is entirely of grace. Salvation is the free gift of God to totally undeserving sinners. 'By grace are ye saved through faith; and that not of yourselves, it is the gift of God'. Man not only does not deserve it, he deserves the exact opposite. He is not only weak and helpless, he is an enemy of God, a rebel against God, and he richly deserves eternal damnation. But God, in spite of that, of His own free rich grace – 'the riches' that the Apostle has been talking about – gives man salvation as a free gift. Salvation is in no sense whatsoever a response on God's part to something that man has first done; it is the exact opposite. The movement is entirely and altogether of and from God, and man contributes nothing at all.

The Apostle has already told us in the fourth verse of the second chapter, that it is 'the goodness of God that leadeth to repentance'. Faith is the gift of God. No man can believe without this gift of faith. Man is 'dead in trespasses and sins', he needs to be quickened. God does it. So as He starts it He continues it. We have seen in chapter 8 that the final perseverance of the saints is solely due to the fact that it is God's from beginning to end, and there is no other explanation.

So you see, as the Apostle contemplates all this he feels that there is nothing that can be done except that a man shall worship and praise and burst out in a kind of heavenly acclamation. And so he does. He says, having thrown out the challenge, 'Who hath known the mind of the Lord? or who hath been his counsellor? Who hath first given to him, and it shall be recompensed to him again? – What are you talking about, says the Apostle – 'Of him, and through him, and to him, are all things: to whom be glory for ever. Amen'.

What does he mean? Well, he works it up like this. God is, first of all, the Source of everything! Who can give God anything? Is not the first verse in the Bible: 'In the beginning God created the heaven and the earth'? He made it all, He owns it all. 'The cattle on a thousand hills' are His says the Psalmist [*Psa.* 50:10]. Everything belongs to Him. Do not think you are giving God anything when you take your burnt offerings and sacrifice; He owns everything – the cattle on a thousand hills, and everything else, they all belong to God. Nobody can give God anything.

Yes but not only are all things 'of God', all things are also 'through God', which means this – that He sustains everything, and that nothing would continue to exist otherwise. This is often stated in the Bible. You find in Psalm 104:28–31, 'These wait all upon thee; that thou mayest give them their meat in due season. That thou givest them, they gather: thou openest thine hand, they are filled with good. Thou hidest thy face, they are troubled: thou takest away their breath, they die, and return to their dust. Thou sendest forth thy Spirit, they are created: and thou renewest the face of the earth. The glory of the Lord shall endure for ever: the Lord shall rejoice in his works'.

Modern man with all his science and his discoveries thinks he knows such a lot; but he is only touching the fringes of things, that is all; nothing more than that. He is excited because he discovers certain things, what he does not know is this, that the great God Who made it all is keeping it all going and sustaining it. If He withdrew His Spirit it would all collapse. This is a work divided between the Persons of the blessed Holy Trinity. In Hebrews 1:3 our Lord is described as 'upholding all things by the word of his power'. You have the same idea in the first chapter of the Epistle to the Colossians. Now the Apostle is summing all this up and he says, 'Of him' – yes, but 'through him' also, 'are all things'.

And finally, it is 'to him' that all things lead. Everything leads to God; everything leads to the glory of God. And this to me is the most thrilling thing of all, the whole of the cosmos is going to display finally the glory of God. 'Of him, through him, to him'. The end of everything is the glory of God.

Even as things are at the present time this is partly taking place. 'The heavens declare the glory of God: and the firmament sheweth his handiwork'. Man does not see that, but it is happening. The same thing is found in Romans 1:19–20.

But then we know that sin has come in and there are briars and thorns, and 'the whole creation groaneth', as he has told us in chapter 8:22. We read again in Hebrews 2:8, 'we see not yet all things put under man'. The world at the moment is chaotic and there are all sorts of contradictions. But, says the prophet Isaiah looking forward, the revelation has been given to him, the day of God is coming, he says 'The earth shall be full of the knowledge of the LORD, as the waters cover the sea' [*Isa.* 11:9]. That is coming! But let us put it again as the apostle has put it to us in this glorious eighth chapter: 'I reckon that the sufferings of this present time are not worthy to be compared with the glory which shall be revealed in us. For the earnest expectation of the creature waiteth for the manifestation of the sons of God. For the creation (the creature) was made subject to vanity, not willingly, but by reason of him who hath subjected the same in hope. Because the creature (the creation) itself also shall be delivered from the bondage of corruption into the glorious liberty' – 'the liberty of the glory' – 'of the children of God. For we know that the whole creation groaneth and travaileth in pain together until now. And not only they, but ourselves also which have the firstfruits of the Spirit, even we ourselves groan within ourselves, waiting for the adoption, to wit, the redemption of our body' [*Rom.* 8:18–23].

Well there it is. The Apostle sees all this coming and as he puts it in 1 Corinthians 15:28, 'And when all things shall be subdued unto him' – that is to say, the Lord Jesus Christ – 'then shall the Son also himself be subject unto him that put all things under him, that God may be all in all'. The glory of God! 'From him, through him, to him, are all things: to whom be glory for ever. Amen.' Now the Apostle, you see, has leapt on and up in his inspired imagination; he sees the glorious end. What he is saying is this: now this is going to be true of everything, the whole cosmos, the whole universe!

Oh! how true it is particularly in this matter of redemption. Nobody has given anything to God in any sense, nobody ever can; the whole of redemption is all of God and has nothing from man. Man had no part whatsoever in the first creation, and he has no part whatsoever in the new creation. As the first creation is altogether of God, the new creation is altogether of God also. God initiated it all. 'Howbeit we speak wisdom among them that are perfect', says Paul in 1 Corinthians 2:6 – 'yet not the wisdom of this world, nor of the princes of this world, that come to nought: But we speak the wisdom of God in a mystery, even the hidden wisdom, which God ordained before the world unto our glory'. He initiated it; it is His idea. Nobody gave a suggestion.

It is all of God – in thought, in concept, in execution. The Son has been sent by God. 'God was in Christ reconciling the world unto himself', and it is all applied to us by the Spirit Whom the Father and the Son have sent into the church in the world. He also quickens us. enlivens us and gives us righteousness and faith. It is all the result of God's gracious free grace and giving.

And why? Well, it is all designed to the glory of God. When God made man at the beginning He made him for His own glory. 'The chief end of man is to glorify God and to enjoy him for ever', says that first answer to the first question of the Shorter Catechism, so rightly. Man was made for the glory of God; and, my friends, it is the same in redemption. What is the object and purpose of our redemption? The Apostle Peter says that it is that 'a chosen generation, a royal priesthood, an holy nation, a peculiar people' might 'shew forth his praises'

– that is, His excellencies, the glory of the one who 'called you out of darkness into his marvellous light' [*1 Pet.* 2:9]. To show 'His' praises, 'His' glory – it is all designed to do this. The only reason why there is such a thing as salvation at all, why any one of us is saved, is the glory of God. 'Of him, through him, to him are all things'.

But we must go on repeating the negative. Man makes no contribution to this whatsoever. The Apostle has stated this many times over. 'Christ died for the ungodly' when 'we were yet without strength' [*Rom.* 5:6]: 'God commendeth his love toward us', to sinners, in Christ's death [*Rom.* 5:8]. But it is even worse than that: it was 'when we were enemies' we were reconciled to God by the death of his Son' [*Rom.* 5:10]. It is all of God. Man makes no contribution. We have seen what man is like: 'We know that the law is spiritual: but I am carnal, sold under sin'. 'In me (that is to say, in my flesh,) dwelleth no good thing' [*Rom.* 7:14, 18]. I have got nothing to contribute in any way whatsoever. The law cannot help me. It is 'weak through the flesh' [*Rom.* 8:3]. Man in his sinful condition can do nothing, he has completely failed; it has been proved. But here is the only answer.

What the law could not do, in that it was weak through the flesh, God 'sending his own Son, in the likeness of sinful flesh, and for sin, condemned sin in the flesh': 'that we might be made the righteousness of God in him' [*Rom.* 8:2; *2 Cor.* 5:21]. You see, man has contributed nothing whatsoever, it is all of God. The calling, the choice, the election, everything – justification to glorification, it is all entirely, utterly, absolutely of God, and man does not contribute anything at all.

So the test of our view of salvation and of our appreciation of it, is simply this: whenever you think of it does it bring you to this doxology? If it does not, I take leave to suggest to you that you know nothing about it. If you, my friend, look back to your 'decision' or anything in yourself, you are unlike the Apostle Paul. If when you contemplate your condition as a Christian, as a saved person, if you do not come to this doxology, I say, there is something radically wrong somewhere. Man makes no contribution at all. I feel like saying what the Apostle has said in the third chapter in verse 4: 'Yea', he says there, 'let God be true, but every man a liar'. And any man who puts forward any claim to anything in himself, whether knowledge or understanding or righteousness or morality or anything, is a liar. It is all entirely, utterly, absolutely of God.

So I put to you a final question. Having gone through this mighty revelation of doctrine, having followed the mighty demonstration of the great Apostle right away through to chapter 11 verse 32, having listened to the Apostle's doxology where he ends by saying, 'To whom be glory for ever and ever . . .' do you say 'Amen' to this?

What does this 'Amen' mean? It means that you confess that you are nothing, that you confess that you are a vile hell-deserving sinner, that you acknowledge gladly that you are what you are solely by the grace of God; that you have ceased to defend yourself, you have ceased to try to excuse yourself, you have ceased to try to justify yourself in any way whatsoever. I go further; that you have ceased to try to pit your mind against God's way. Are you still arguing against election? If you are you have not said your 'Amen' to all this. Do not forget the mighty demonstration of chapters 9–11. The purpose of God according to election! Are you still standing up and putting your mind and your opinion against it? If so you are not saying your 'Amen' to this great doxology. The man who says his 'Amen' is the man who says, I am nothing, He is all. I know nothing, I can do nothing, I have nothing. I am simply a vile sinner, I owe all things to the grace and the glory and the mercy of God and I give it Him. I give it Him with my lips, I confess Him, I say I am nothing, I say it is all of Him – I do it by my life. I am ready to say what Paul says, not only here but again to the Corinthians: 'Of him (of God) are ye in Christ Jesus, who of God is made unto us wisdom, and righteousness, and sanctification, and redemption: That, according as it is written, He that glorieth, let him glory in the Lord'. And I say 'Amen' to it. What can we say? There is nothing to say except what the Apostle says: 'To whom be glory for ever'!

*Glory be to God the Father,*
*Glory be to God the Son,*
*Glory be to God the Spirit,*
*Great Jehovah, Three in One.*
*Glory, Glory –*
*While eternal ages run.*